IMAGES
of America

ASHLEY VALLEY

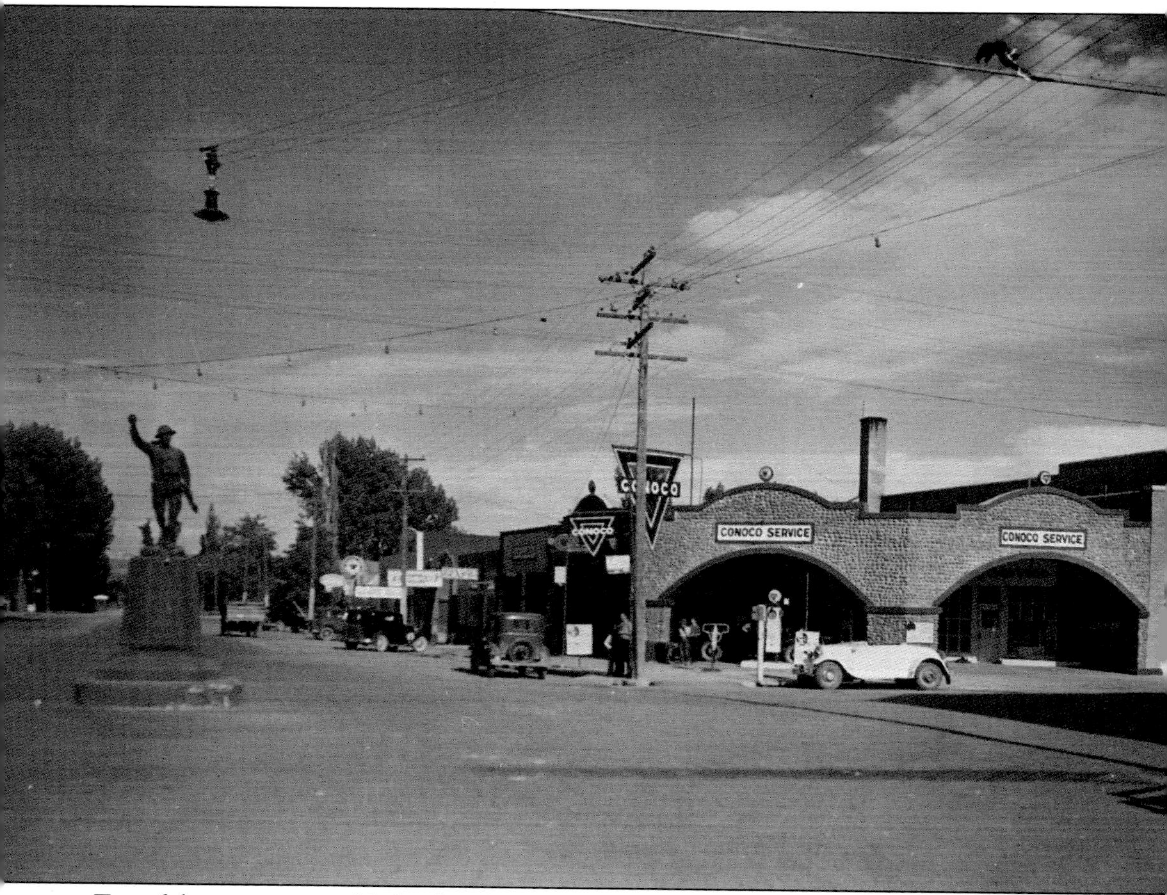

Two of the most memorable landmarks for the local valley were located in the heart of Vernal at the intersection of Main Street and Vernal Avenue. The *Doughboy* is a war memorial that was placed in the center of town in 1924 to honor World War I veterans; it has since been relocated to a spot in front of the courthouse. The Cobble Rock Station was built in 1925 with modern convenience that provided one-stop ease for local residents and travelers. (Courtesy of Uintah County Library Regional History Center.)

On the Cover: Representatives of the Capital Brass Foundry of Salt Lake City came to Vernal one week prior to Armistice Day to deliver and supervise the placing of the bronze *Doughboy* and the brass plates with the names of 350 Uintah County war veterans. The old truck to the right is from the Vernal Milling and Light Company. The Uintah State Bank Building is in the background. (Courtesy of Uintah County Library Regional History Center.)

IMAGES
of America

ASHLEY VALLEY

Regional History Center Staff

ARCADIA
PUBLISHING

ISBN 978-0-7385-8507-9

Published by Arcadia Publishing
Charleston, South Carolina

Printed in the United States of America

Library of Congress Control Number: 2011929767

For all general information, please contact Arcadia Publishing:
Telephone 843-853-2070
Fax 843-853-0044
E-mail sales@arcadiapublishing.com
For customer service and orders:
Toll-Free 1-888-313-2665

Visit us on the Internet at www.arcadiapublishing.com

This book is dedicated to the early Ashley Valley settlers who left a rich history for others to enjoy.

Contents

ACKNOWLEDGMENTS

The Regional History staff would like to give thanks to Doris Karren Burton for her vision and vigorous work to begin the Regional History Center. It is said to be the best center in the Western region and the only one of its kind in the state of Utah. Doris aggressively and tirelessly found funding and donations to increase the historical archives located in the history center. Thank you to all other volunteers and staff that have contributed to the continuing growth of the center.

We would like to recognize Leo Thorne for his passion in capturing the history of the Ashley Valley and surrounding areas through the lens of his camera and his daughter Rhoda DeVed for making it possible to obtain the Leo Thorne Collection. A thank-you goes to the *Vernal Express* for its donation of thousands of photographs that were used in the newspaper. Thanks are extended to the many people who have donated and added to our photograph collections. We would like to give acknowledgment to the University of Utah Marriott Library for housing much of our collection on its server and website.

A thank-you goes to the past library director, Evan Baker, and Sam Passey, the current library director, who have eagerly participated and pushed forward the work in the history center. The Uintah County commissioners have been behind the history center 100 percent, and we are grateful for their continuing support. We would like to recognize and give thanks to Lee Cheves and the Uintah County Library Board for their encouragement on our behalf.

All photographs in this publication are courtesy of the Regional History Center unless otherwise noted.

We would like to give a final thank-you to our patrons and to anyone who has donated to our history center.

The Regional History Center staff members include Ellen Kiever, Elaine Carr, Michelle Fuller, and Susan Merrell.

INTRODUCTION

Nestled at the foot of the Uinta Mountains, Ashley Valley is situated in eastern Utah's Uinta Basin. Fur traders and trappers passed through the valley in the early 1800s. One particular fur trader, William Ashley, took a liking to the area and left his name on the walls of Red Canyon in 1825. Ashley Valley, Ashley Creek, Ashley Town, and many other places and things took the name *Ashley*. This valley surrounded by mountains was once the home of dinosaurs and many years later, the people known as the Fremont Indians. Later settlers discovered proof of their existence.

After being employed at the Uintah Indian Reservation in Whiterocks, Utah, Pardon Dodds, along with John Blankenship and Morris Evans, entered the Ashley Valley in 1873. Dodds built the first cabin near the Ashley Creek and constructed the first irrigation ditch from that same stream. He brought his cattle from Whiterocks through Deep Creek and on into the valley, where feed and water were plentiful.

An early expedition party sent out by territorial governor Brigham Young called the area unfit for opening up. This delayed permanent settlement until 1876, when pioneers began trickling into the valley. Clearing the waist-high grass, sagebrush, and other wild vegetation from the landscape required a lot of grit from early settlers.

It was discovered that the land offered more than previously thought. The soil was rich with nutrients and soon began to grow grass, grains, fruits, and vegetables. Water sources in the form of Ashley Creek and the Green River ran through the valley from the surrounding mountains. Due to the abundance of grazing land and water, sheep and cattle did well in this area, and livestock became a growing industry for early settlers.

Small communities with homes and businesses sprang up, including Dry Fork, Maeser, Ashley, Vernal, Glines, Naples, Davis, and Jensen. Families grew, and residential streets multiplied. Schools and churches dotted the landscape. Businesses of all kinds opened their doors to a growing community.

Besides the rich soil, valuable minerals and oils were discovered in surrounding mountains. Copper, iron, and phosphate were found in the Uinta Mountains north of the valley. Forests provided logs for building, and many sawmills started up. To the south, Gilsonite, oil, and oil shale opened up a promise of prosperity. Asphalt was discovered west of Vernal and made it possible for streets in the city of Vernal to be paved. By 1904, the Uintah Railway came into the southern part of Uintah County; it brought the mail, freight, and visitors to the valley. Wool, honey, oil, and Gilsonite were among some of the commodities sent from the valley to other parts of the country.

The valley people helped each other through hard and happy times—from the hard winter of 1879 when food was scarce, the Meeker Massacre scare, the outlaw presence in the valley, the flu epidemic of 1918, and the effect that the world wars placed on the local citizens. The community also suffered through economic ups and downs of boom and bust cycles. With hearty optimism, local residents stood together during hard times and became stronger and more resilient.

Folks looked for occasions to celebrate with parades, rodeos, picnics, dances, plays, and sporting events. Cultural performances were presented at an opera house constructed by Jake Workman.

Prominent citizens stepped into leadership roles and brought growth and prosperity to the valley. The people of the Ashley Valley have always been proud, patriotic, and had great passion for their community.

Visitors and tourists began to frequent the area with its wealth of things to do and see. The Dinosaur National Monument located just east of Vernal offers visitors a chance to see dinosaur fossils displayed in the quarry where they were first discovered. With the building of the Flaming Gorge Dam and Reservoir, boating and trophy fishing have become popular recreations for many. For the adventurous, the Green River offers plenty of white-water rafting with an ample amount of calm stretches to view the rugged beauty that the canyon walls present. The Uinta Mountains are another source of enjoyment. Lakes and streams dot the mountaintops for excellent trout fishing. Wild game wanders the mountain ridges providing opportunities for the avid hunter.

Today, when visitors enter the valley, they will see modern growth mixed with small-town appeal. They will feel welcomed by a warm, inviting community. They will notice the clean, landscaped streets. In the summer months, one's senses are overwhelmed with the vivid colors and smells of a city in bloom. Community pride and hard work earned Vernal national honors for its beautiful community in 2004.

The original settlers have all passed on, but pioneering still occurs in the valley. A great part of the Ashley Valley is made up of descendants of those hardy folks who first claimed this land as their own.

People are still building and exploring new ways to use the resources that are available to them in this bounteous land. They are enterprising people with pioneering spirit and dreams of bettering their community for future generations.

One

In the Beginning

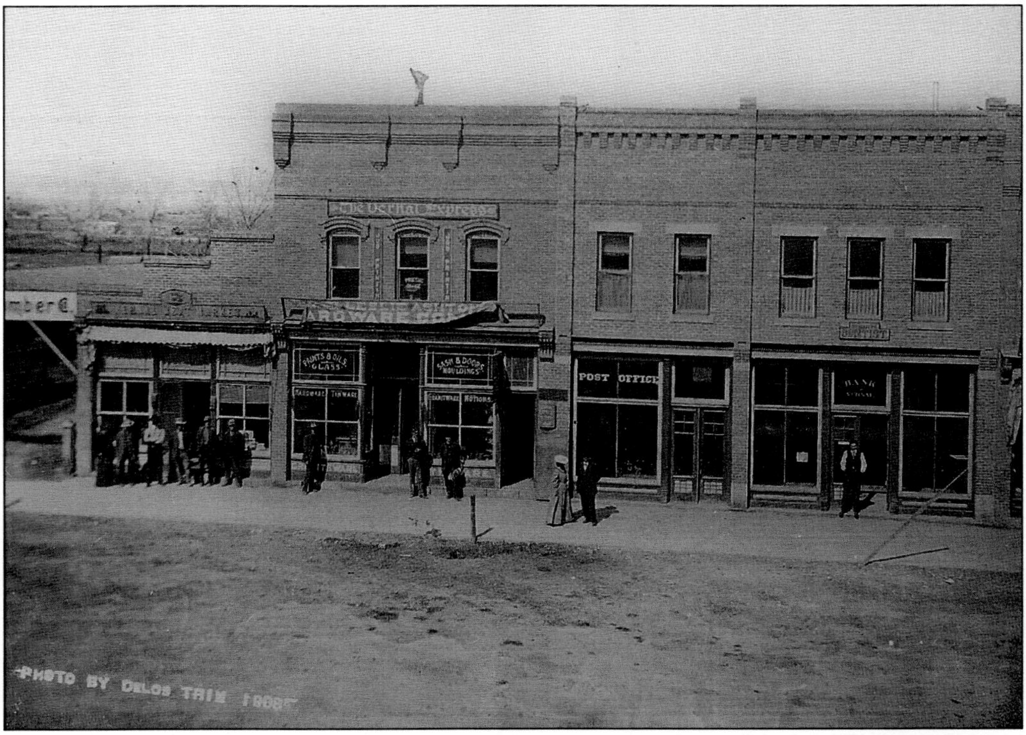

On a sunny afternoon in 1908, citizens of the community gather on the north side of Uintah Avenue in front of the Vernal Meat Market, Leslie Ashton Hardware Store, Vernal Express office, the post office, and the Bank of Vernal. Uintah Avenue later became Main Street. Early photographer Delos Trim took this image.

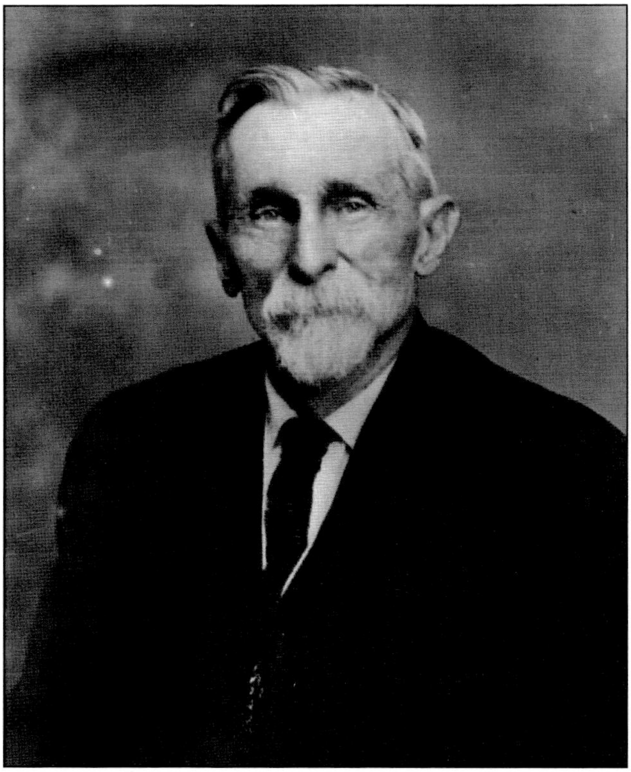

Pardon Dodds was born on March 8, 1837. He was the first Indian agent for the Uintah Indian Reservation, and he established the Whiterocks Indian Agency in 1868. In 1869, Dodds retired from the agency. He moved his cattle into the Ashley Valley and built the first log cabin north of Ashley Creek. He built the first irrigation ditch from the creek, which is still referred to as Dodds Ditch. Dodds included a storeroom on his home, and after purchasing supplies he ran a trading post for trappers and Indians. Dodds met and married Minnie Hatch from Heber; they are pictured in front of the home that Dodds built. In 1880, the legislature appointed Pardon Dodds as a selectman. He died September 9, 1921, at 84 years old.

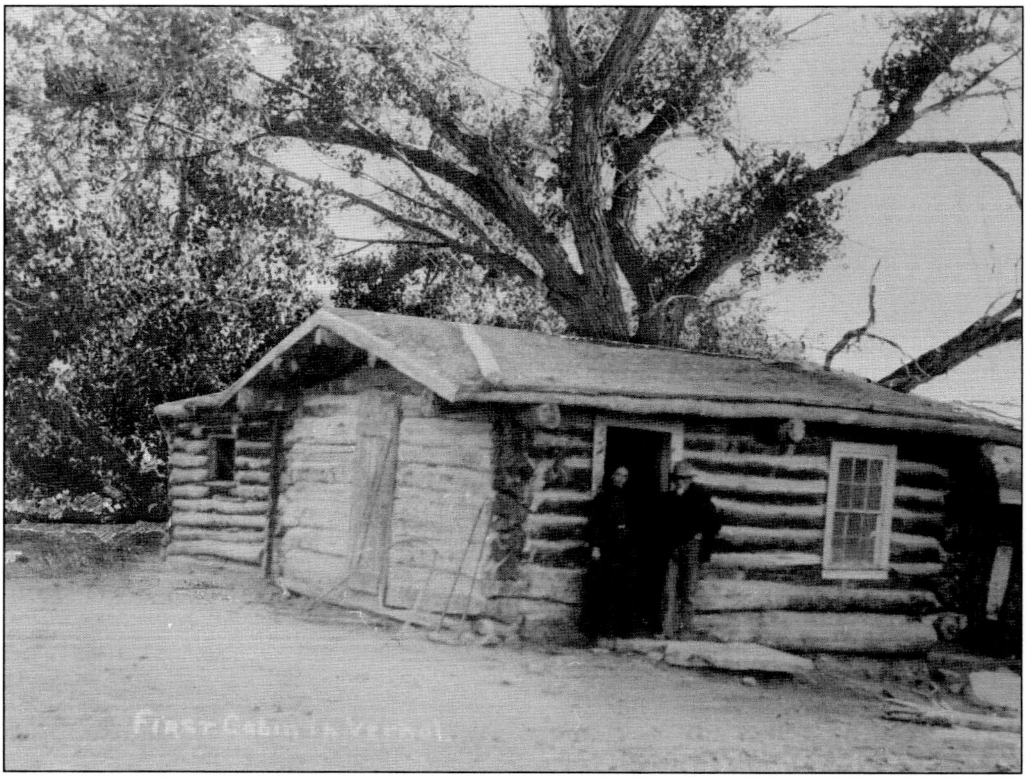

George Findley Britt, often called Finn, was one of the first settlers to arrive in Ashley Valley. He came to the valley along with his brother Wilbur in 1877. Finn married Maria Merkley, and they raised their family in the valley. He worked for the government as a commissary manager. Finn died in 1943.

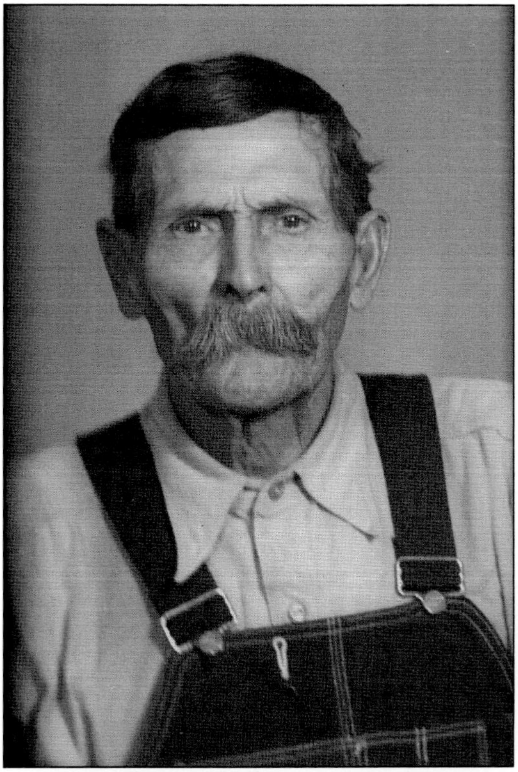

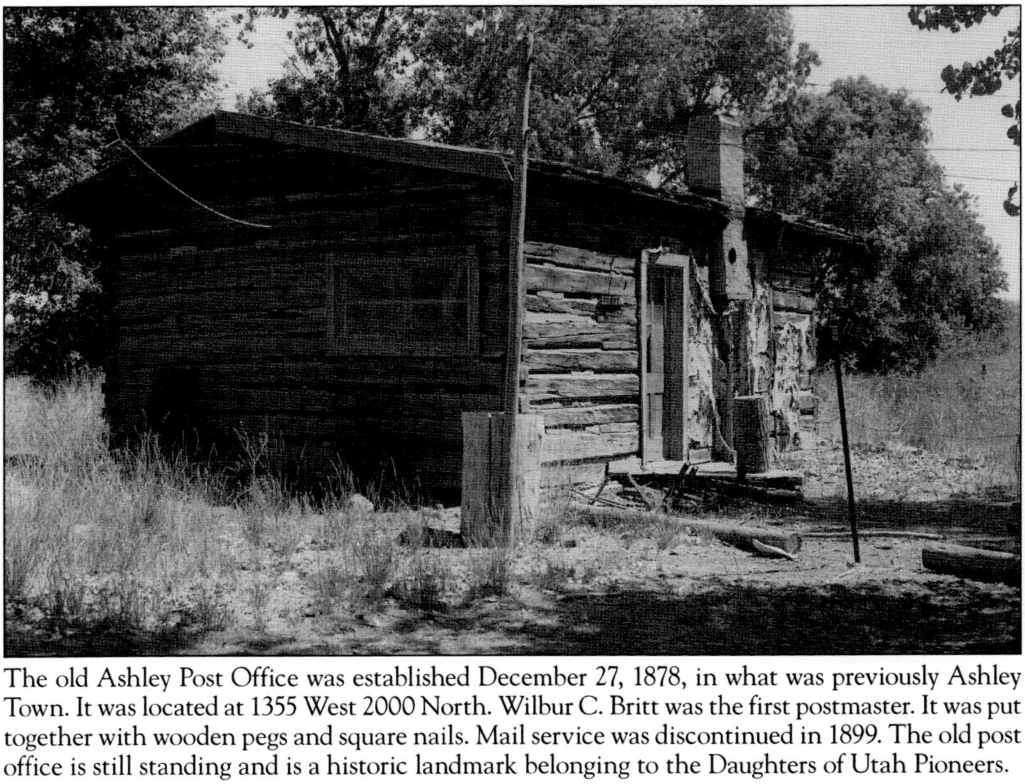

The old Ashley Post Office was established December 27, 1878, in what was previously Ashley Town. It was located at 1355 West 2000 North. Wilbur C. Britt was the first postmaster. It was put together with wooden pegs and square nails. Mail service was discontinued in 1899. The old post office is still standing and is a historic landmark belonging to the Daughters of Utah Pioneers.

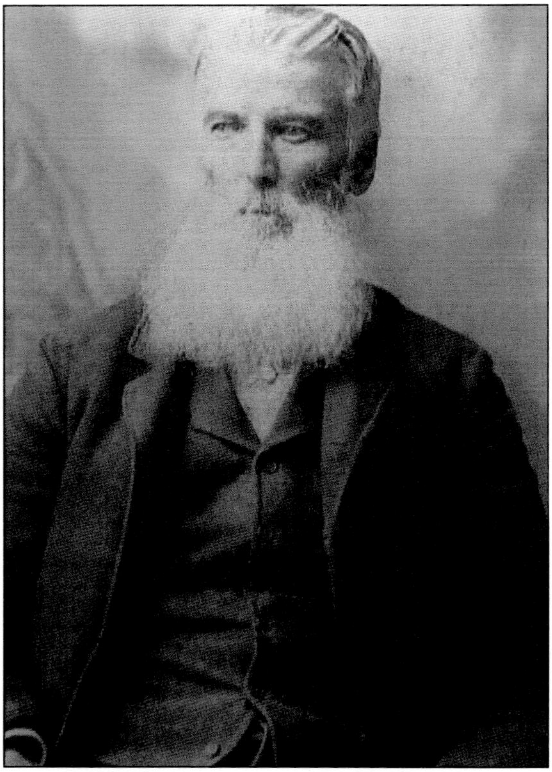

Matthew Caldwell served in the Mormon Battalion in 1847. He saw action in the Walker, Tintic, and Utah Black Hawk Wars. When he and his family arrived in the Ashley Valley, they made Mountain Dell their home. Matthew was appointed to be the first postmaster in that area. He was active in politics, being chairman of the Democratic Party in the community. Matthew was a polygamist with five wives. His fifth wife, Nancy Mariah Caldwell, lived with him in Mountain Dell. Matthew died at his home in Mountain Dell (Dry Fork). Many of his posterity remain in the valley.

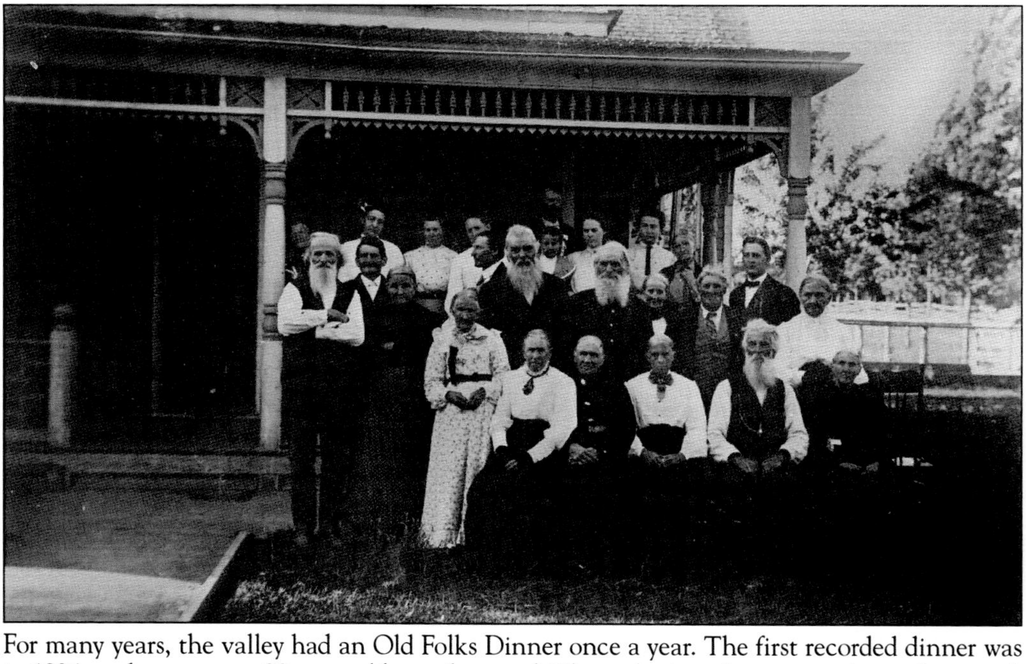

For many years, the valley had an Old Folks Dinner once a year. The first recorded dinner was in 1894, and guests over 80 years old were honored. The gathering places were always decorated, and a fine meal was served. Matthew Caldwell is pictured in this early Old Folks Dinner on the first row. Standing on the far left in the second row are Dr. Harvey Coe Hullinger and Clarisa Jane Taylor.

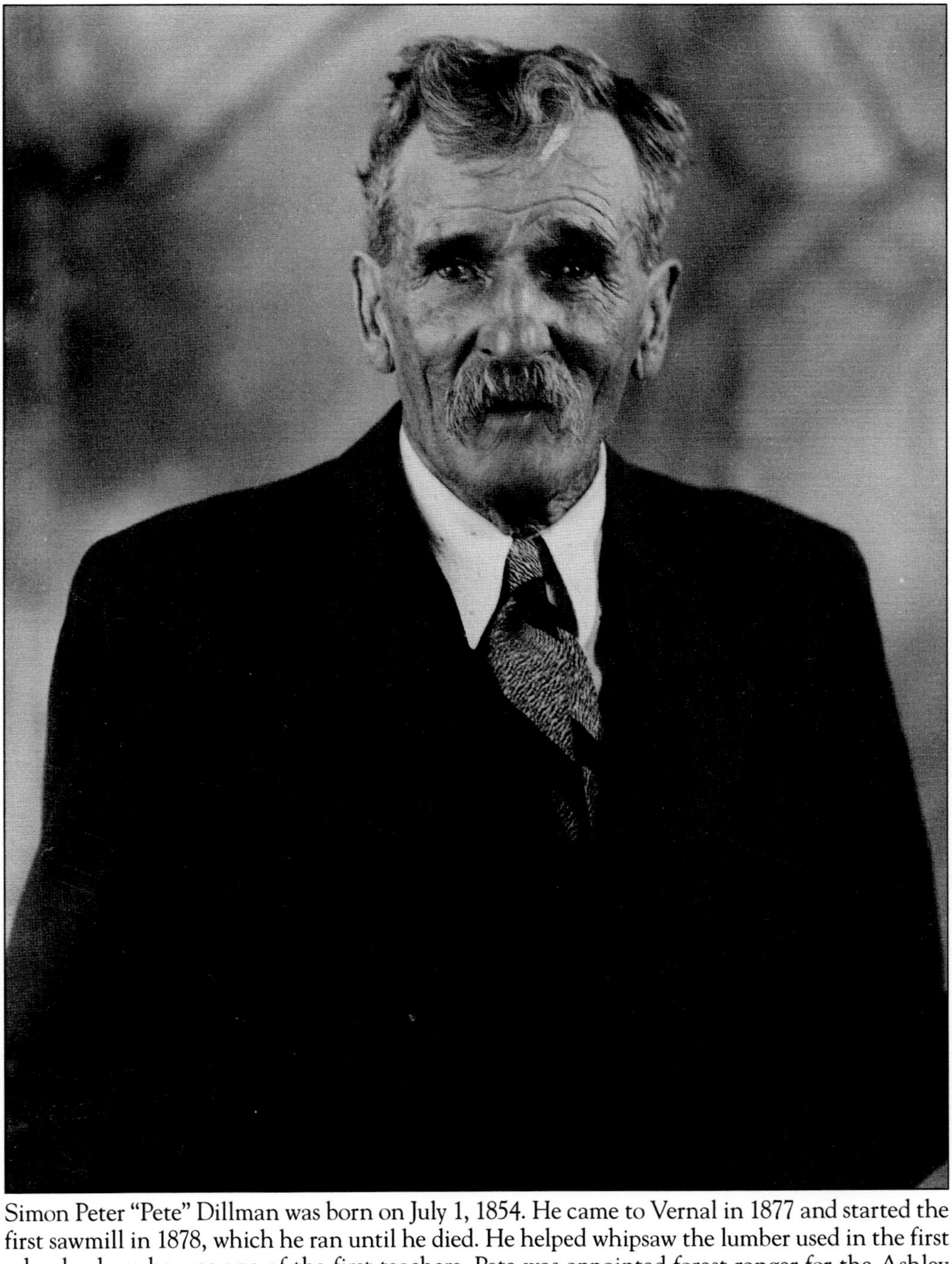

Simon Peter "Pete" Dillman was born on July 1, 1854. He came to Vernal in 1877 and started the first sawmill in 1878, which he ran until he died. He helped whipsaw the lumber used in the first school, where he was one of the first teachers. Pete was appointed forest ranger for the Ashley National Forest and was the first government Indian farm supervisor at Whiterocks. In 1884, he contracted and supervised building of the road from Fort Duchesne to Vernal. He owned the first drug store, which opened in 1886 on South Vernal Avenue. During the early days, he was instrumental in capturing outlaws in the area. Solomon Trim and Pete opened the first funeral parlor in Ashley Valley. Pete helped beautify the valley by planting numerous orchards and gardens. At 79 years old, he had his left leg amputated. He died August 1, 1939, at 85 years old.

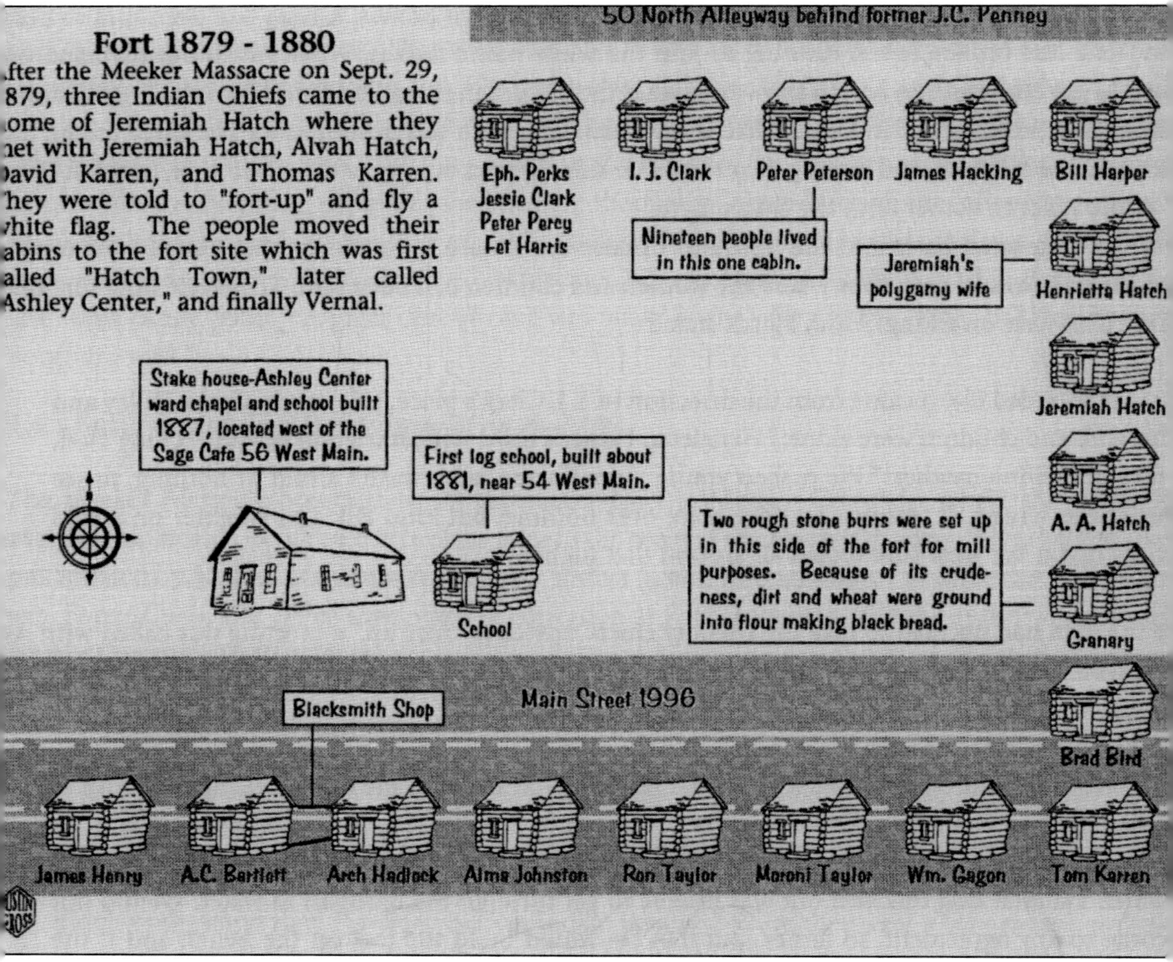

The Bench settlers selected their fort site. They took their log cabins apart and numbered the logs before reassembling them at the site. The plan was to place the houses in a square with 16-square-foot buttresses between the cabins, which would give them protection if any Indians attacked. Cedar posts were used to construct the buttresses. The people completed three sides of the square fort when the government gained control of the Indians; therefore, the fort was left in a U-shape. It was sometimes called "Fort Scared to Death." This rendition of the early fort in Vernal was created by Justin Gross in 1996, while he was working at the Regional History Center on the work-release program through Uintah High School.

Two

LAW AND ORDER

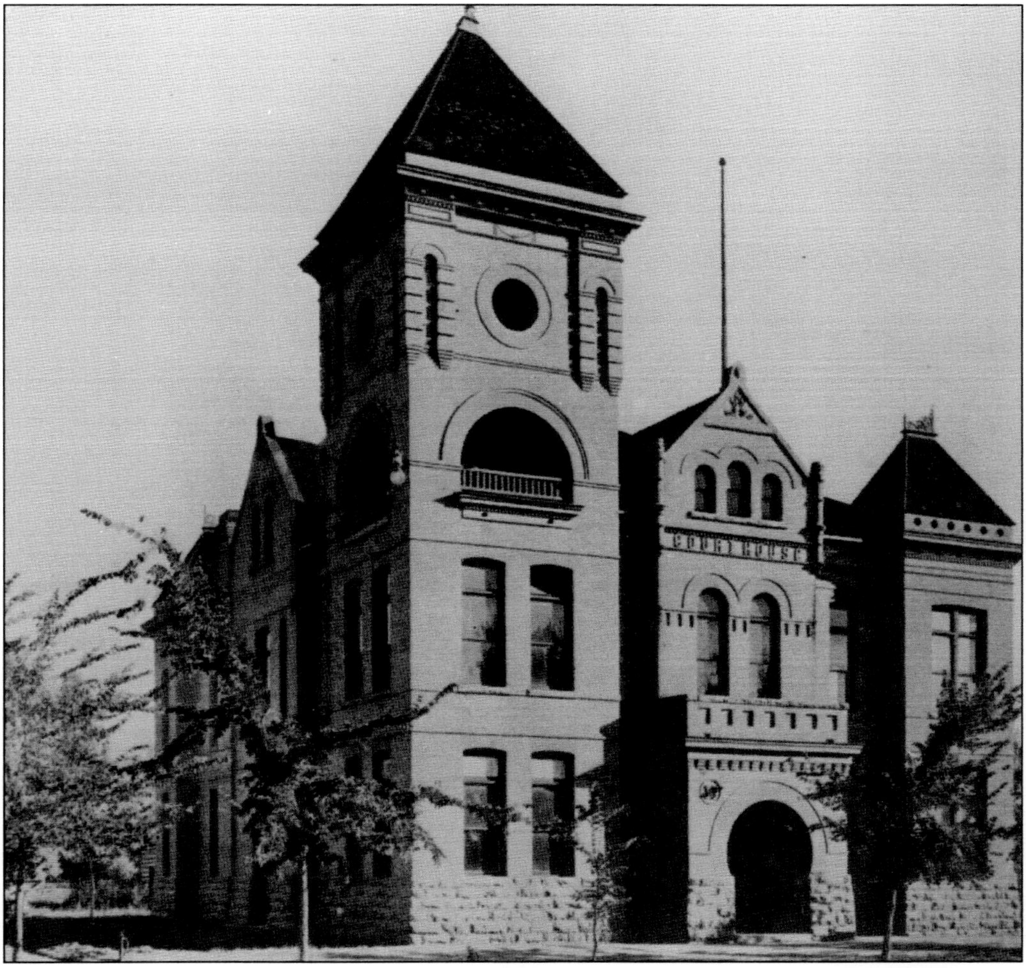

The Uintah County Courthouse was built in 1900. The two-story building was located around 150 East Main Street in Vernal. In 1910, the center of justice saw its first murder trial. For 59 years, the courthouse grounds were a community gathering spot. Picnics were common, and families and neighbors came together to celebrate events and share stories. In 1959, the courthouse was torn down and replaced with a new building.

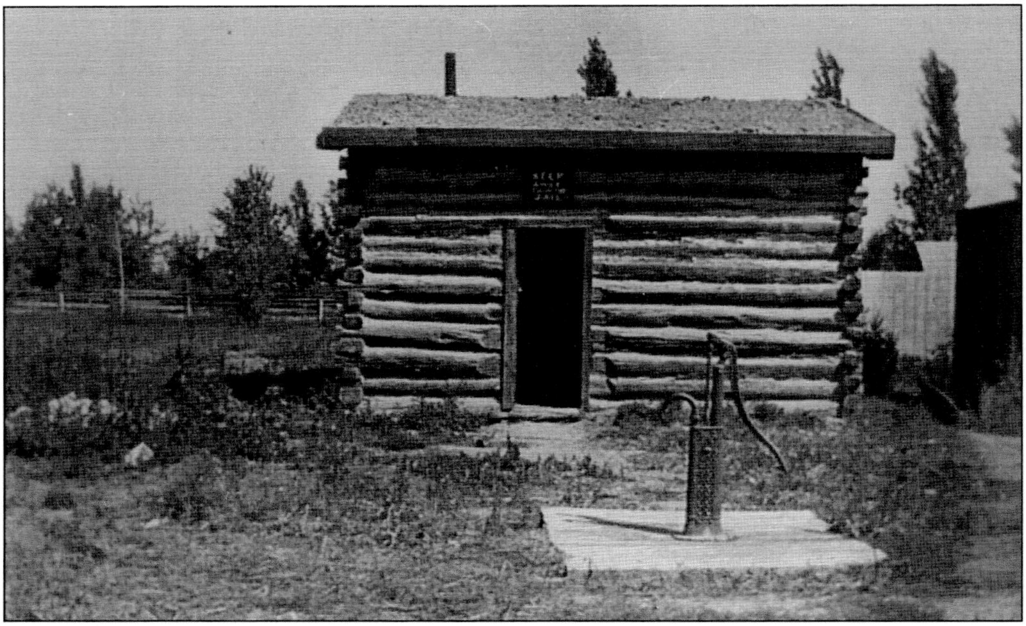

In 1887, logs and rocks were built around two iron cages, or cells, that were located in Ashley Town. The jail was in good condition except that weapons could be slipped through the windows or through an opening dug between the logs. Consequently, the sheriff was compelled to keep guard day and night when he had a prisoner. The sign over the door reads, "Keep away from the JAIL."

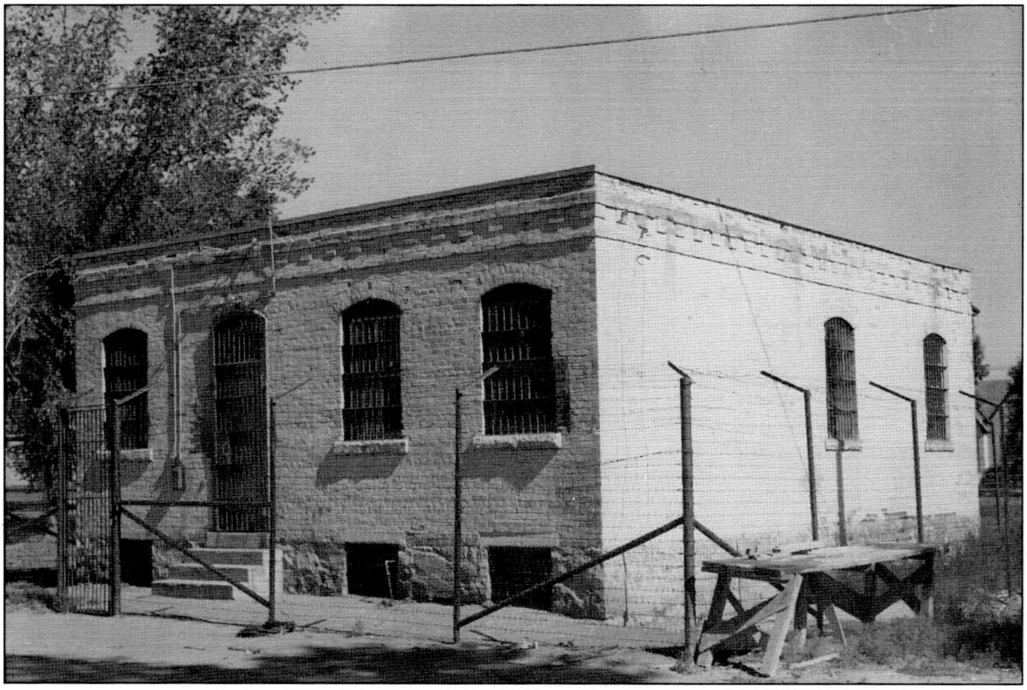

After the county seat was moved to Vernal, the old jail was taken apart and moved to the present courthouse grounds where it was used until this brick jailhouse was built in 1910. The new jail was used until the second courthouse was built in 1959. The jail was then housed within the courthouse, and the brick jail was torn down.

City Jail Burglarized and Between 100 and 200 Bottles of Booze Stolen

A week ago Sunday night the city jail was broken into and nearly 200 bottles of booze were taken therefrom. To be more specific, Sheriff Richardson claims the loss of 199 bottles from his vintage. City Marshal Byron Eaton deserves the credit of unearthing the whole affair, which as near as we can learn is as follows: On Sunday night, February 22, Don Crawley and Royal Potter broke into Hadlock's blacksmith shop and took therefrom a bolt cutter and proceeded to the city jail where they cut the lock and gained entrance to the stock of booze kept in the bastile.

They first fortified themselves by imbibing some of the goods, and then filled up a gunnysack and carried the stuff to the basement of the Vogue theatre, gaining entrance through an open door to the furnace room of the Uintah State Bank.

Marshal Eaton found the blacksmith shop broken into as he went his rounds early Monday morning and then found the bolt cutters at the rear of the Uintah State Bank. He knew something had happened, and soon after received word from the sheriff that the jail had been broken into.

Keeping a still head it was no long before he secured from Potte first and then young Crawley al the facts pertaining to the whol matter, together with informatio regarding the place where they ha concealed the liquor. Marshal Ea ton, as a result, has secured abou 50 or 60 full bottles and enoug broken bottles to make up about 100 but fails to find the other 99 whic the sheriff claims are lacking.

The case was turned over to th county, and Prosecuting Attorney Wallace Calder filed a crimina charge against Potter, to which h waived examination, and it is under stood he will plead guilty when h appears before Judge Morgan nex week for trial. The least sentenc the Judge cas impose for the crim charged is one year in the Stat Penitentiary.

Young Crawley will be handle by Juvenile Judge Hansen, on ac count of his age.

In the meantime the officers ex pect to haul in others connecte with the crime, as they have informa tion pointing to the guilt of othe more responsible persons.

This article ran in the *Vernal Express* in 1920.

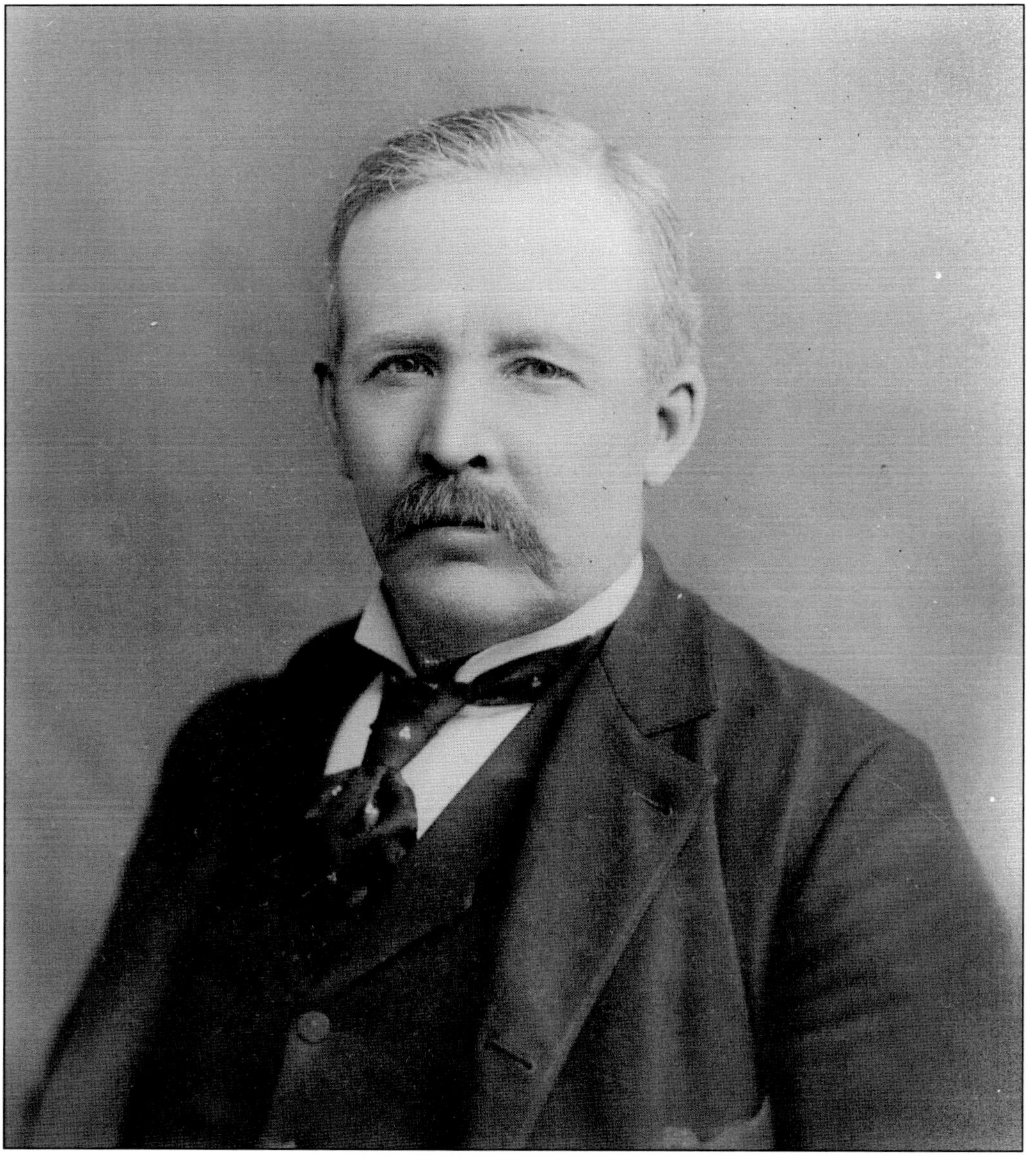

William "Billy" Gibson was born in April 1845, in Scotland, and came to America in 1852. When he was 19 years old, he married Mary Lambert. The couple had three children. He came to the Ashley Valley in 1877. When Uintah County was first formed in February 1880, Gibson was appointed constable and acting sheriff. William was a small man but was strong and fearless. He possessed extraordinary physical endurance, was a natural leader in adventures, and was the bitterest of foes to all lawbreakers. In November 1895, he was elected to the first legislature and participated in Utah becoming a state. William chose the site for his family's graveyard at the point in Steinaker Draw, where he had first viewed the Ashley Valley. William died on December 11, 1932, and went to rest at his chosen spot on the hill. When the Steinaker Dam was built, his grave was dug up, along with seven others. The bodies were relocated to the Vernal Cemetery.

John Theodore Pope was born in 1860, in Farmington, Utah. He married Charlotte Ann Stock in 1880 and came to the Ashley Valley in 1884. John was elected sheriff in 1890, and in 1895 he served as sheriff and city marshal. During Pope's time as sheriff, which also happened to be the worst outlaw times in the area, he had to kill some men to enforce the law while protecting himself. Due to money disputes with city officials, Pope resigned in 1899. He spent several years practicing law and later became involved in mining ventures. Pope was a hard man who stood alone against incredible odds. He used his guns and risked his life to bring civilization to a lawless time. Pope died on January 1, 1943. He was 83 years old.

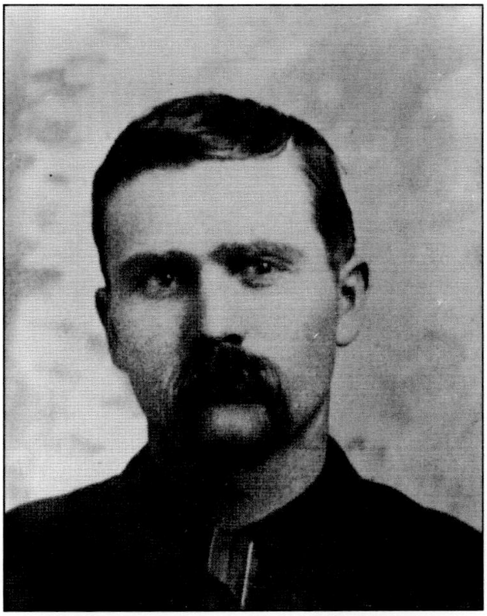

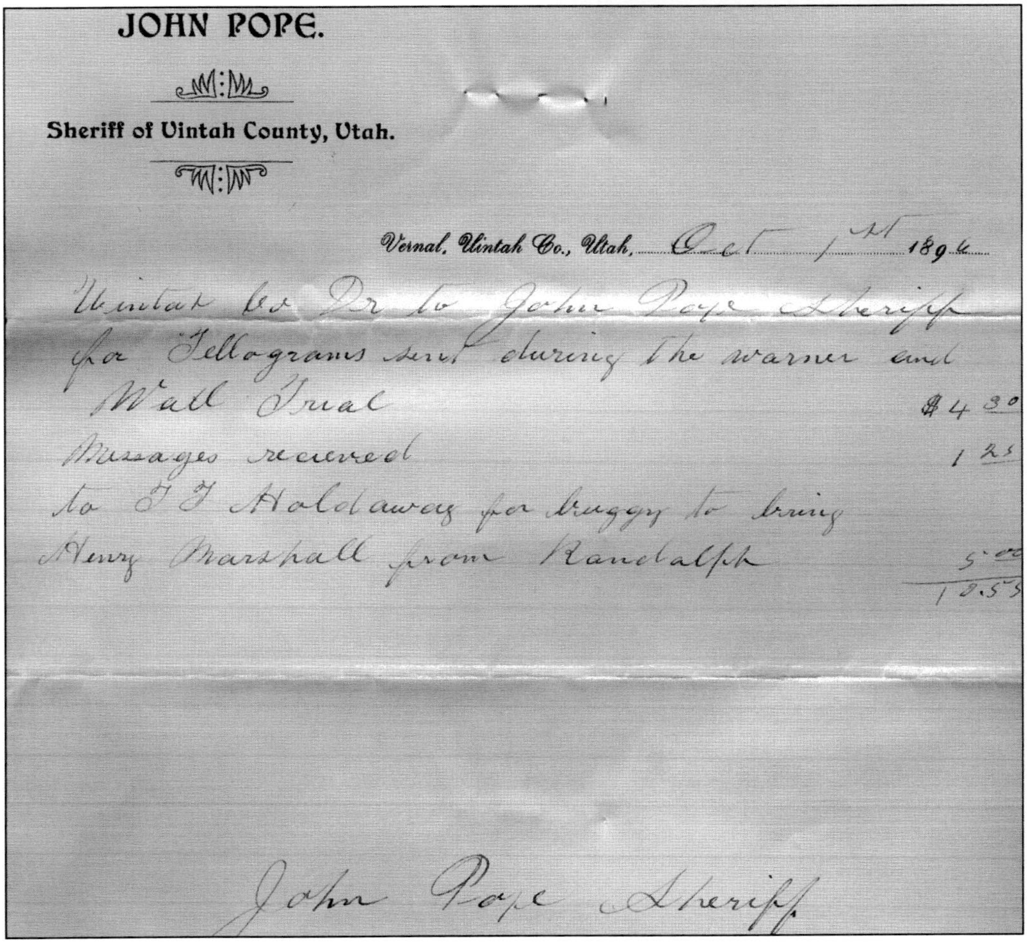

JOHN POPE.

Sheriff of Uintah County, Utah.

Vernal, Uintah Co., Utah, Oct 1st 1896

Uintah Co Dr to John Pope Sheriff
for Tellograms sent during the warner and
Wall Trial $4.30
Messages received 1.25
to T T Holdaway for buggy to bring
Henry Marshall from Randalph 5.00
10.55

John Pope Sheriff

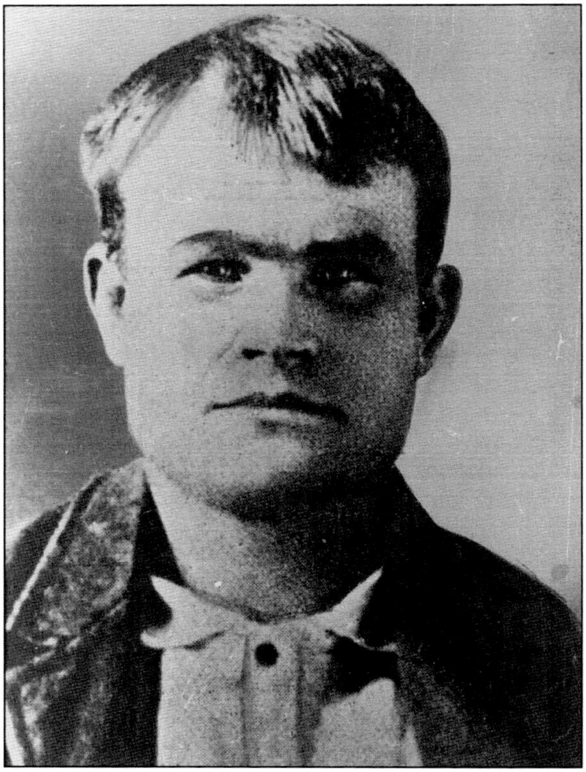

In the early days of the Ashley Valley, some notable outlaws spent their time in Vernal and surrounding areas. The most notorious of these outlaws were Butch Cassidy (left) and Elza Lay from the Wild Bunch. They frequented the Overholt and other saloons until the law came around, at which time they would leave town for a while. They were friends with many families in the valley. Allen and Matilda Davis, along with their children, were close friends with the two outlaws—even hiding them and assisting in their getaways from the law. Elza married their eldest daughter, Maude; the Lays later divorced.

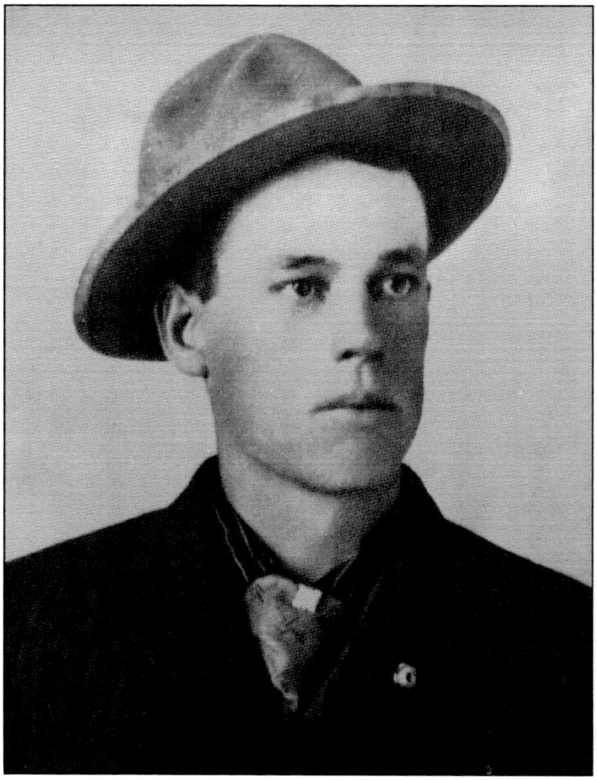

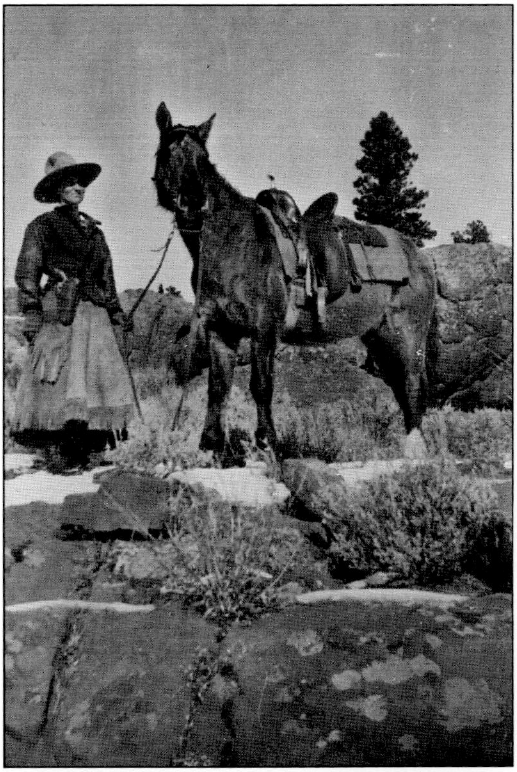

Ann Bassett Willis (right), known as Queen Ann, and Josie Bassett Morris were the notorious "Bassett Sisters" who came into the Brown's Park area in 1878. They bordered on the outlaw life and were friends with many who led such lives . Ann became interested in cattle at an early age and was later deemed "Queen of the Cattle Rustlers." She married Frank Willis and passed away in 1956. Josie attempted married life five times before settling on single life in the log cabin she built near Jensen, Utah. She lived there alone for 50 years. She took care of her own needs, including killing and dressing out wild game and, occasionally, a stray cow that wandered by. She made and bootlegged whiskey but claimed to have never consumed it. Josie died in May 1964.

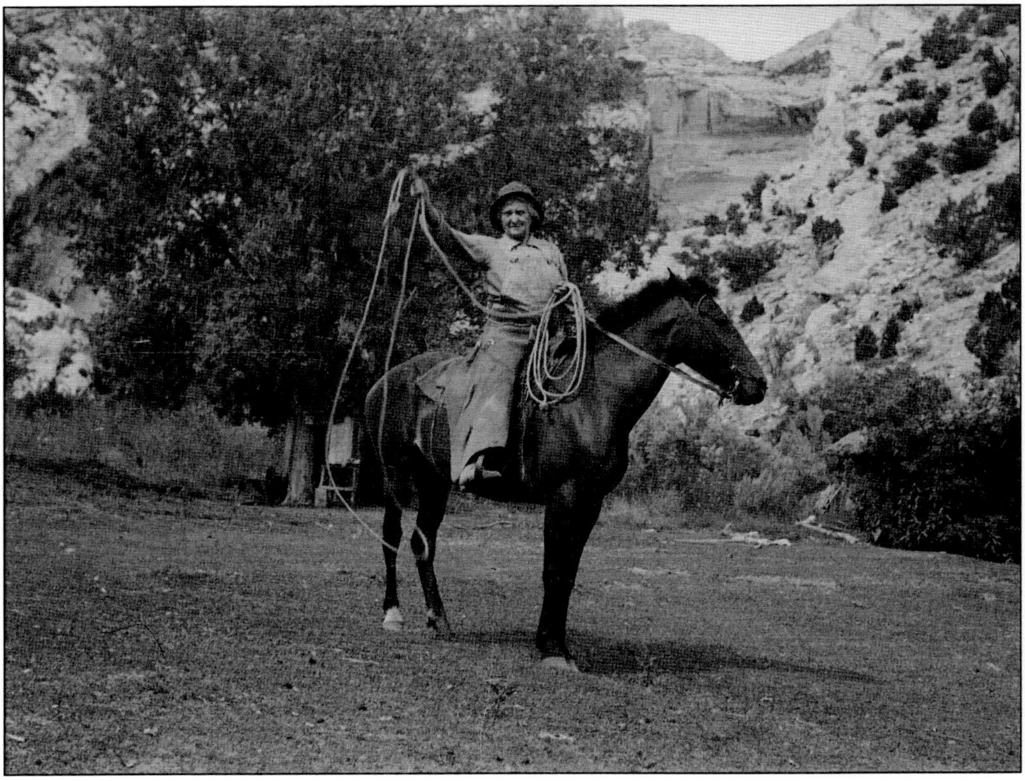

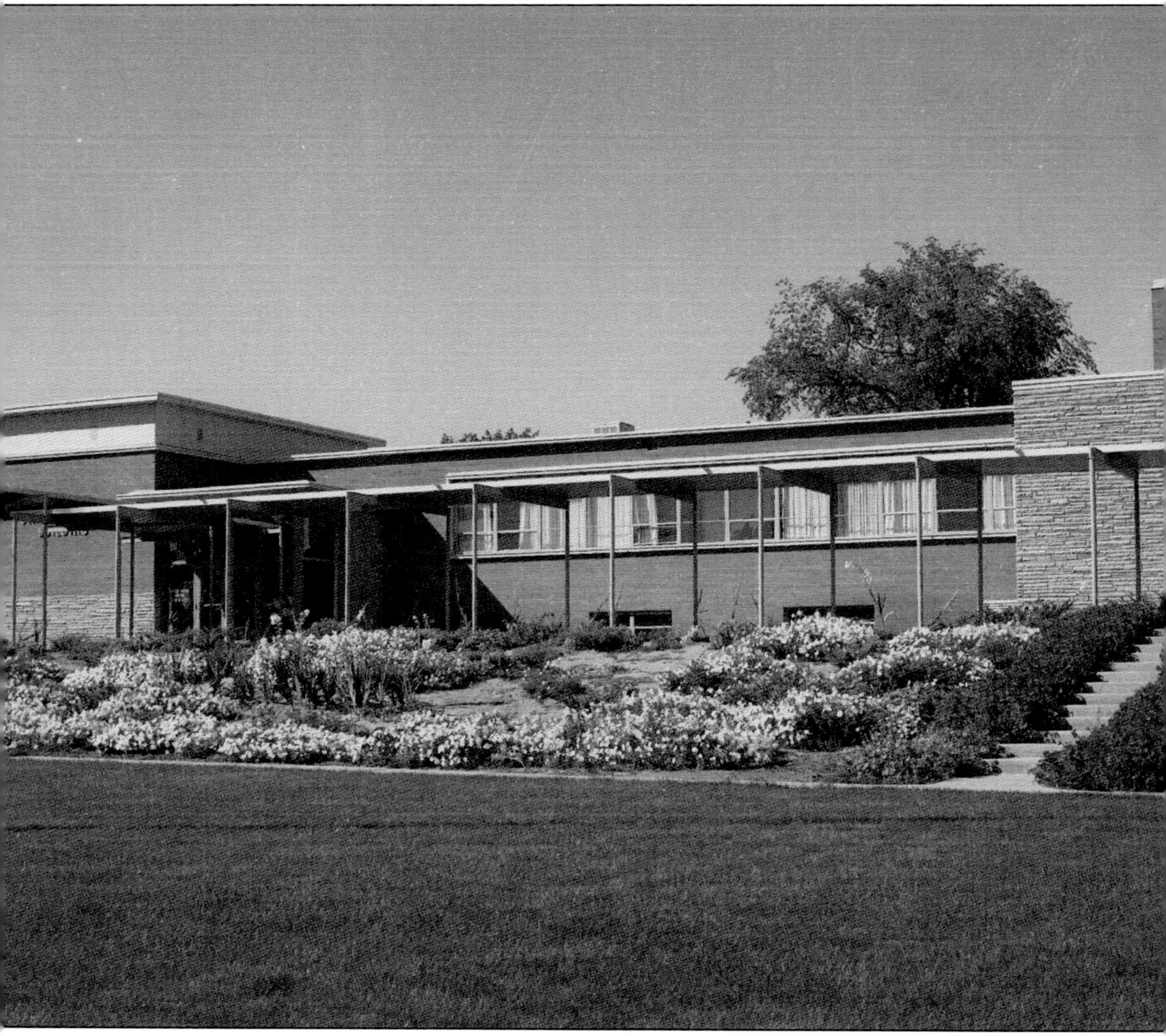

In June 1959, Uintah County's new $394,000 courthouse was dedicated. The structure replaced the old building that was erected in 1900. With the old courthouse removed and landscaping complete, the courthouse and the Utah Field House Museum made an imposing addition to Vernal City. They are both located on Main Street, also known as Highway 40. The new building represented many years of planning and unselfish work by leaders of the county.

Three

Land of Opportunity

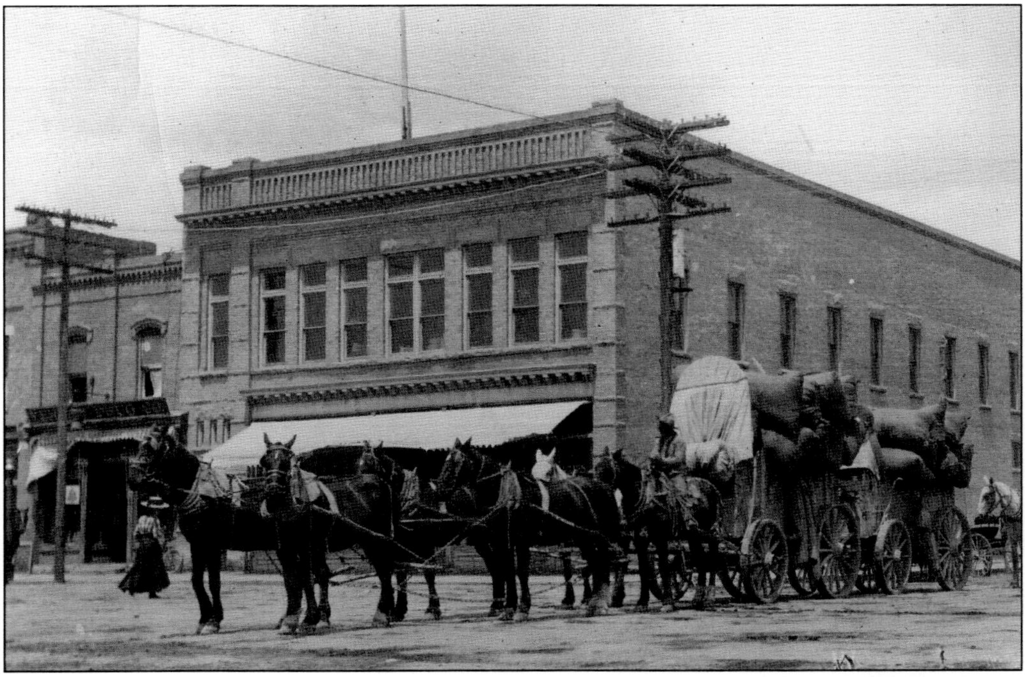

Shortly after the first settlers came to the valley, it was evident that the sheep industry could be a favorable source of wealth. Sheep husbandry was one of the main industries for the area during the early 1900s. Here, horse-drawn freight wagons loaded with wool pass through the Vernal Avenue–Main Street intersection in 1912. The wagonloads of wool were taken to Watson, Utah, where they were loaded onto the Uintah Railway; the Ashley Co-op is seen in the background.

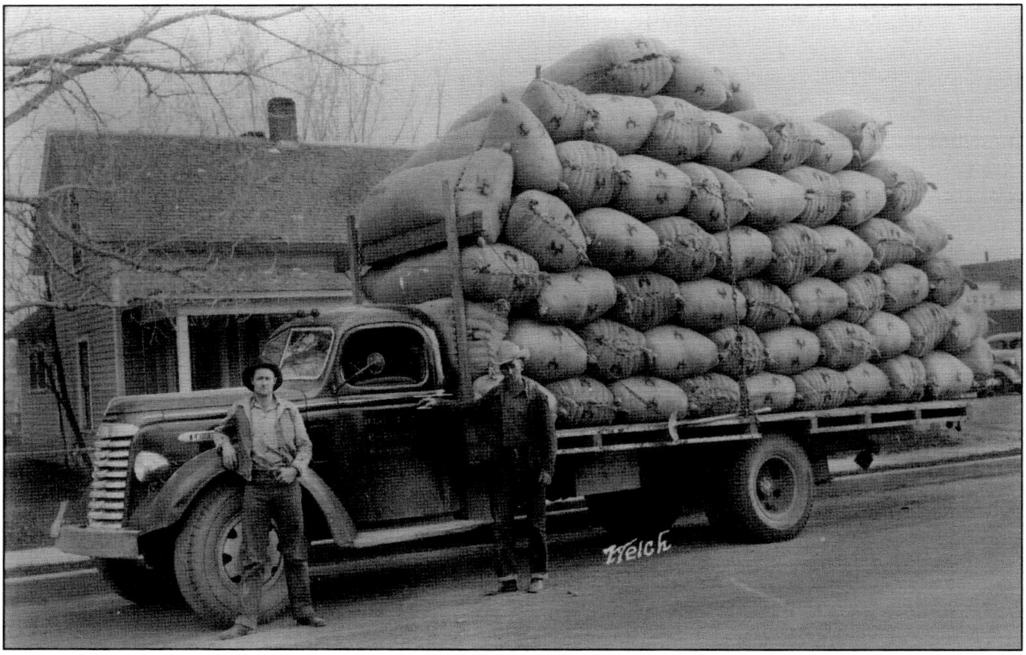

Wool was later freighted by truck. The wool was driven to Price, Utah, or Craig, Colorado, where it was loaded onto train cars. Truck drivers Acel Rowley (left) and Lynn Hall stand next to a truckload of wool. (Courtesy of Myke Hall.)

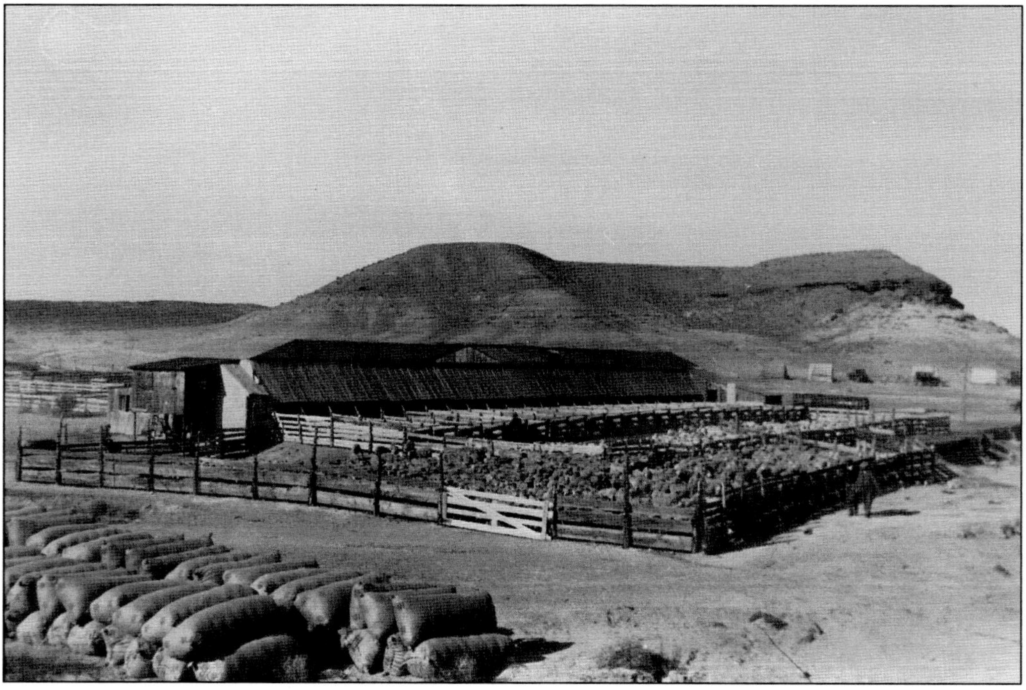

Sheep men took their herds to sheepshearing plants in the spring. Many sheepshearers came into the valley to work at the large plants along with local shearers. A good shearer turned out an average of 175 sheep a day. The Alhandra Shearing Plant was near the Green River and was one of the larger operation plants.

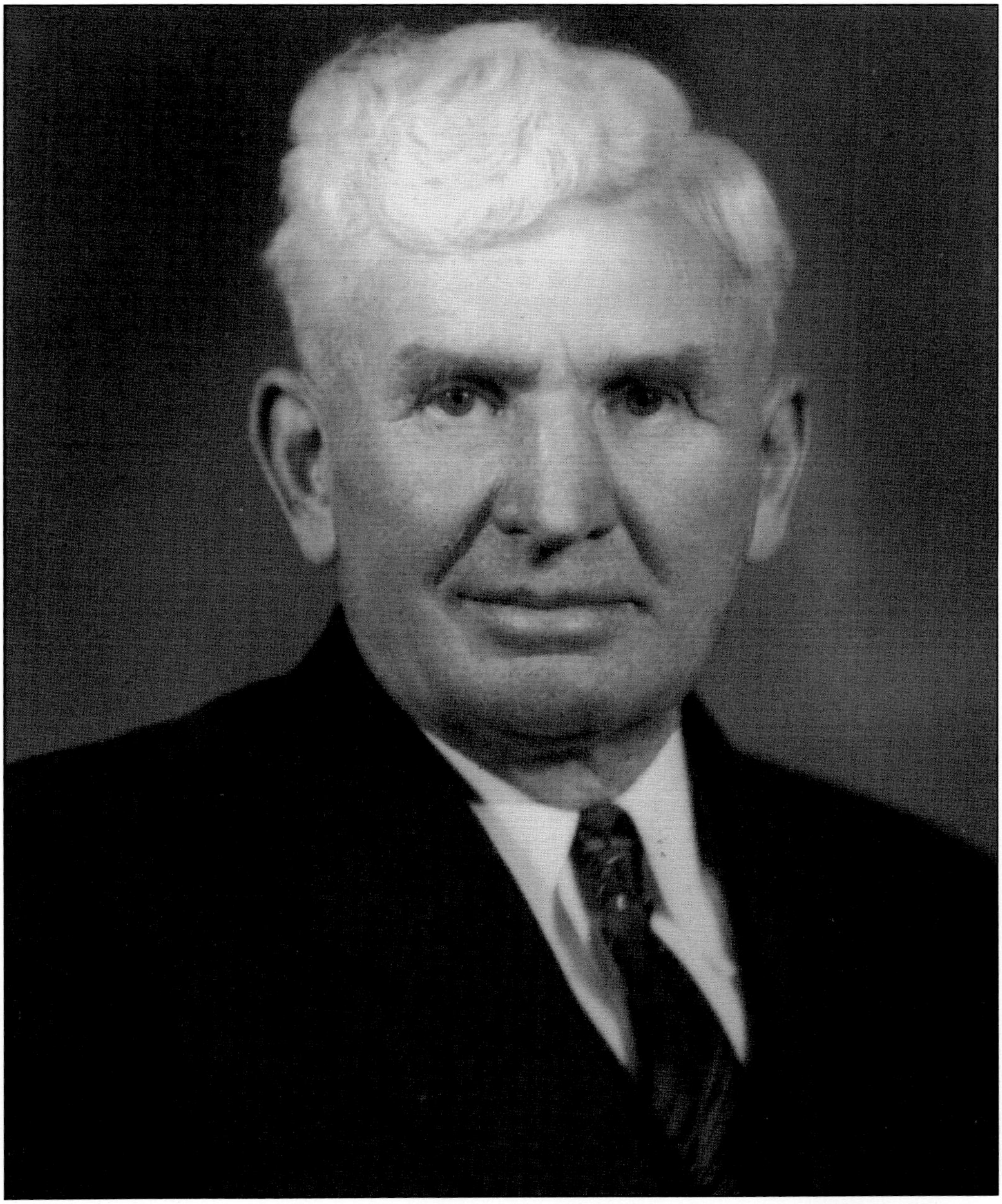

William Siddoway came to the Ashley Valley in 1888, at 20 years old. He married Emily Dunster, and they had nine children. William was very involved in the sheep industry, and he served on the county and state levels of the Wool Growers Association. Other woolgrowers economically benefitted from William's effort in negotiating better prices for local wool clips. He obtained one of the first grazing permits, allowing him to run 9,000 sheep on the forest and Bureau of Land Management lands. Besides the sheep business, William was one of the incorporators of Vernal Milling Company, Vernal Power and Light Company, Vernal Drug Company, Vernal Amusement Company, Uintah Abstract Company, and the Leslie Ashton Hardware Company. At the time of his funeral, Walter Woolley said there was not a public building in Vernal during that time without his time, money, and ingenuity invested in it. He was a county commissioner and served as president of the board of education for 20 years. William died in 1950.

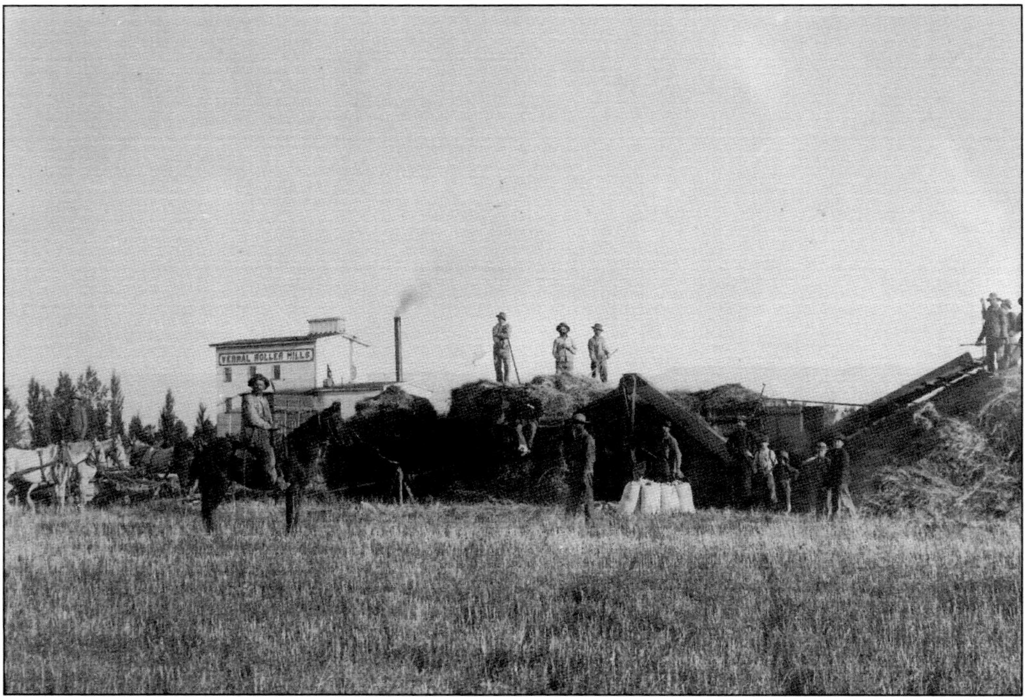

Farming was an important industry in the area, including raising grain. The farmer depended on the grain crop to supply his family with flour; it was also used as feed for livestock. During the fall, the wheat was cut, shocked, and left to dry. Many hauled their grain to large piles where it was then threshed. The valley had several horse-powered threshing machines, but many were steam-powered. After the grain was threshed, it was placed in gunnysacks or granaries. Much of the grain was taken to mills, such as the Vernal Roller Mill.

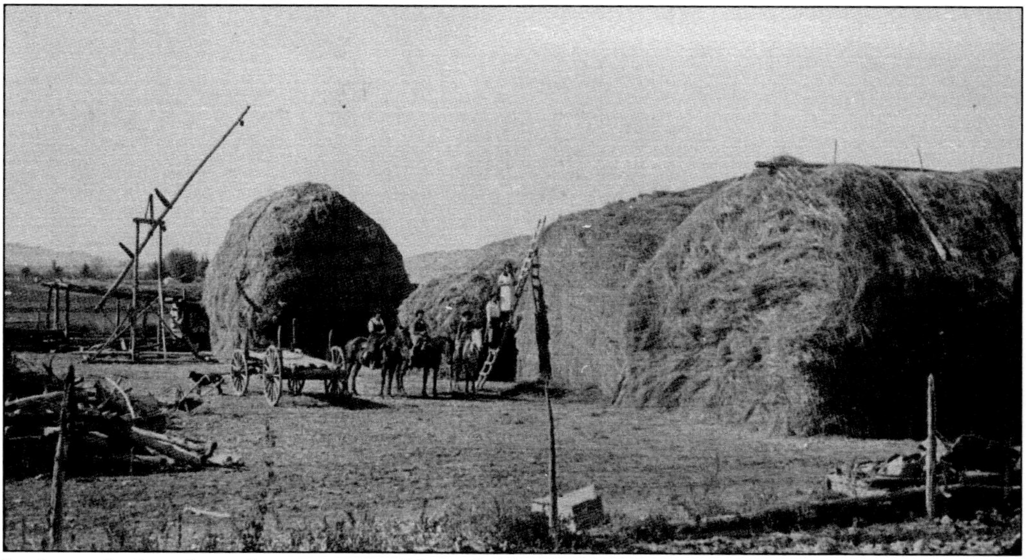

In the early days, loose hay was moved from fields on wagons. The hay was piled into large stacks with the use of a hay derrick (seen at far left). There were several types of derricks used in the valley, such as a Jackson hay fork, a tripod derrick, a crane derrick, and an A-frame derrick, which became the most popular for local farmers.

William Pitt Reynolds was born April 3, 1816, and came to the Ashley Valley in 1880. He and his sons built the first flour mill. He served a term as county prosecuting attorney and was a prominent man in the community. Reynolds died on November 13, 1900.

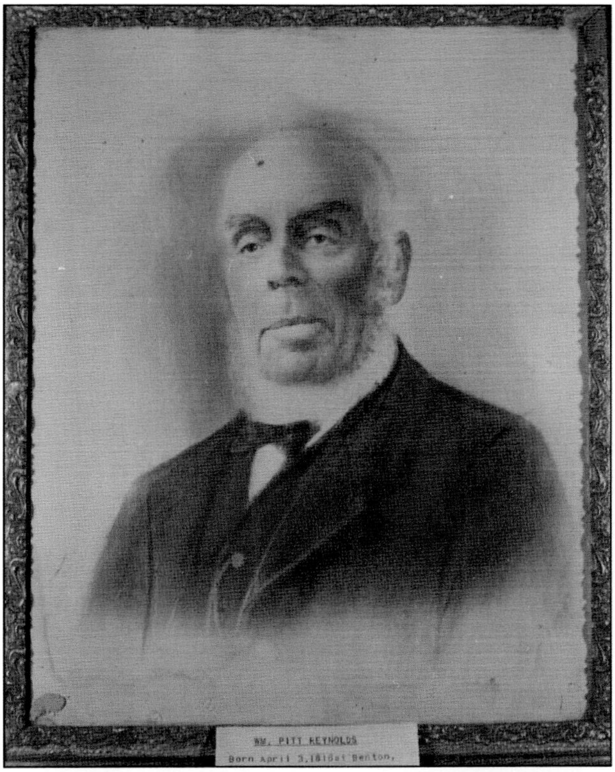

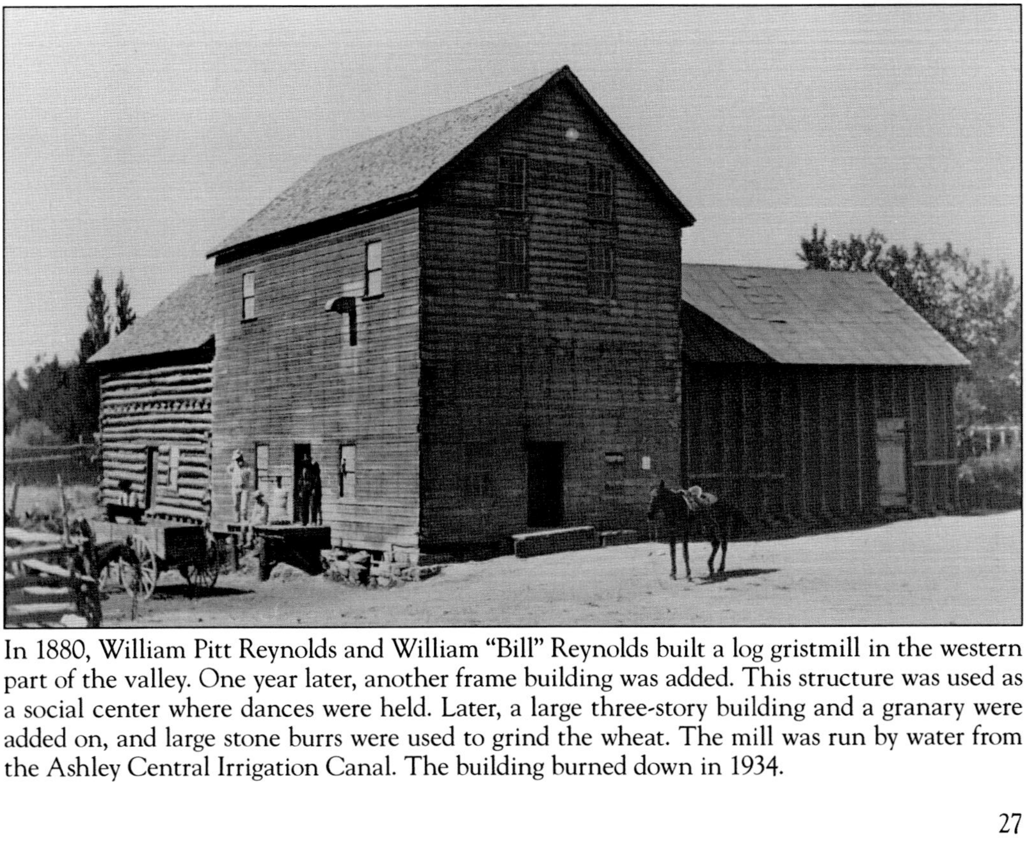

In 1880, William Pitt Reynolds and William "Bill" Reynolds built a log gristmill in the western part of the valley. One year later, another frame building was added. This structure was used as a social center where dances were held. Later, a large three-story building and a granary were added on, and large stone burrs were used to grind the wheat. The mill was run by water from the Ashley Central Irrigation Canal. The building burned down in 1934.

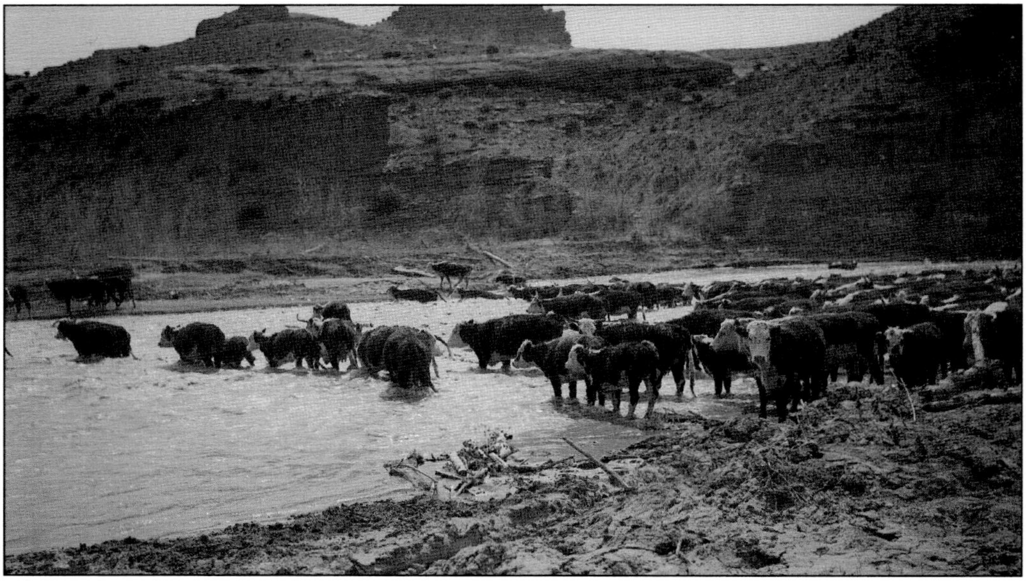

The cattle industry was well established as early homesteaders, such as Pardon Dodds and John Blankenship, brought cattle into the valley. They found the Ashley Valley was a fertile place with an abundance of feed and water, which made it ideal for grazing their livestock on the open range. In early days, livestock was marketed as feeder stock, where the stock was fattened and shipped to Eastern and Western markets. The completion of Highway 40 promised opportunities for local people to fatten their own stock and sell directly to buyers. They used local feeds and made sales at local livestock shows. The first Uintah Basin Livestock Show was held in 1938. Alvin Weeks was the first president, and the event was a great success. Judges and attendees claimed it to be the best in the state. More than 200 entries were entered in the show from surrounding areas in the basin.

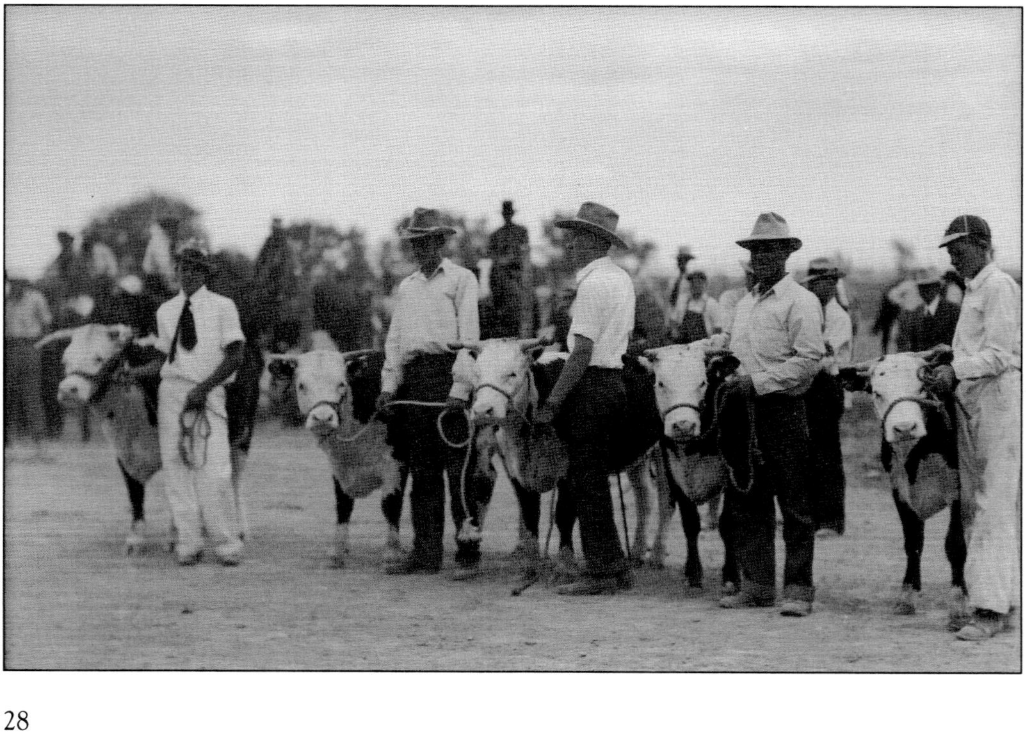

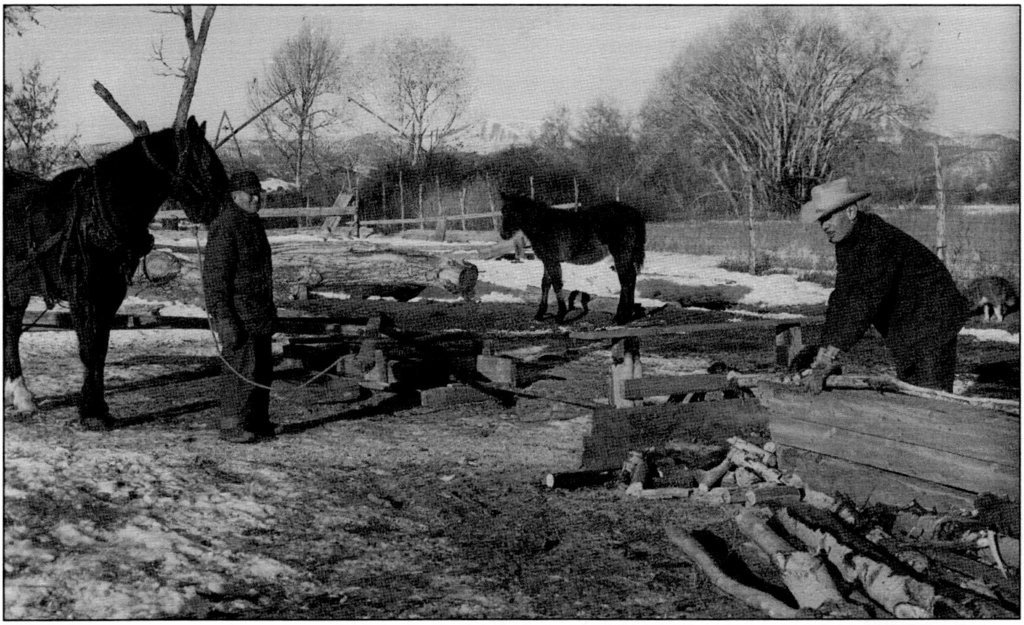

In 1962, a 44-year-old horse-powered machine was still performing for Allen Jones (left) and his son Darrell as they cut lumber. The horse is attached to a long pole and walks in a circle providing a one-horsepower motor that turns a wheel system and drives a circular saw or any other attachment. The Jones farm is located at 1314 North 2500 West, Vernal, Utah.

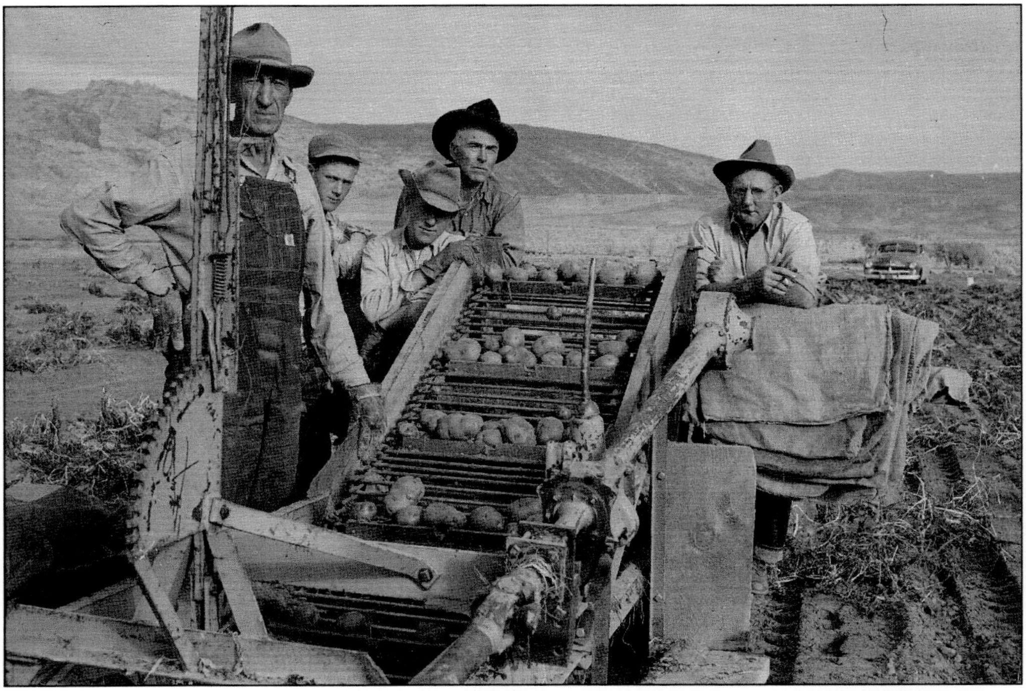

Potato digging became easier for Bob (left) and Neal Thorne in 1953, when they built a contraption on the end of their potato digger. Instead of the potatoes dropping onto the ground from the digger, they would go from the digger into a box where they traveled up an elevated belt that loosened the dirt, and then dropped into a bag. The digger was able to bag 500 pounds a day.

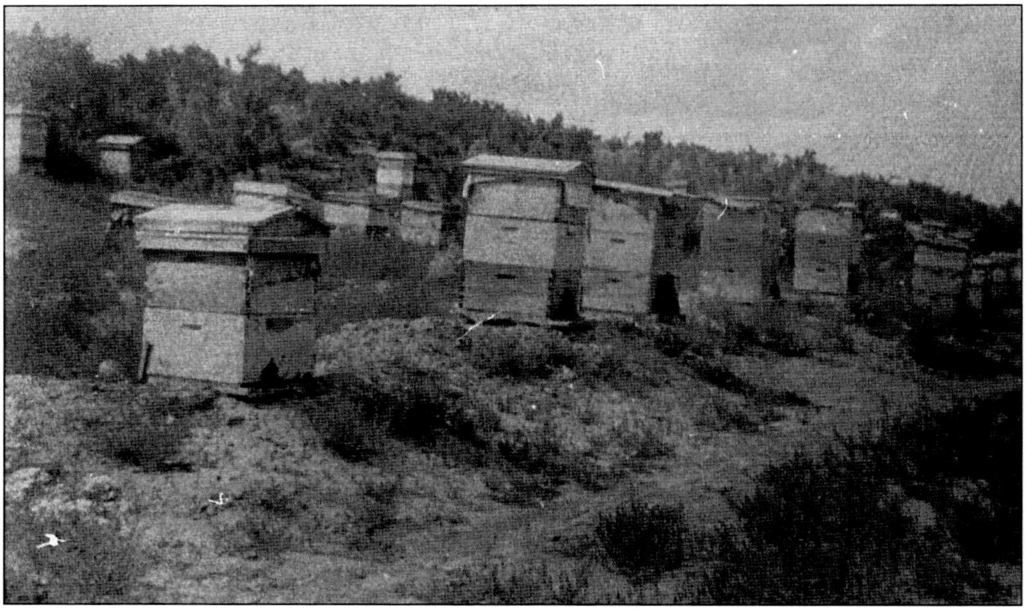

Before the 1900s, the bee industry was one of the main sources of wealth in the area. The honey that was produced among the finest of quality and flavor in the world. In 1896, the county bee inspector encouraged all beekeepers to form an association to discuss the best methods of handling bees. In early 1900, they extracted over 318,300 pounds of honey. In 1913, they extracted over 600,000 pounds of honey, valued at $30,000. The International Beekeeper's Association awarded Vernal first prize for its honey on various occasions. In 1943, Byron Goodrich, Mr. Vernon, Joseph Yack, and William Turner operated large apiaries. Below, Goodrich is selling honey from the back of his pickup truck.

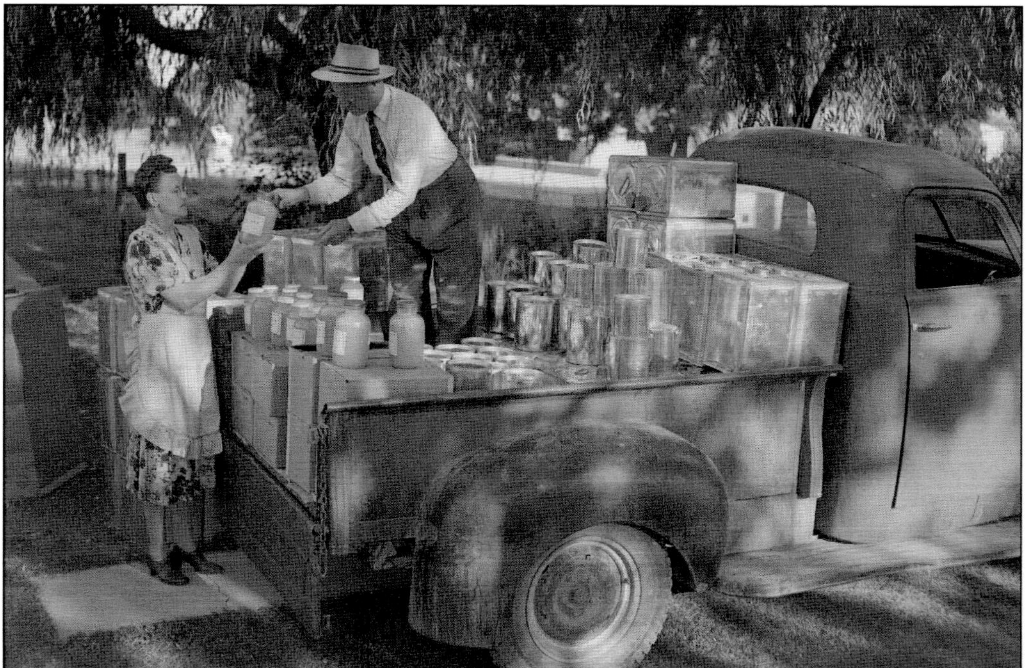

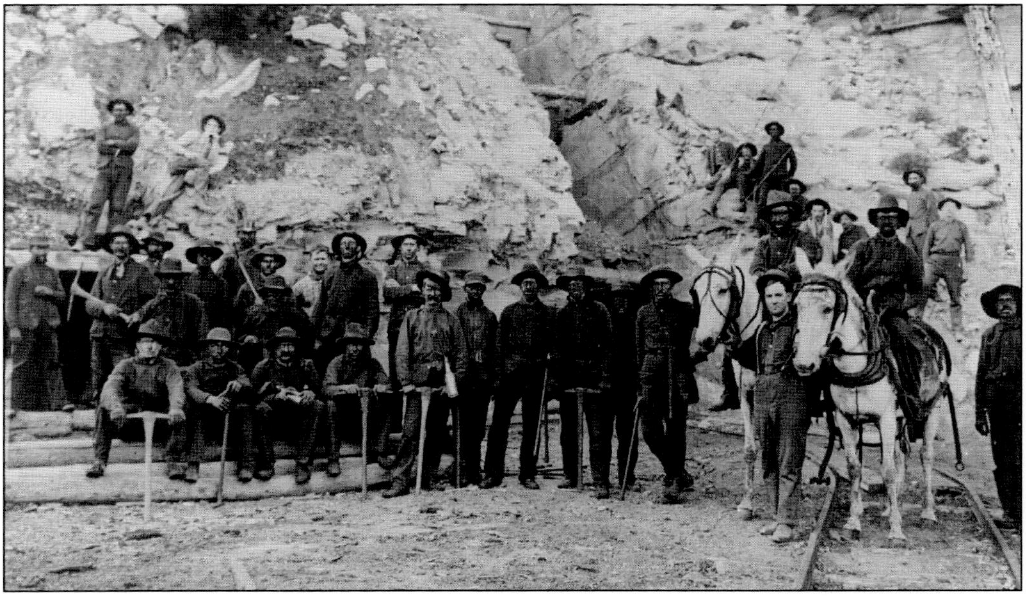

In 1908, Gilsonite miners pose for a group photograph near the Black Dragon Mine in Dragon, Utah. Many early residents worked at the Gilsonite mines south of the Ashley Valley. Gilsonite is a solid hydrocarbon that is found in deep narrow veins. It has a similar appearance to coal, but instead of burning, it melts into a rubbery substance. It is used in many different products such as shingles, ink, and rubber. Gilsonite can only be found in large quantities in the Uinta Basin and is still mined today by the American Gilsonite Company.

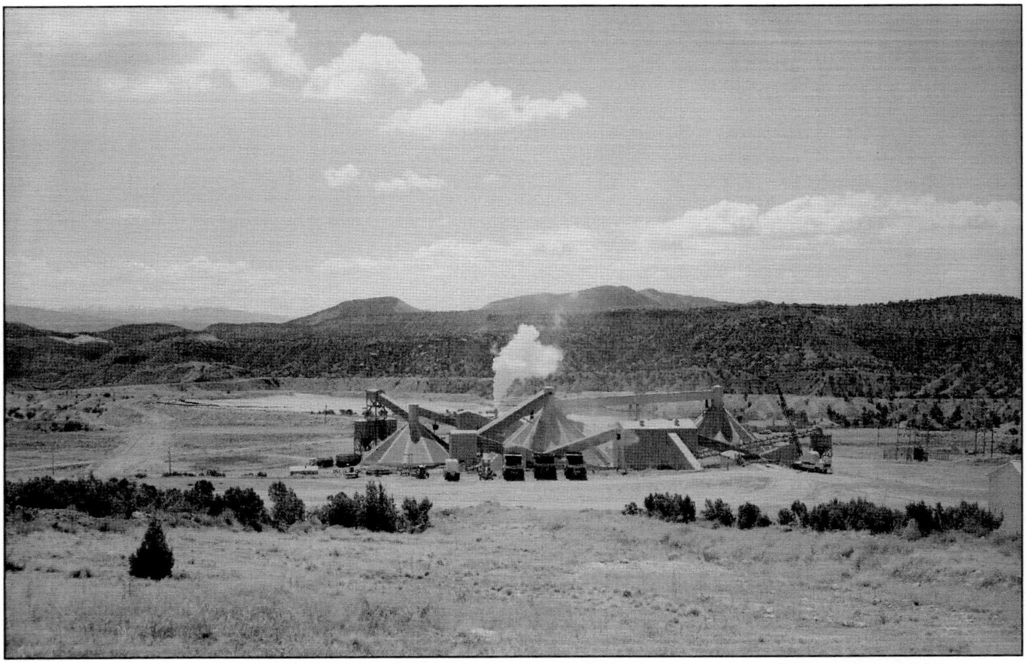

The San Francisco Chemical Phosphate Plant opened for operation in December 1960; it was located 15 miles north of Vernal in the Brush Creek area. The plant began working three shifts, 24 hours a day, and was hauling 35 to 50 tons of ore an hour. The phosphate plant was later bought by Stauffer Chemical and is now owned by the J.R. Simplot Company.

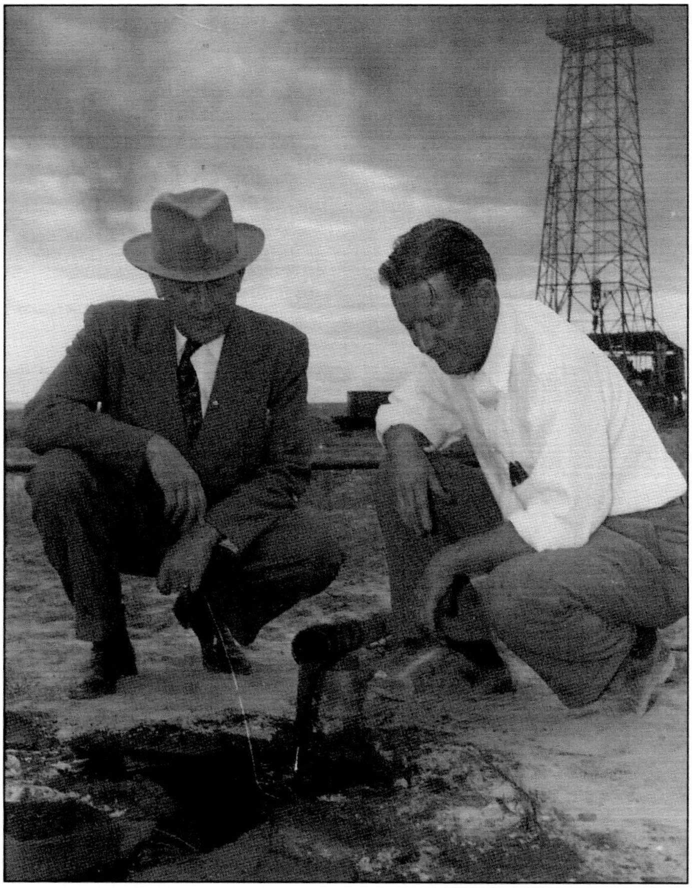

Drilling for oil in the Ashley Valley began in 1900, when John Pope drilled the first well 1,000 feet deep, but there was no promise of success. Through the years, others drilled and began to see some results. In 1925, a 10-million-cubic-foot gas gusher was struck between Vernal and Jensen near Ashley Creek. The Ashley Field was the first major producer of gas in the county and in Eastern Utah. Other rich mineral resources, such as oil, oil shale, tar sands, phosphate, and asphalt, have been discovered along with natural gas. The rich minerals of the Ashley Valley have provided both positive and negative experiences in the economical development of the valley. In 1948, J.L. Douglan (left) and J.W. Collins watch as rich, dark oil runs from a pipeline.

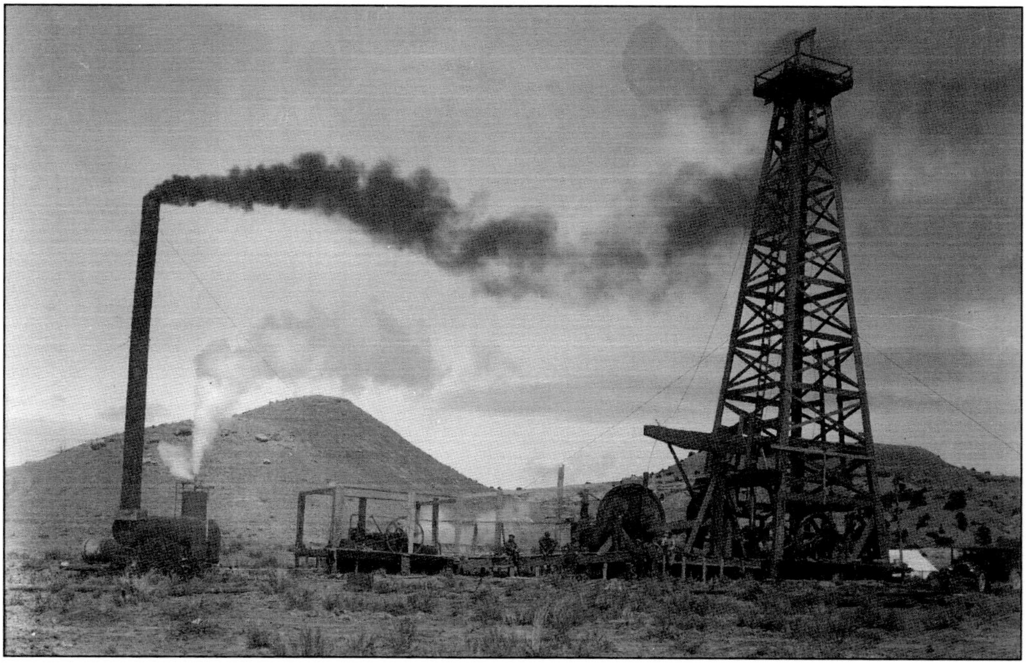

Four

Growth and Prosperity

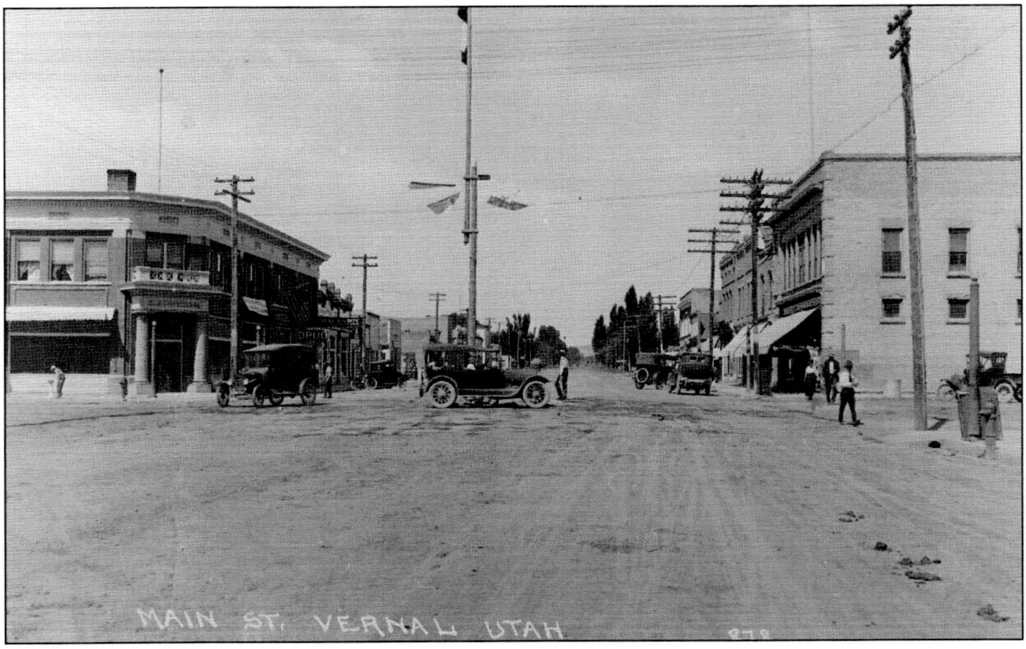

Uintah and Vernal Avenues formed the main intersection of Vernal. This was the center of business and a busy place for people to shop and visit with neighbors. This Main Street photograph is looking west with the Bank of Vernal and the Coltharp Building on the left and the Ashley Co-op on the right. Uintah Avenue was later renamed Main Street.

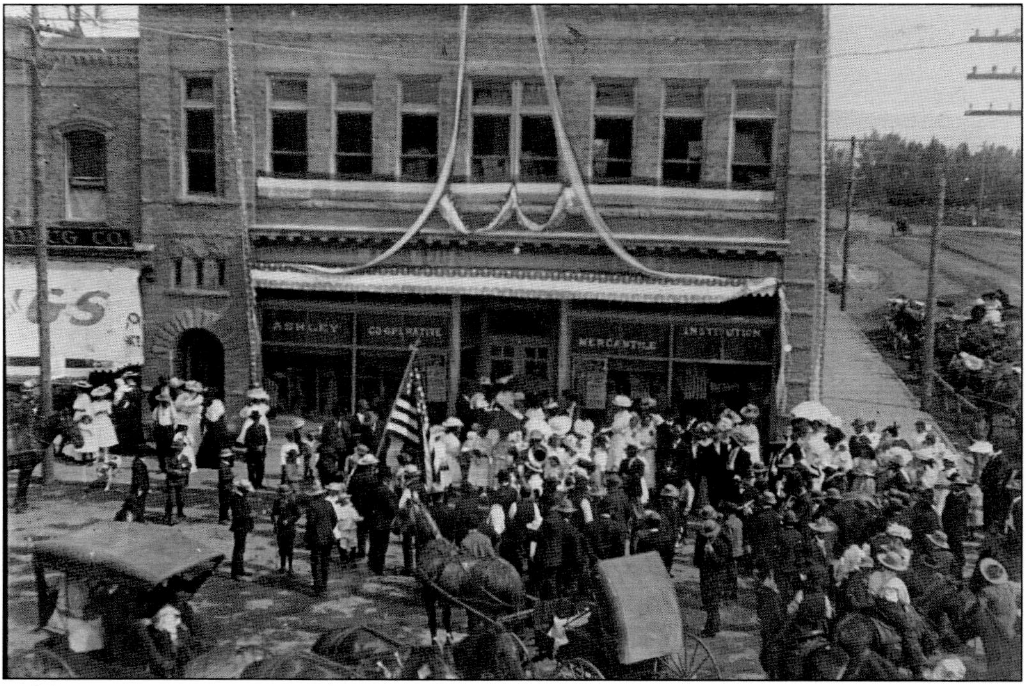

Ashley Co-operative Mercantile was the foremost business in the valley and located in the heart of town. It was first built in 1881 as a one-story log structure. The company replaced this with a rock building; in 1900, it was rebuilt into a two-story brick edifice that is still standing today. The store not only sold general merchandise, but it also acted as Vernal's first bank. The original incorporators were Samuel R. Bennion, George Davis, Enos Bennion, Charles Bartlett, Jeremiah Hatch Sr., Margaret Caldwell, Nellie Ashton, Leslie Ashton, William Ashton, Lynn Ashton, George Davis Merkley, Nelson Merkley, Nathan C. Davis, James Hacking, Charles Carter, Josephine Carter, Isabella Davis, George Billings, Margaret Carroll, and Elizabeth Guymon. The Ashley Co-op rented space to various businesses such as Vernal Drug, Vernal Express, Leslie Ashton Hardware, and many others. (Ashley Co-operative token courtesy of Lee Cheves.)

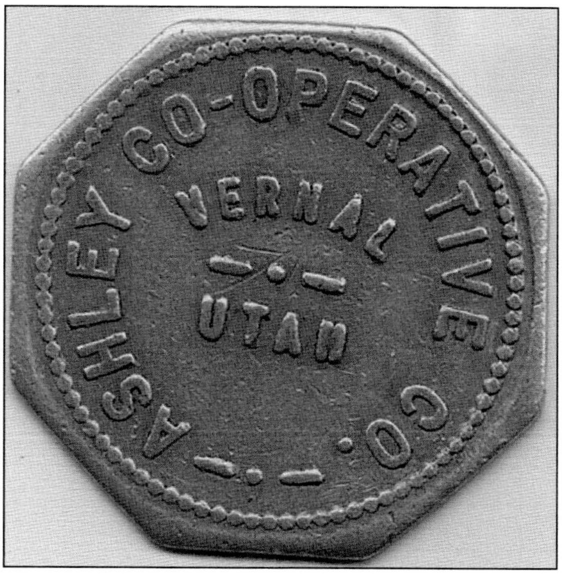

Leo C. Thorne was born in 1883. In 1906, he began his long career in photography when he began developing film. In 1907, Thorne purchased a studio and never looked back. Not only did he photograph people, but he also traveled the valley photographing anything and everything. He was a charter member of the Lions Club and a civic leader of the community. Leo played an important part in Ashley Valley and surrounding areas by capturing local history through photographs. His daughter and son-in-law continued the photography business after Leo passed in 1969.

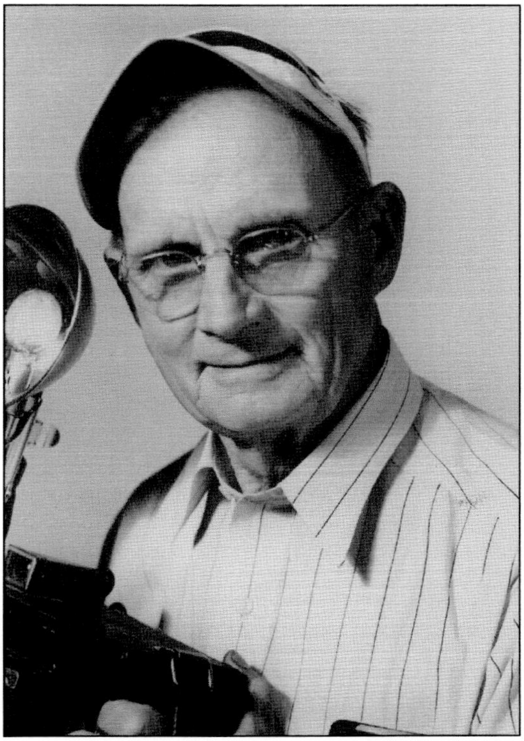

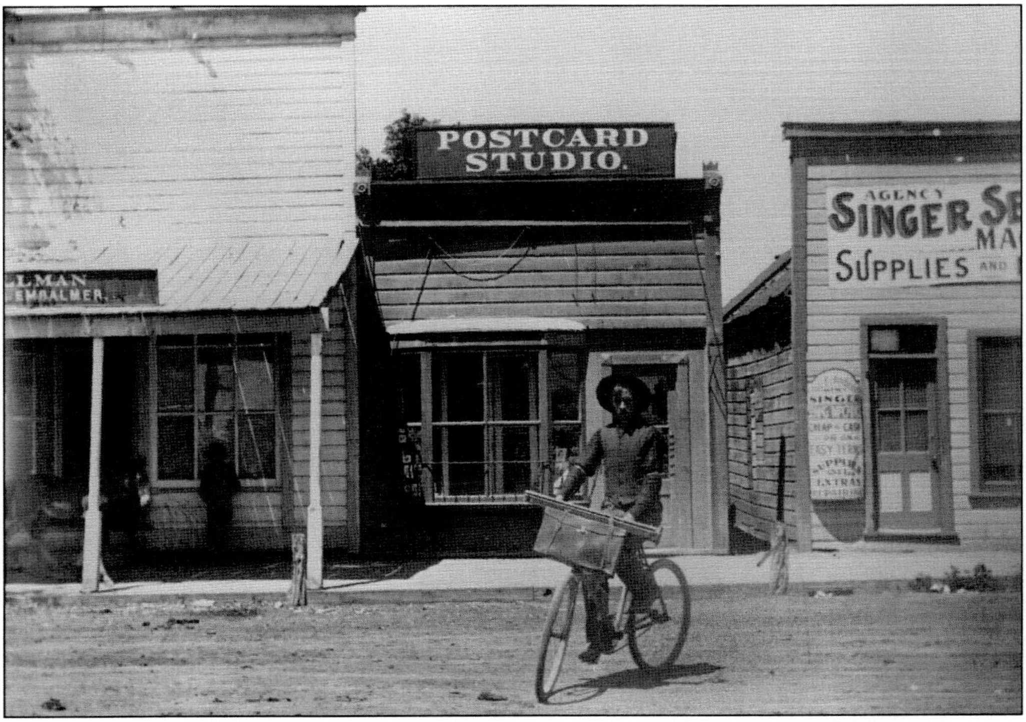

A young Leo Thorne sits on his bicycle in front of his Postcard Studio on South Vernal Avenue. With his camera and tripod strapped to the handlebars of his bicycle, Leo was often pedaling off to take a picture. Dillman Embalming and Singer Sewing Supplies are on either side of his store.

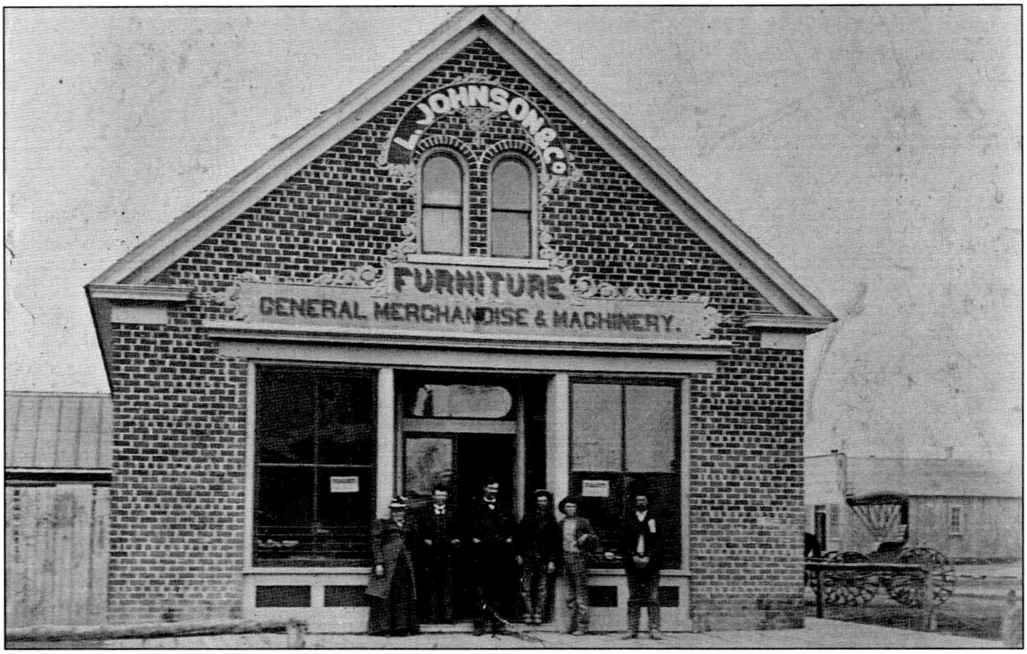

Lycurgus Johnson, an early entrepreneur, opened a general merchandise store with his sons Alfred and Snellon. It was located on the southeast corner of Main Street and Vernal Avenue. The store sold furniture, general merchandise, and machinery. Standing in front of the building are, from left to right, Rube Collett, Cora Johnson, Roy Colton, and three unidentified men.

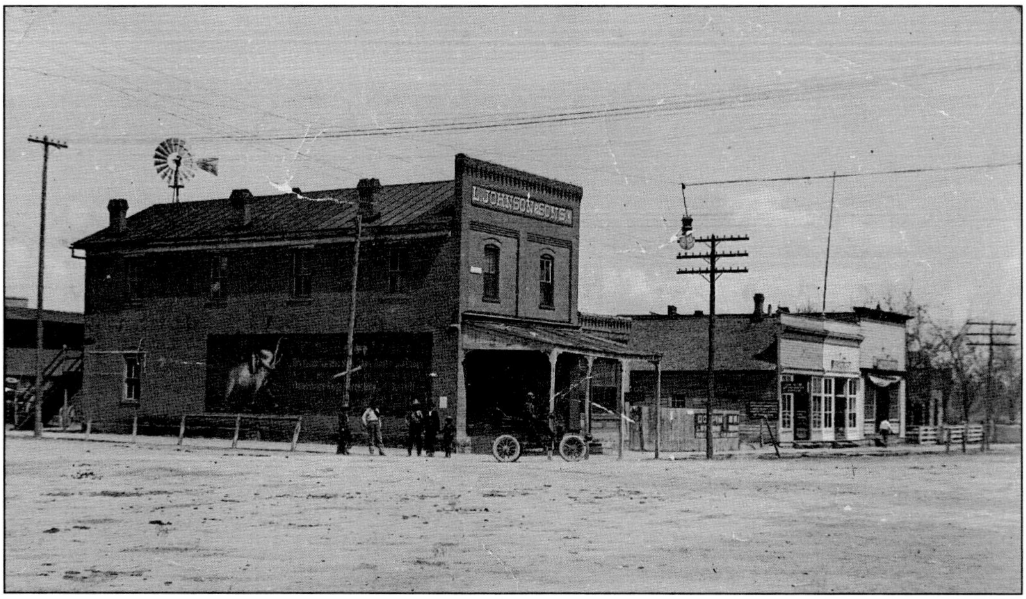

In 1886, Lycurgus Johnson moved the L. Johnson and Sons store to the northeast corner of Main Street and Vernal Avenue to the Big Elephant Store, where he continued his general merchandise business. Johnson's office building was located there, as were county court sessions before the courthouse was built. Also on the block were Colpin Drug Company, Drew and Martin Hides, and Uintah Saloon. The Big Elephant Store was torn down in 1913, and the Uintah State Bank was built at this location.

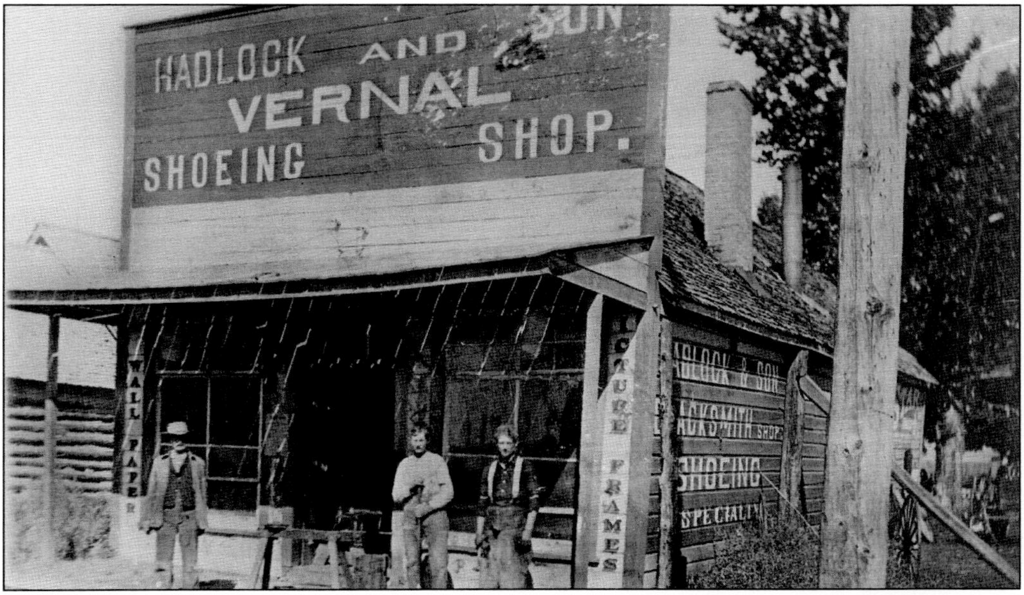

From 1900 to 1930, around 20 different blacksmith shops existed in Vernal. As horses were still the only way of travel at the time, blacksmiths and livery stables were needed to care for the animals. Operating for more than 30 years, the Hadlock and Sons Blacksmith Shop was one of the longest-running blacksmith shops.

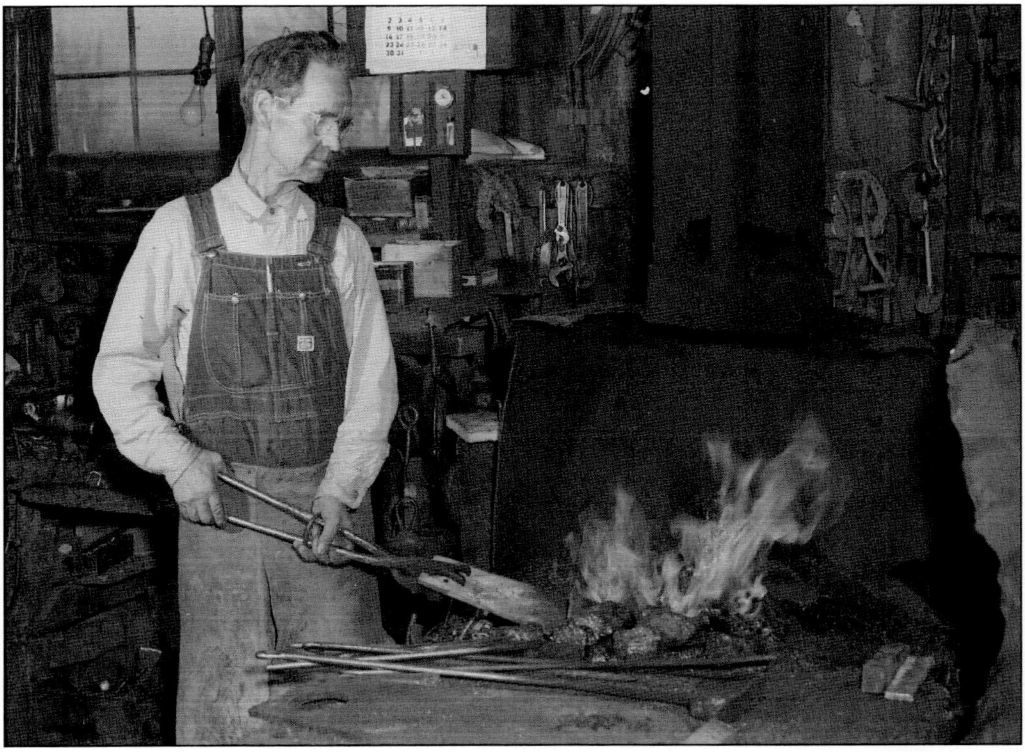

In 1910, Joseph Collier opened a blacksmith shop in the Naples Store. By 1920, he owned the only blacksmith shop in Naples and continued his business until 1955. Collier served the community for 45 years and died in 1959.

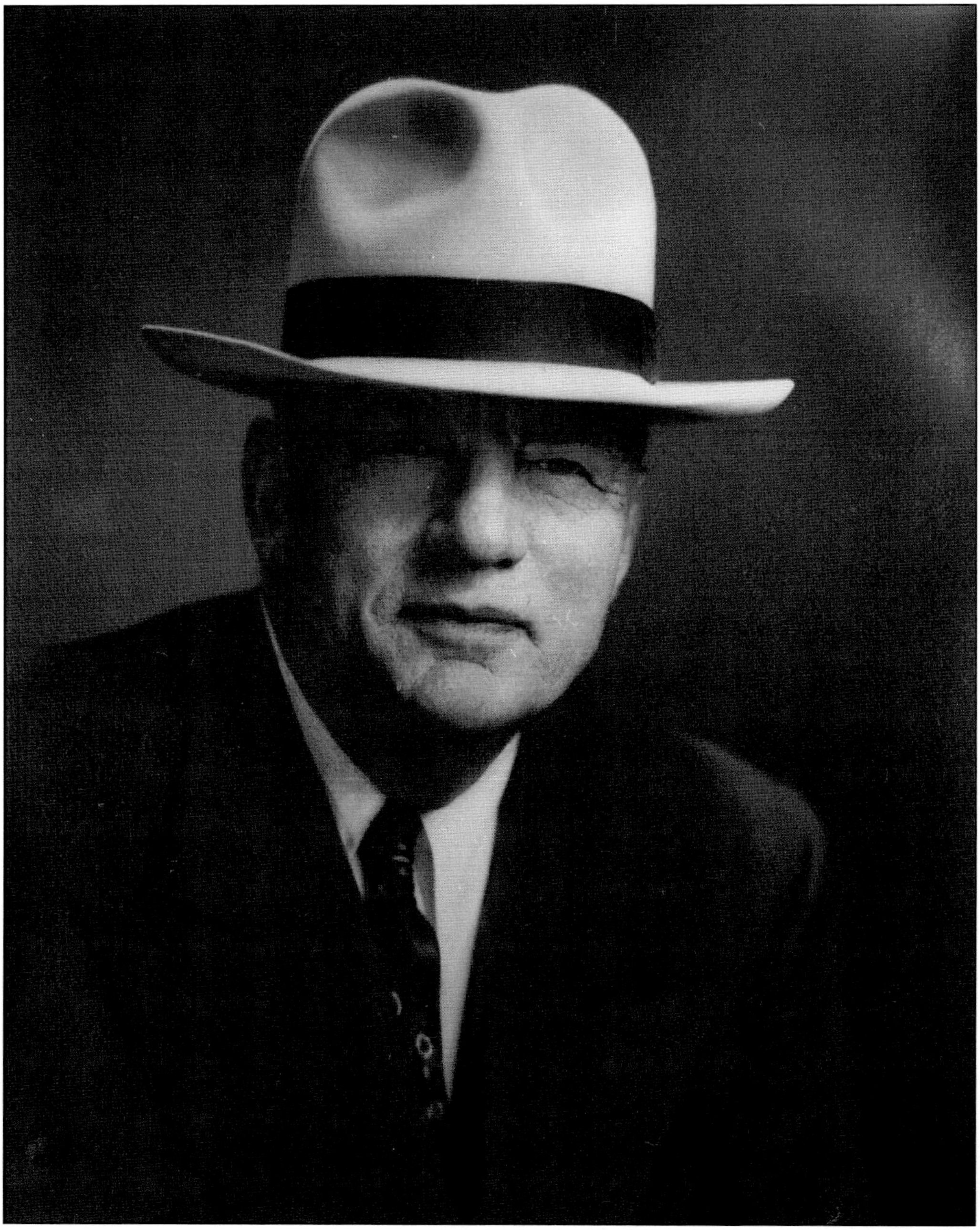

William Horace Coltharp was born February 26, 1884, to William Porter and Sarah Coltharp. He was one of the pioneers of the sheep industry in the area and a prominent young businessman in the valley. In 1917, he built the Coltharp Building, which was to house the Bank of Vernal, in honor of his father. This same quality of vision and foresight caused him to organize and promote the Uintah Power and Light Company, where he was the president for 20 years. William became involved in the oil industry and furthered oil exploration in the area. He was one of the founders of the local Texaco Oil Company. He served as Vernal City councilman and county commissioner. William was known for his many works of charity and acts of kindness. He died on April 14, 1956.

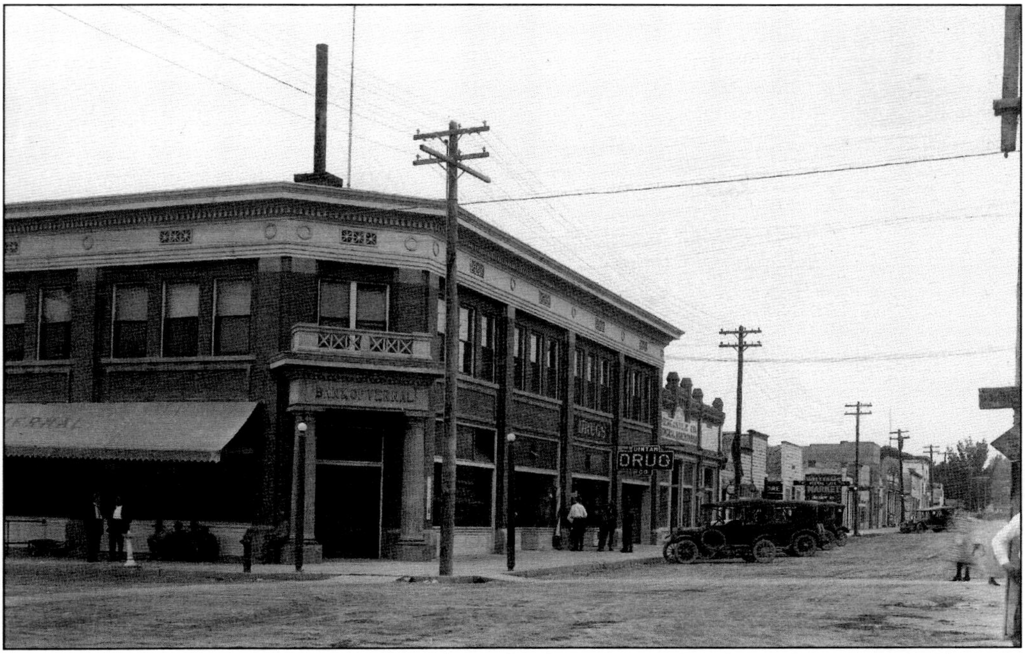

The Bank of Vernal, known as the parcel post bank, was completed in February 1917. The new bank was built in place of the Coltharp Mercantile Company. Only the best materials were used for the structure, including brick that were made in Salt Lake City. Unfortunately, the freight for the 80,000 bricks would be four times the cost of the brick. William Coltharp utilized the lower-rate parcel post service for the brick to be delivered. The bricks were wrapped in paper in 50-pound packages and mailed in numerous shipments. The 407-mile route took the bricks from Salt Lake City to Mack, Colorado, and Watson, Utah, by train, and then to Vernal by freight wagon. The Bank of Vernal became known as the "bank sent by mail."

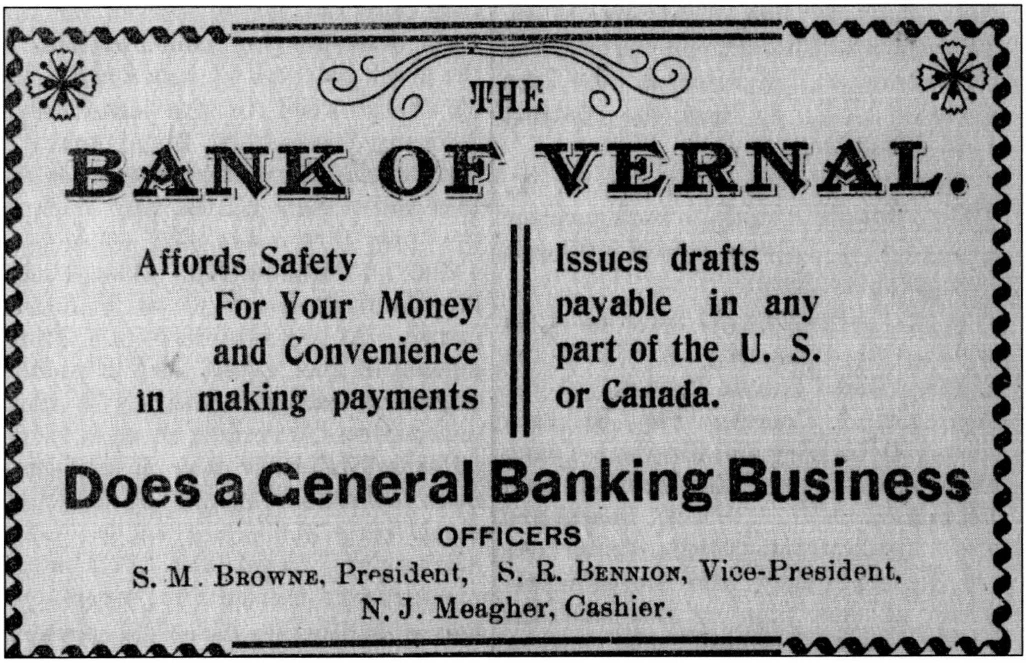

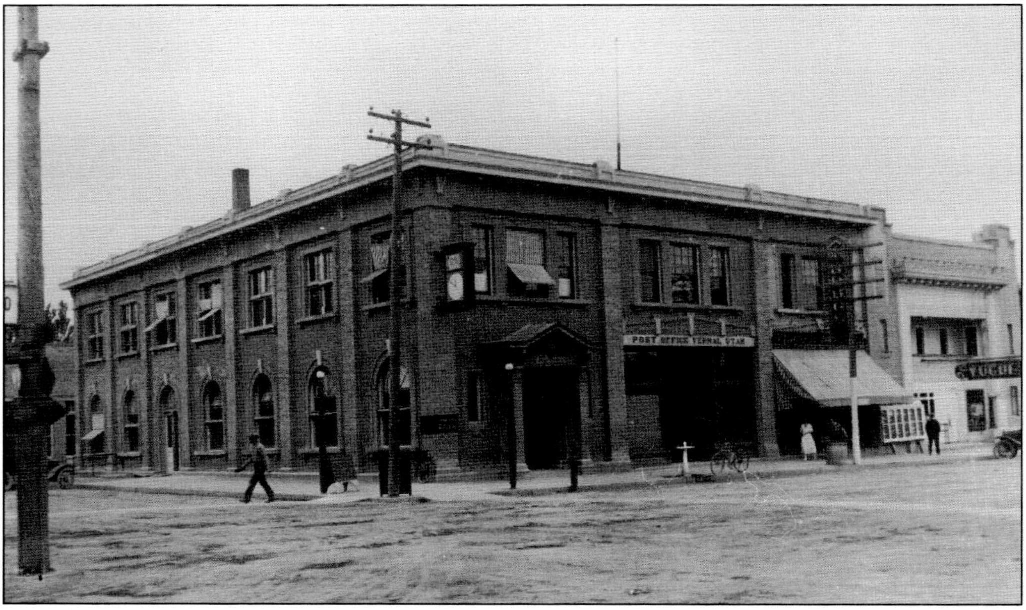

Uintah State Bank opened for business in 1910 in the L.H. Woodard Building on South Vernal Avenue. William H. Smart was the bank's first president, and Enos Bennion took over the position the following year. The bank moved into its new building (above) on the northeast corner of Main Street and Vernal Avenue in 1914. A fireproof and antiburglary safe was installed with a time lock feature. The Vernal Post Office and the Vernal Drug Store were housed in the new bank building.

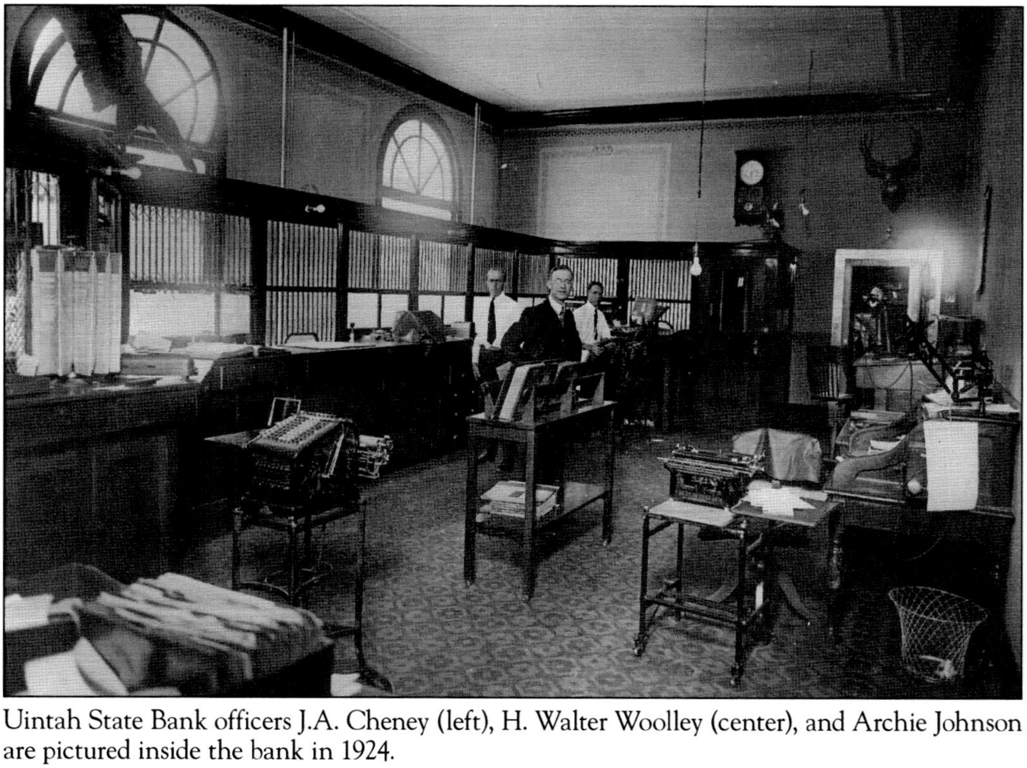

Uintah State Bank officers J.A. Cheney (left), H. Walter Woolley (center), and Archie Johnson are pictured inside the bank in 1924.

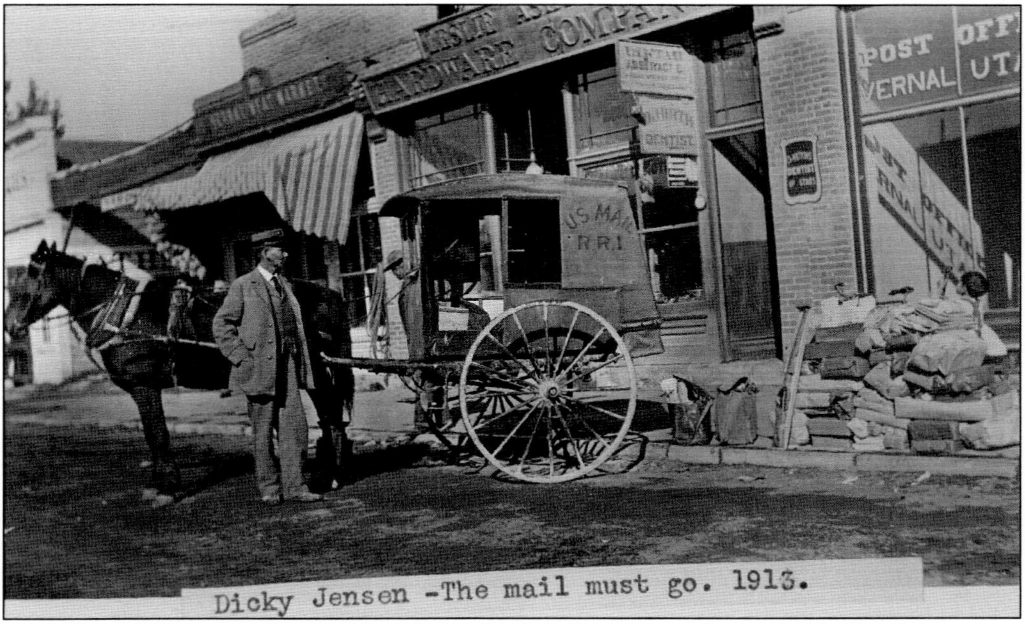

In 1913, Dickie Jensen, an early Vernal postman, stands next to the mail buggy parked in front of the post office on the north side of Main Street. Shortly after parcel post began, packages are stacked in front of the post office ready to be delivered. Jensen was also a noted saddler.

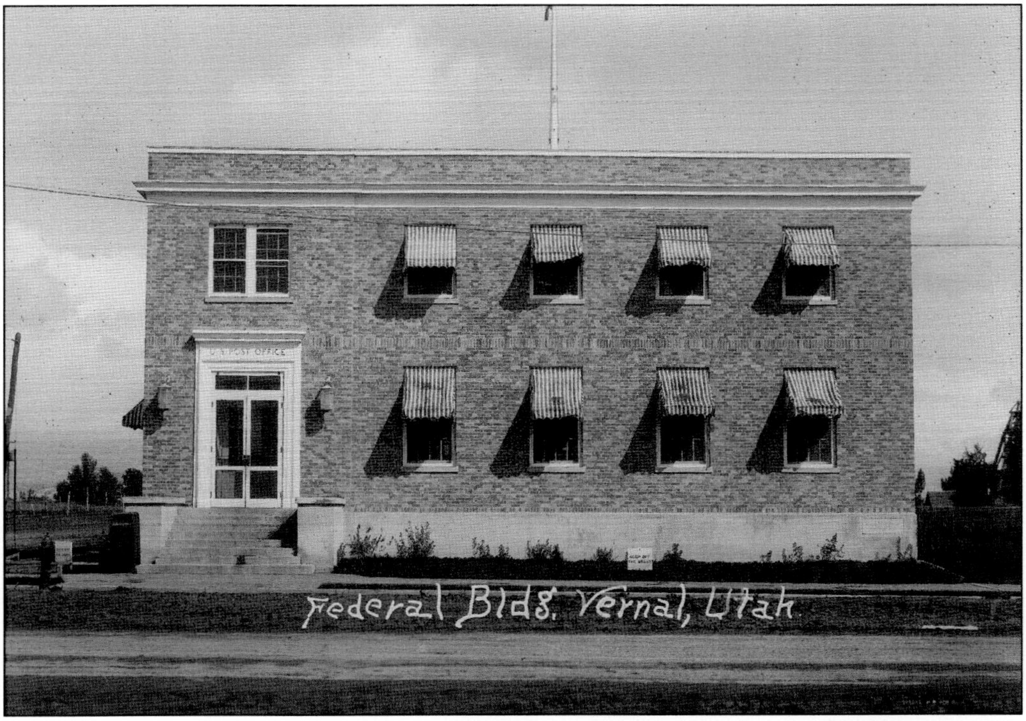

A new, modern federal building located on the 100 West Main Street corner and housing the Vernal Post Office opened for business in November 1925. The beautiful new structure was the largest federal building in the United States that was located in an inland city. Edward J. Young Jr. was the postmaster at the time.

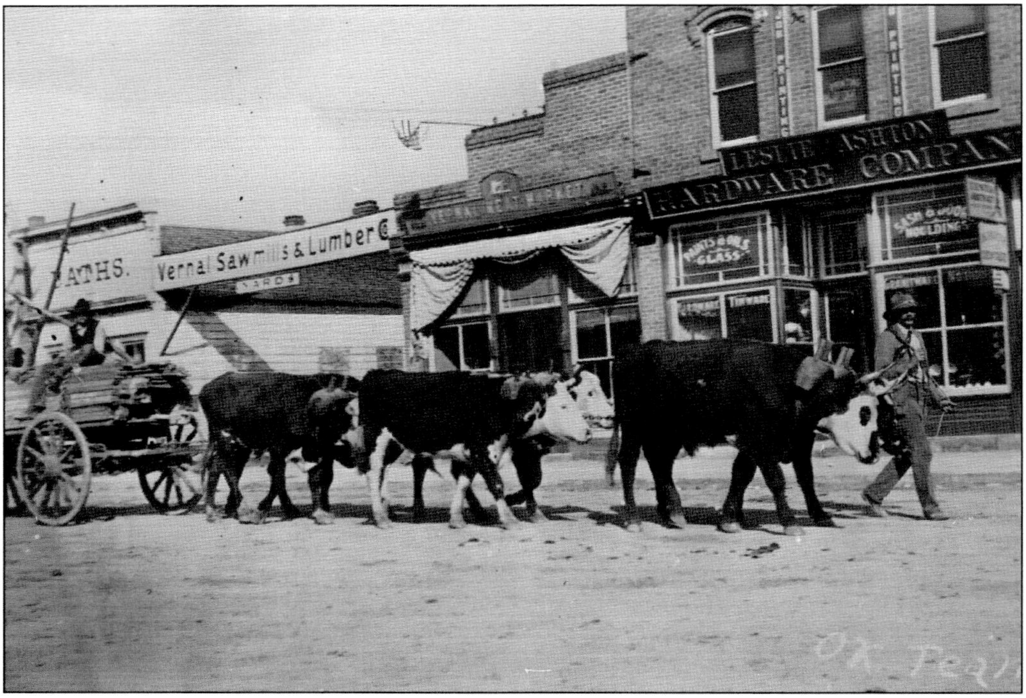

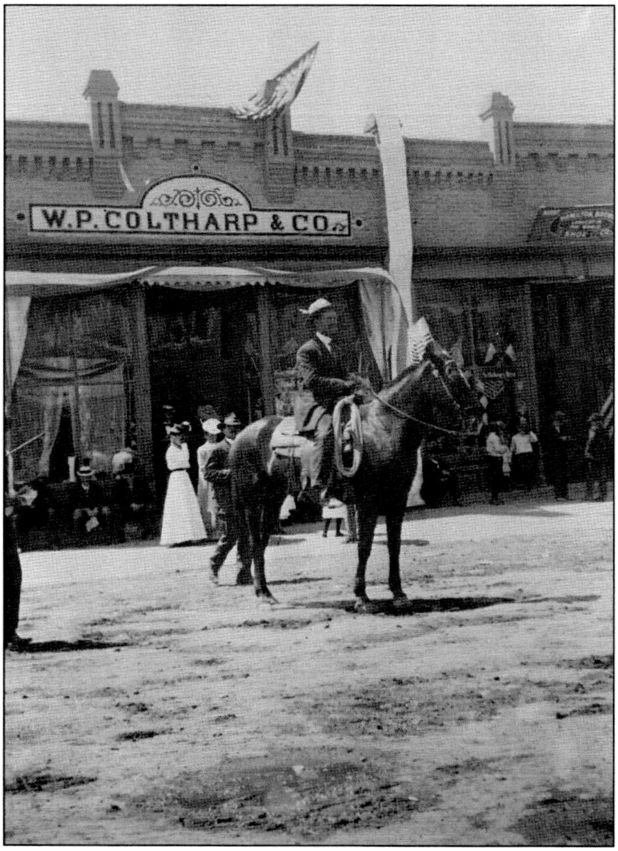

Leslie Ashton opened a hardware store on Main Street in 1895. The business supplied residents with hardware and building materials. Heber Luck is seen leading an ox team, which is pulling a wagon loaded with lumber. Joe Luck is riding on top of the load.

Hy Meeks sits on his horse in front of the W.P. Coltharp Company. William Porter Coltharp established the company in 1893; it was located on the south side of Main Street. The store sold quality clothing and shoes for men and women. The building later housed the Bank of Vernal.

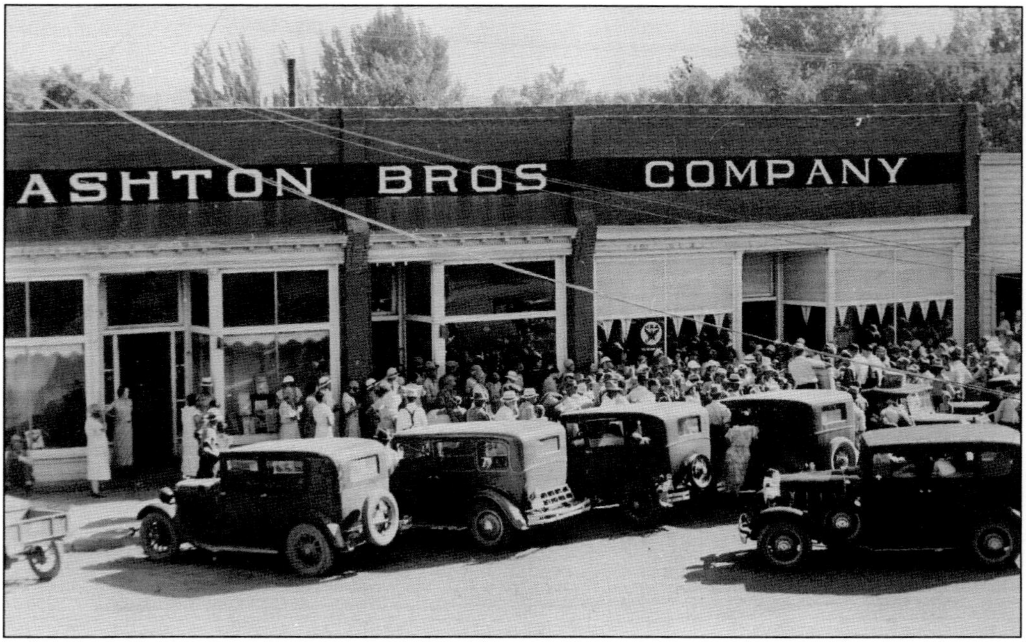

Leslie Ashton's son Rae Ashton moved from Roosevelt to Vernal in 1924 with his wife, Eva. He relocated the Leslie Ashton Hardware store to the Coltharp Building on the south side of Main Street and changed the name to Ashton Brothers Company. The above image was taken during the grand opening sale in 1924. Rae managed the general merchandise store and his two sons, Ralph and Stewart, later took over the management. Ashton Brothers became a quality department store for many years until it closed in 1985. Below, Rae Ashton is pictured behind the counter in this early photograph of the store.

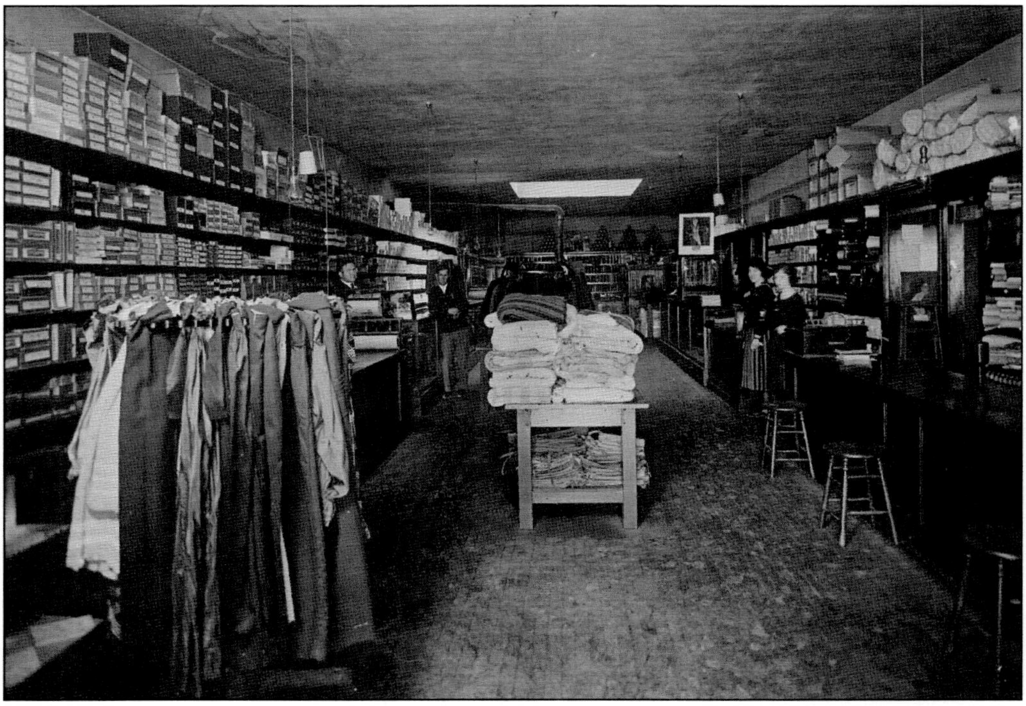

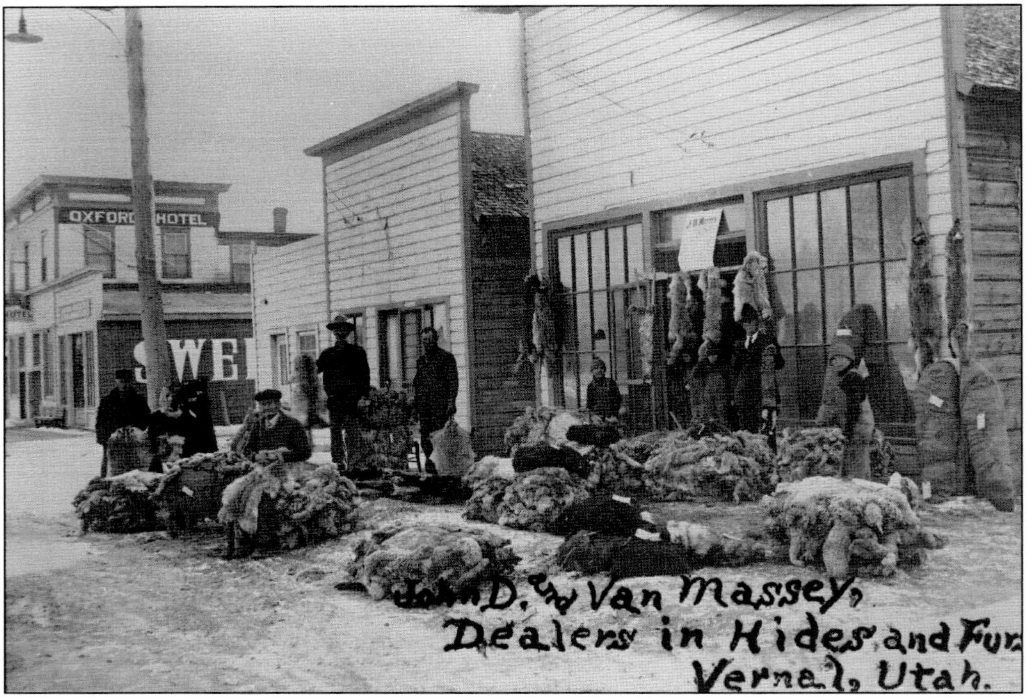

Van Massey settled in the Ashley Valley during the early 1900s. He was employed as a farmer, a veterinarian, and a government trapper. Massey purchased the old Hullinger Store building for $2,600 and opened a hide and fur company named John D. Massey and Son; it was later called the Uintah Fur Company. The business was located near 120 West Main Street. Identified in the photograph are John D. Massey (seated on the hides) and Nick Meagher (in the suit).

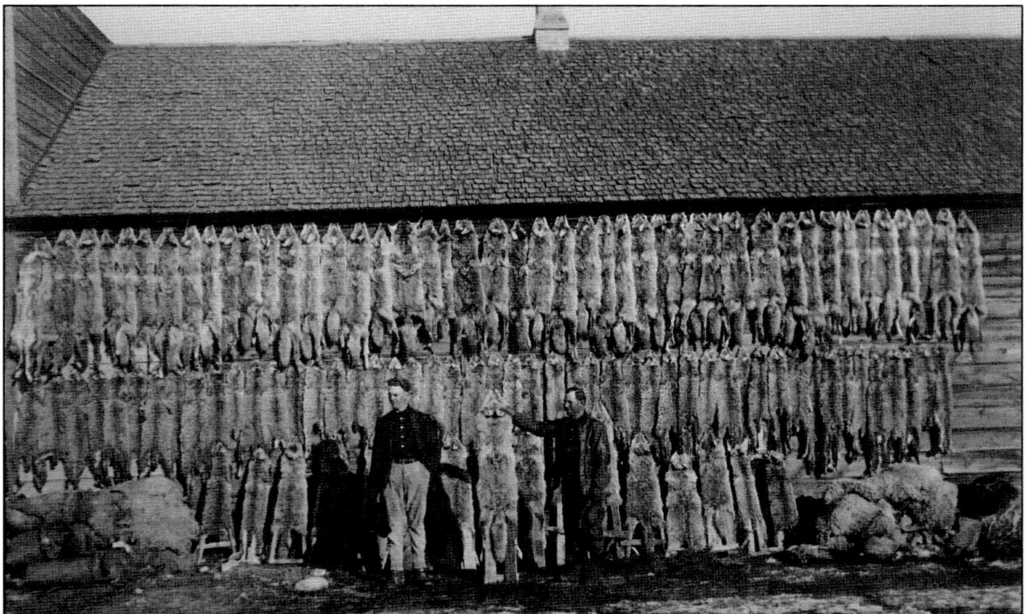

Acel Rowley (left) and Van Massey stand in front of three rows of coyote hides at their fur and hide business. The pelts are hanging on the building to dry.

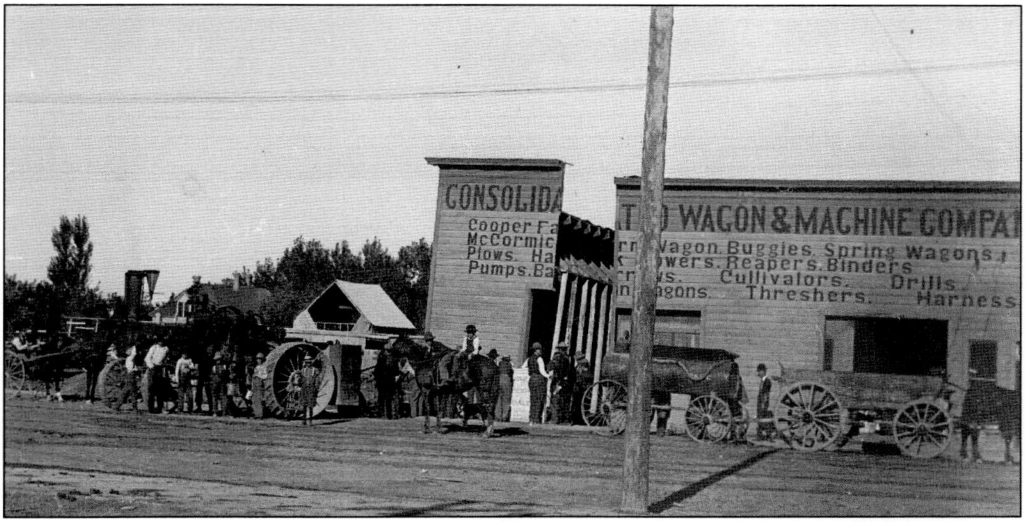

The original Consolidated Wagon and Machine Company was located on Vernal Avenue between Uintah Avenue and First North. A new building was later put up in 1908, next to part of the old structure. It was built of 250,000 bricks manufactured by the Swain Brothers, and the total cost of the edifice was $8,000. The business provided locals with various farming equipment and feed supplies. The building was also known to hold large gatherings such as dances with live musical entertainment.

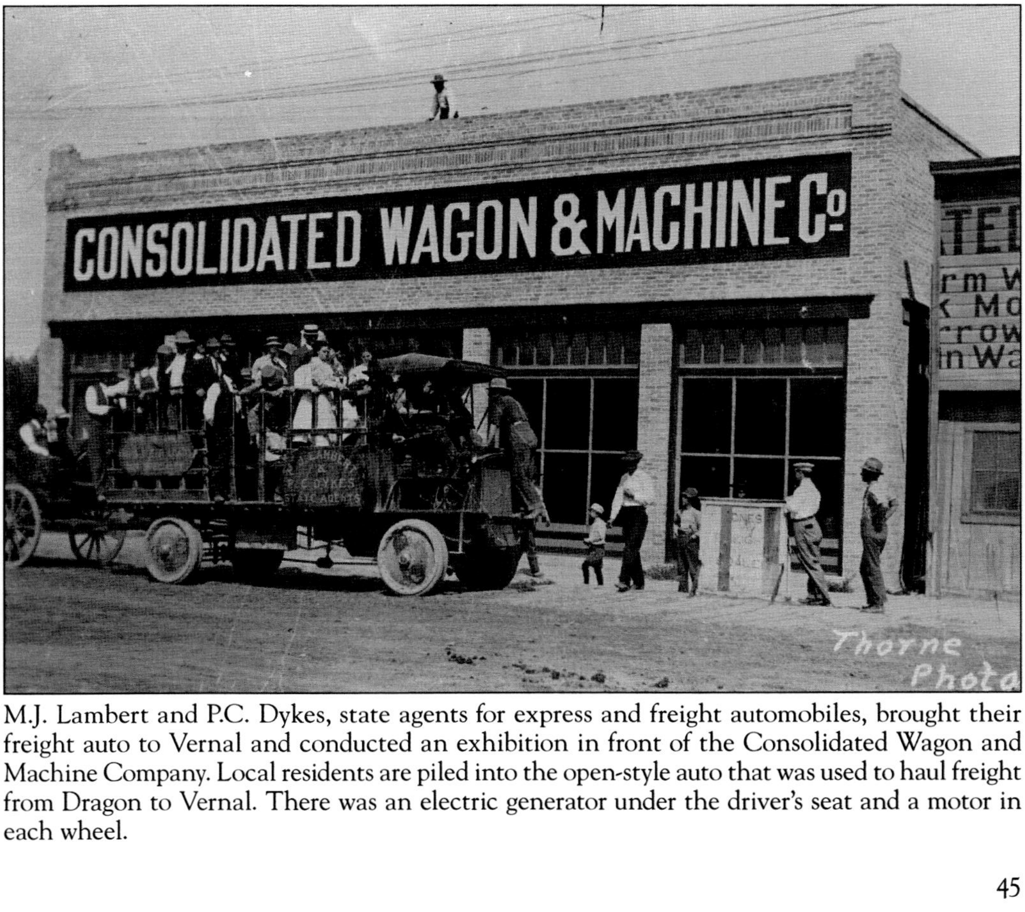

M.J. Lambert and P.C. Dykes, state agents for express and freight automobiles, brought their freight auto to Vernal and conducted an exhibition in front of the Consolidated Wagon and Machine Company. Local residents are piled into the open-style auto that was used to haul freight from Dragon to Vernal. There was an electric generator under the driver's seat and a motor in each wheel.

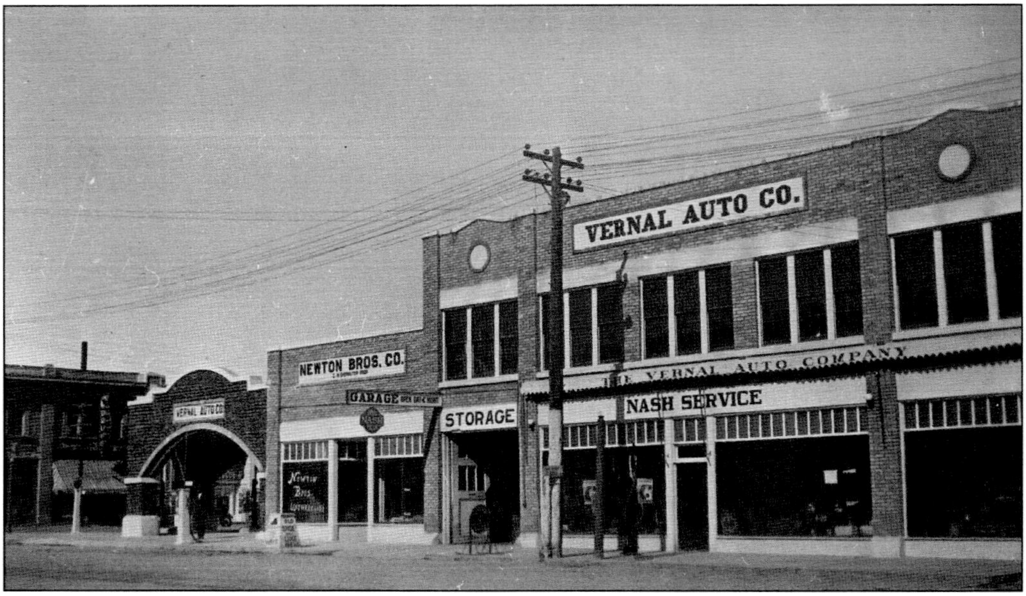

The Vernal Auto Company block was a three-building complex that housed the Cobble Rock Station, the Newton Brothers Saddle Company, and the Vernal Auto Company. Vernal Auto Company was separated into three bays. The large central bay was divided from the outer bays by strong brick pillars. The left bay had vehicle access to the second floor storage, which could house up to 150 automobiles

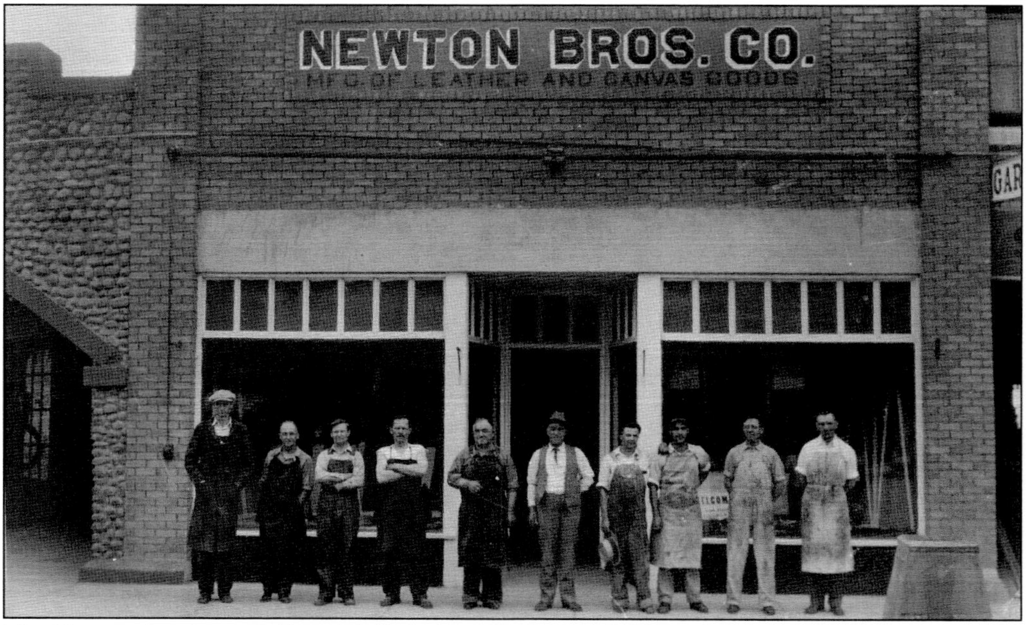

The Newton Brothers, William "Bill" and Isaac "Ike," opened a shoe shop in 1905 next to Cobble Rock Station on Vernal Avenue. Although Bill was left blind from a childhood accident and Ike was born with a physical handicap disability, they worked hard together to make a successful company. They used mostly hand tools but later expanded the enterprise with modern equipment to do business on a larger scale. Bill and Ike are pictured (fourth and fifth from left) in the center with their employees.

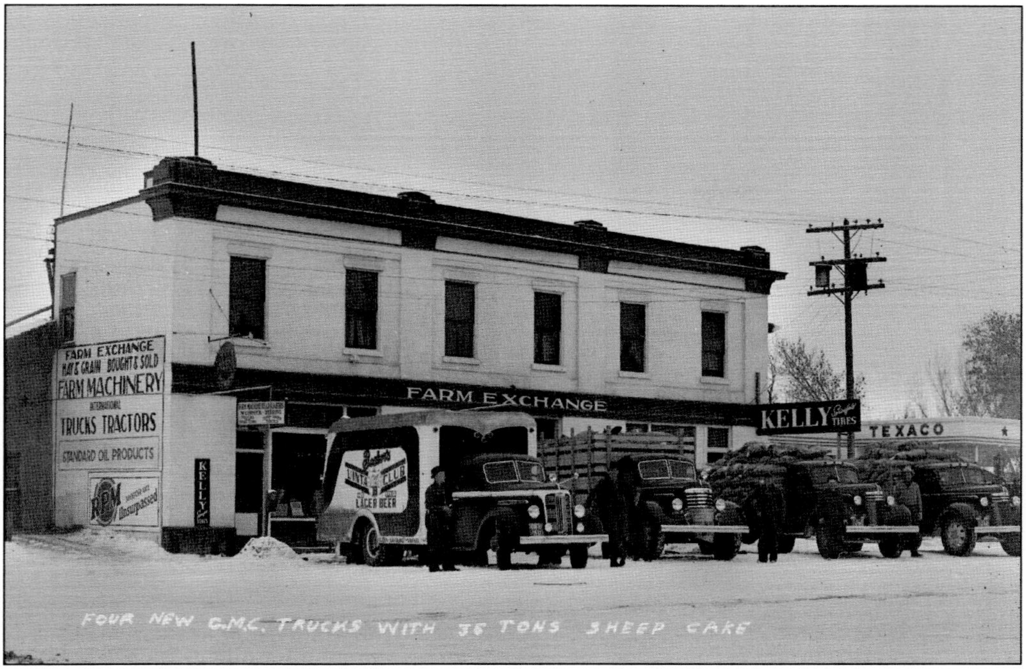

The Farm Exchange was the outgrowth of the Farm Bureau, which A. Theodore Johnson managed from 1919 to 1935. In 1937, he sold the business, located at 200 West Main Street, to T.G. Alexander, who remodeled the building inside and out. This 1948 photograph shows men standing in front of new GMC trucks loaded with 36 tons of wool.

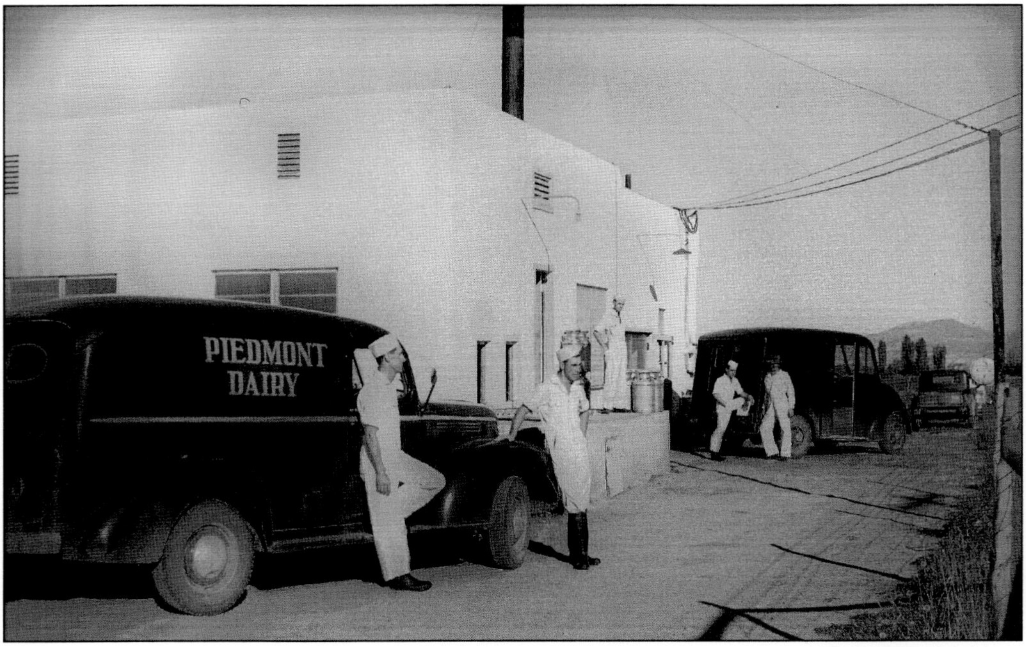

Oakley Larson and Clifton Perry opened the Piedmont Dairy near the Maeser Store in 1947. The dairy was set up to bottle grade A pasteurized milk, buttermilk, and chocolate milk and to make cottage cheese and ice cream. The men operated the dairy until 1954, when Meadow Gold Dairy leased the building—and later bought it. Meadow Gold is still operating in this location.

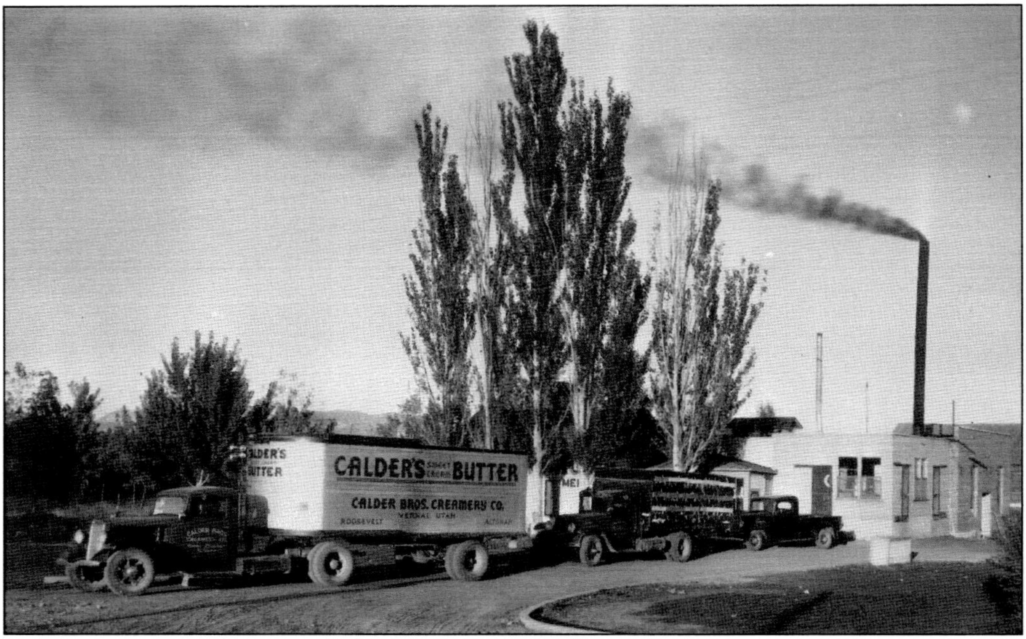

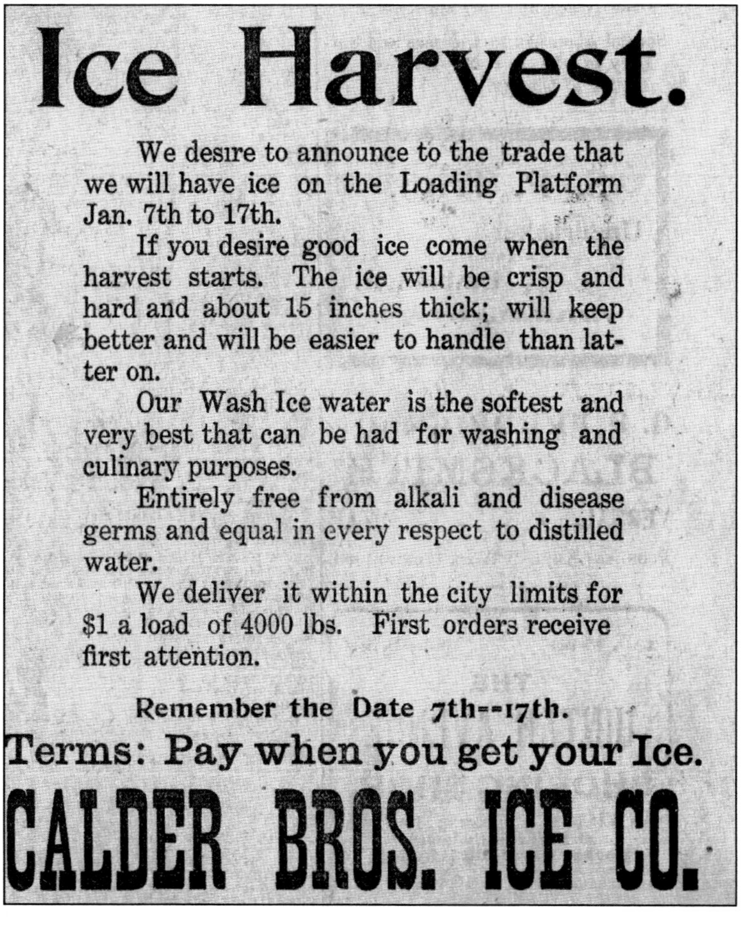

Pontha and Hyrum B. Calder started the Creamery as an ice business in 1904. They built Calder's Pond on North Vernal Avenue. During the winter, they cut the frozen ice into large blocks. The ice from Calder's provided refrigeration for many people in their homes. In 1910, with the success of the ice company, they branched out into two other areas. Soda pop was made in the bottling works division and came in several flavors. The creamery made and sold milk, cheese, butter, and cottage cheese; it was also said to make the best ice cream in the world. This advertisement for ice ran in the *Vernal Express* on January 14, 1907.

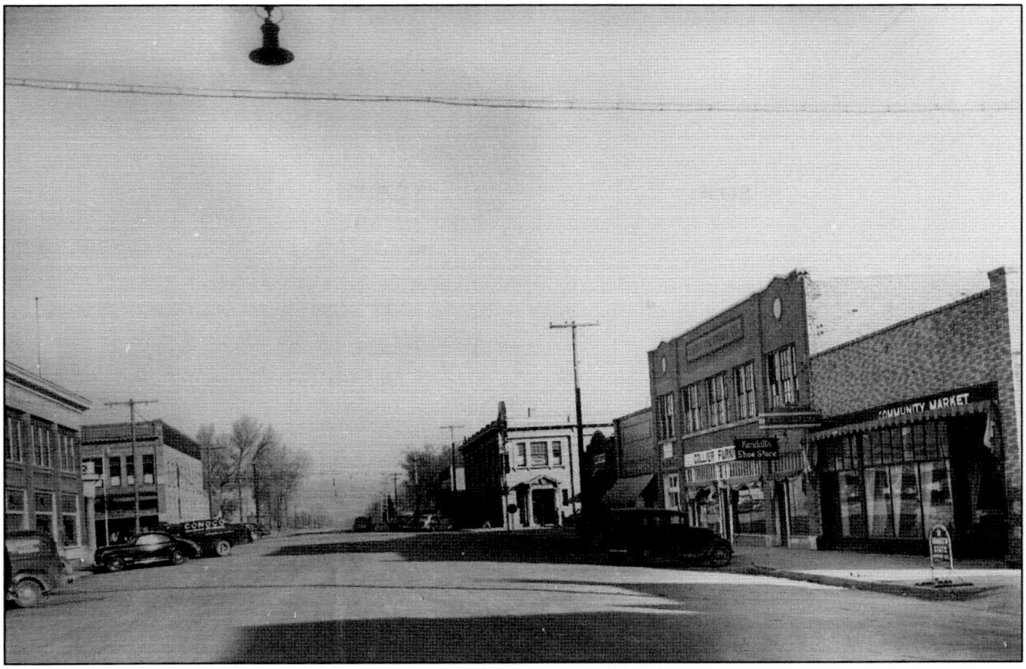

This photograph was taken on South Vernal Avenue looking north. The smooth native rock asphalt pavement had been recently laid along this busy street in 1941. On the left side are the Bank of Vernal and Ashley Co-op, and on the right side are Community Market, Kendall's Shoes, Collier Furniture, Cobble Rock Station, and Uintah State Bank.

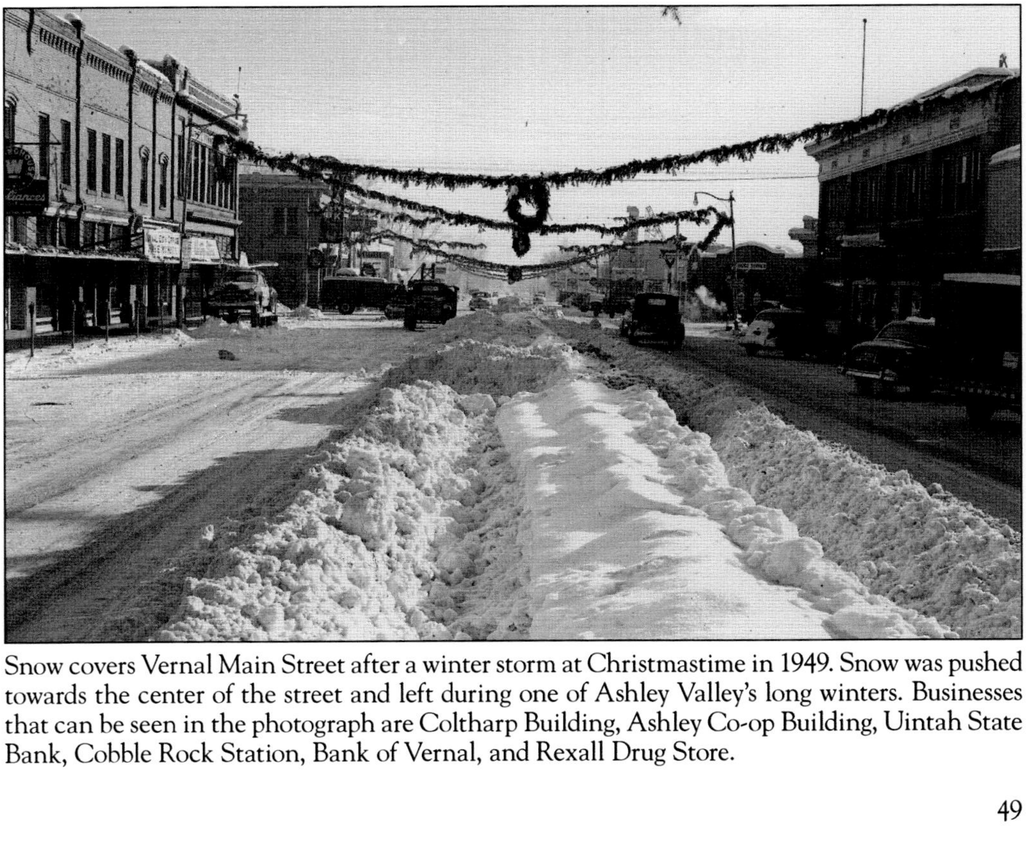

Snow covers Vernal Main Street after a winter storm at Christmastime in 1949. Snow was pushed towards the center of the street and left during one of Ashley Valley's long winters. Businesses that can be seen in the photograph are Coltharp Building, Ashley Co-op Building, Uintah State Bank, Cobble Rock Station, Bank of Vernal, and Rexall Drug Store.

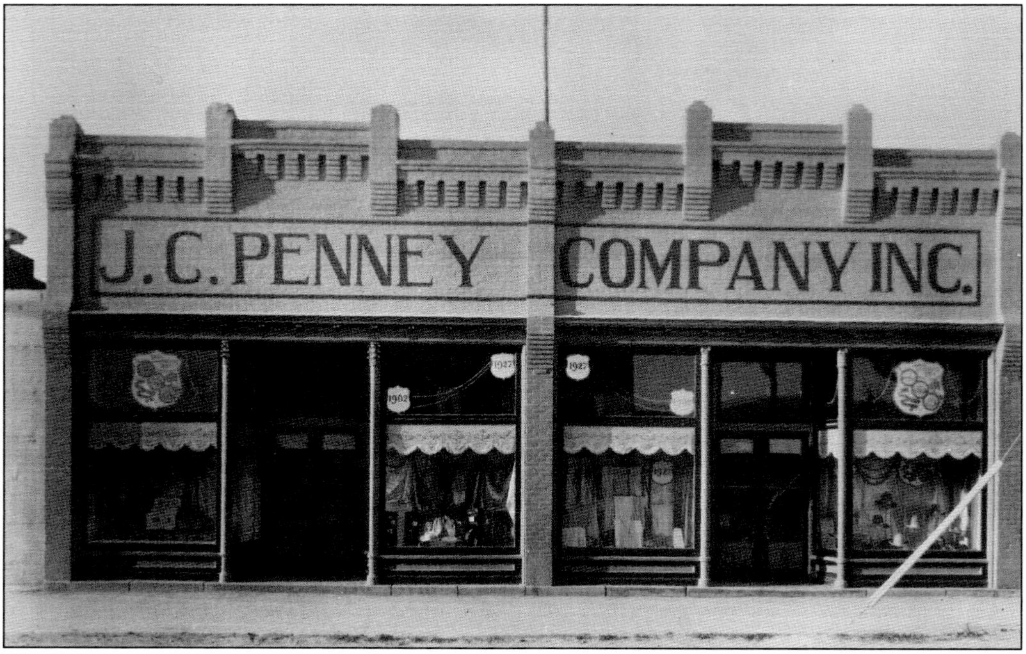

The J.C. Penney Company opened in 1927. This was J.C. Penney's 25th store to open in Utah. It was located in the former Acorn Mercantile at 100 West Main Street. In 1932, J.C. Penney replaced the Ashley Co-operative. Penney's was a quality store that continued in the community until 1990.

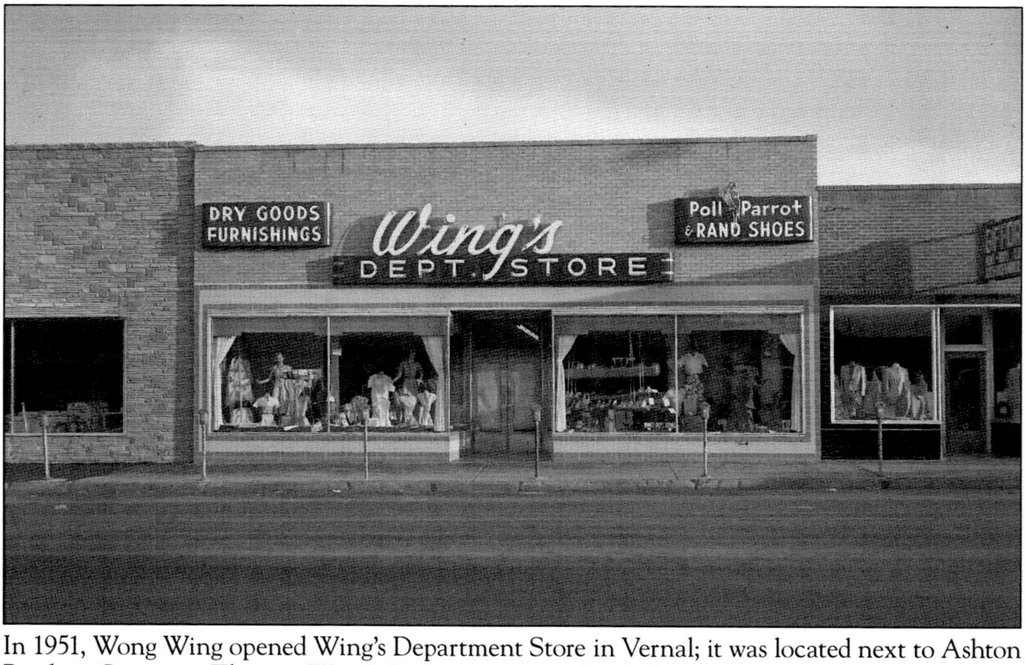

In 1951, Wong Wing opened Wing's Department Store in Vernal; it was located next to Ashton Brothers Company. The new Wing's Store was equipped with fluorescent lighting and illuminated showcases. The luxurious new store offered clothing and shoes to outfit the whole family. Mrs. Wing managed the shoe department and used an X-ray machine to insure the best fittings. Ashton's bought the store out in 1960.

William S. Ashton, James Shaffer, and Augustus C. Emert bought out Harmston's inventory and began the Vernal Drug Co. on South Vernal Avenue. In 1897, the store was moved to a new two-story brick building at 4 West Main Street. In 1907, Vernal Drug Co. was incorporated and moved to the Calder Building. In 1917, the drugstore moved into the new Uintah State Bank building. Rice Cooper bought the business and ran it for many years until his son Glenn took over. In 1957, a new building was constructed several doors down. The drugstore was furnished with a fountain and said to make the best sundaes and milk shakes. The Vernal Drug Co. had been in operation longer than any other county drugstore when it closed in 1991.

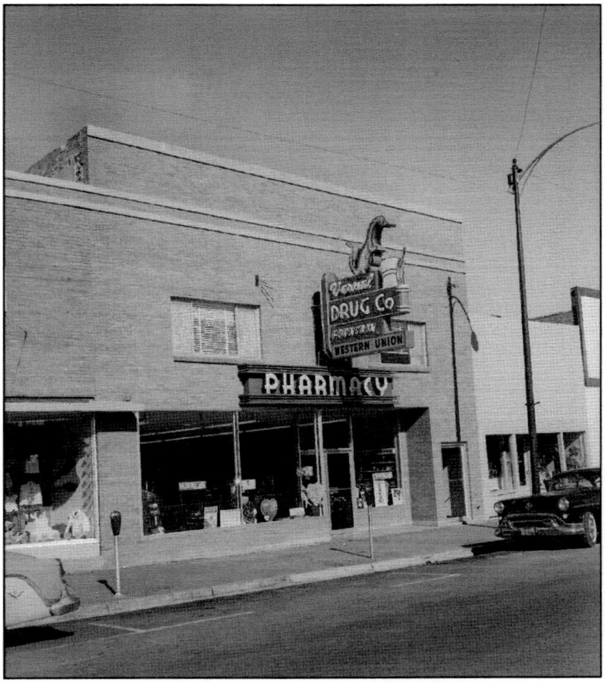

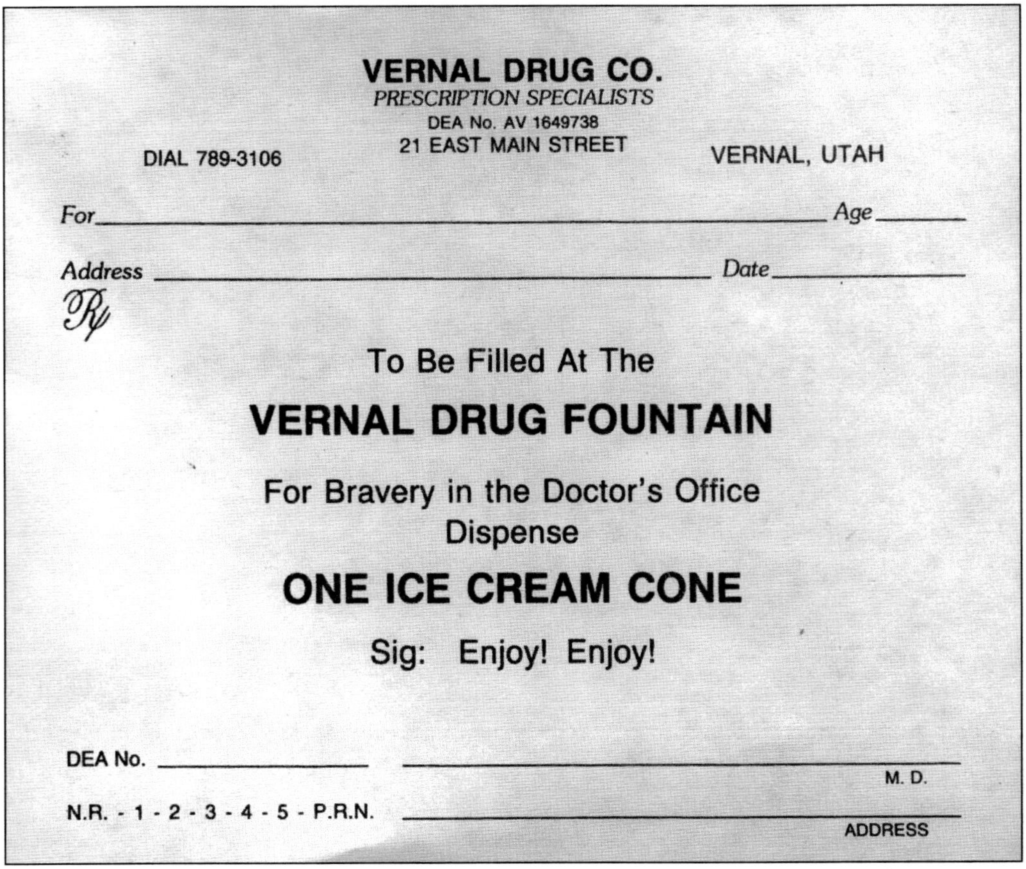

VERNAL DRUG CO.
PRESCRIPTION SPECIALISTS
DEA No. AV 1649738
21 EAST MAIN STREET

DIAL 789-3106 VERNAL, UTAH

*For*____________________ *Age*______

Address ____________________ *Date*______

℞

To Be Filled At The

VERNAL DRUG FOUNTAIN

For Bravery in the Doctor's Office
Dispense

ONE ICE CREAM CONE

Sig: Enjoy! Enjoy!

DEA No. __________ ____________________ M. D.

N.R. - 1 - 2 - 3 - 4 - 5 - P.R.N. ____________________ ADDRESS

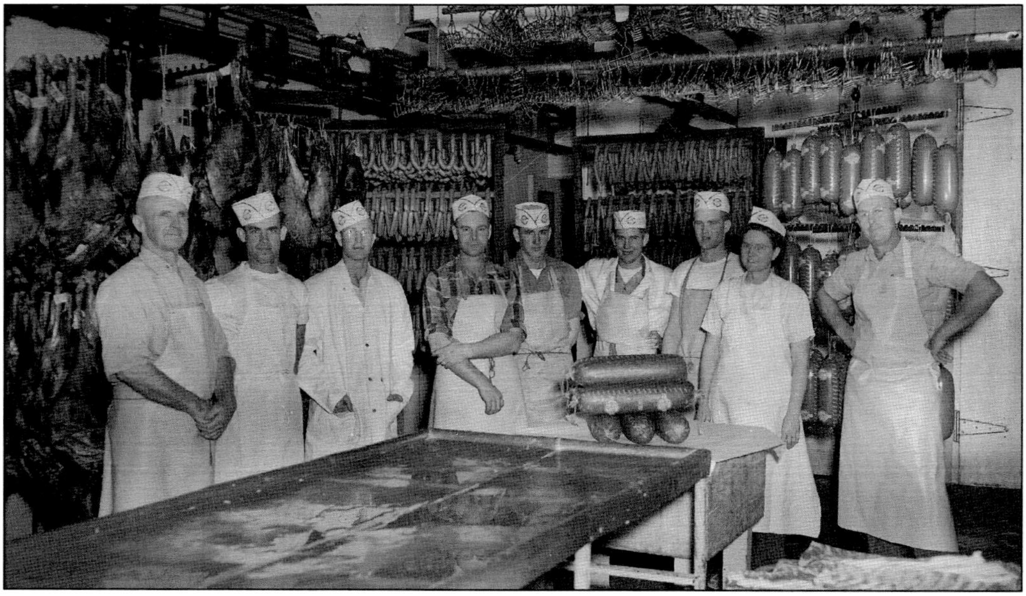

During 1944, Uintah Packing Company began as a small meat-curing plant at 135 West Main and developed into a successful operation at 400 North Vernal Avenue. The packing plant was owned by LaRell Anderson and is still operated by his son Don Anderson. Pictured in this photograph are, from left to right, Fred Anderson, Deloss Reynolds, Jack Powell, Heber Haws, Fran Richens, unidentified, Carl Dow, Mrs. Smith, and LaRell Anderson.

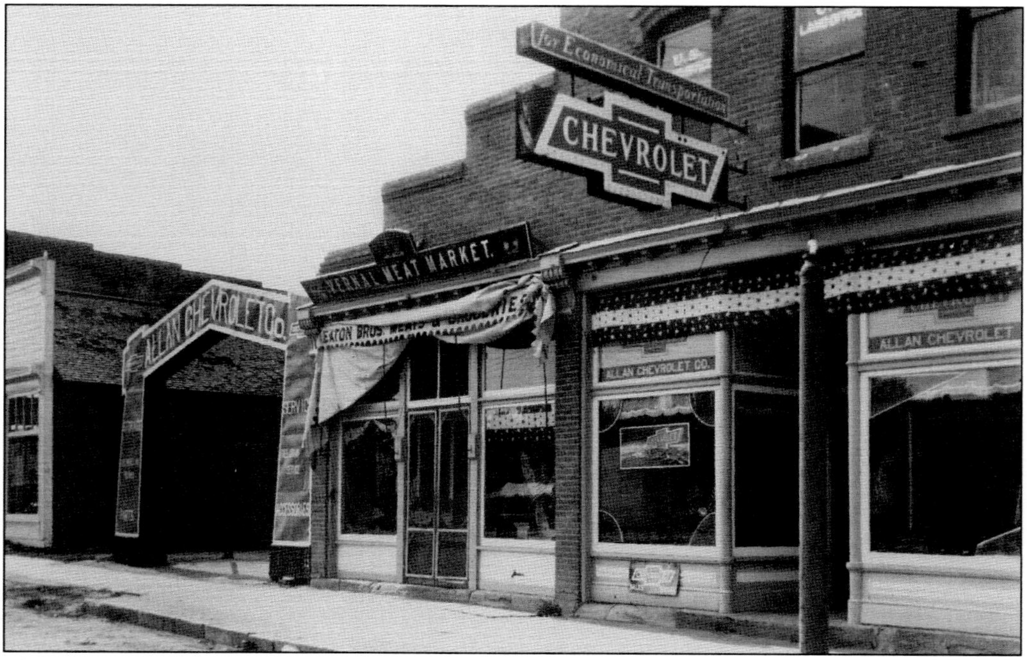

The Vernal Meat Market was located in the Calder Building. It had several owners before Orlando, Ernest, Irvine, and Elmer Eaton, known as the Eaton Brothers, bought the business from John Glines. They learned to butcher and cut animals from their father, Joseph Eaton. A specialty was their pickled pigs feet. The Eaton Brothers operated the business for 31 years. Allan Chevrolet was located next to Vernal Meat Market and was owned by L.H. Allan.

Five

Hometown Hospitality

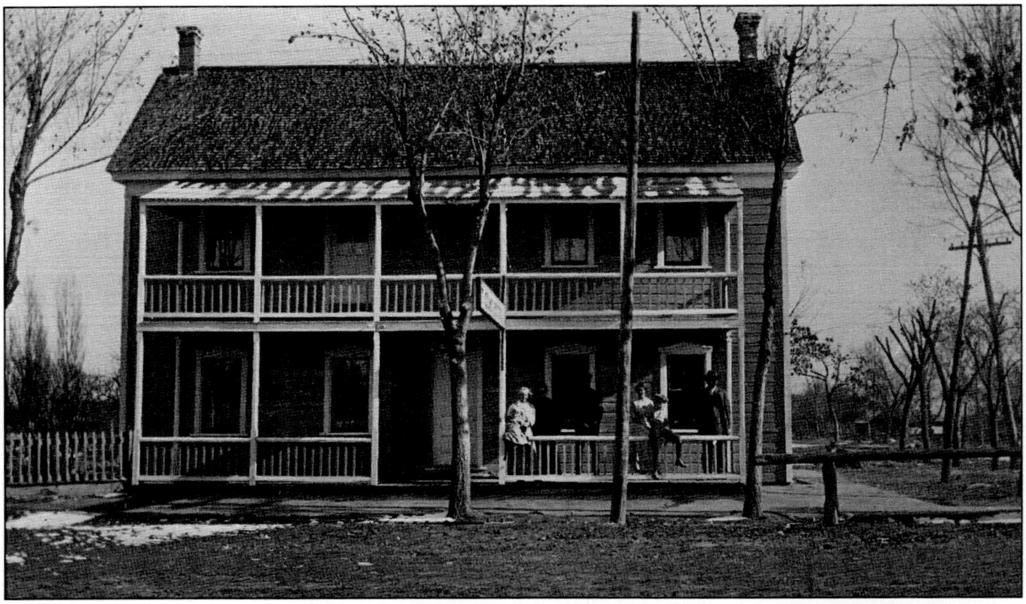

The Vernal Hotel was the first large hotel to operate in the city for an extended period of time. Joseph Hardy owned the lodging, located on the northeast corner of 100 South and Vernal Avenue. Running the hotel was a tough job since almost everyone wore a six-gun strapped to his belt; a saloon was located in the vicinity. The hotel was destroyed by fire in 1936.

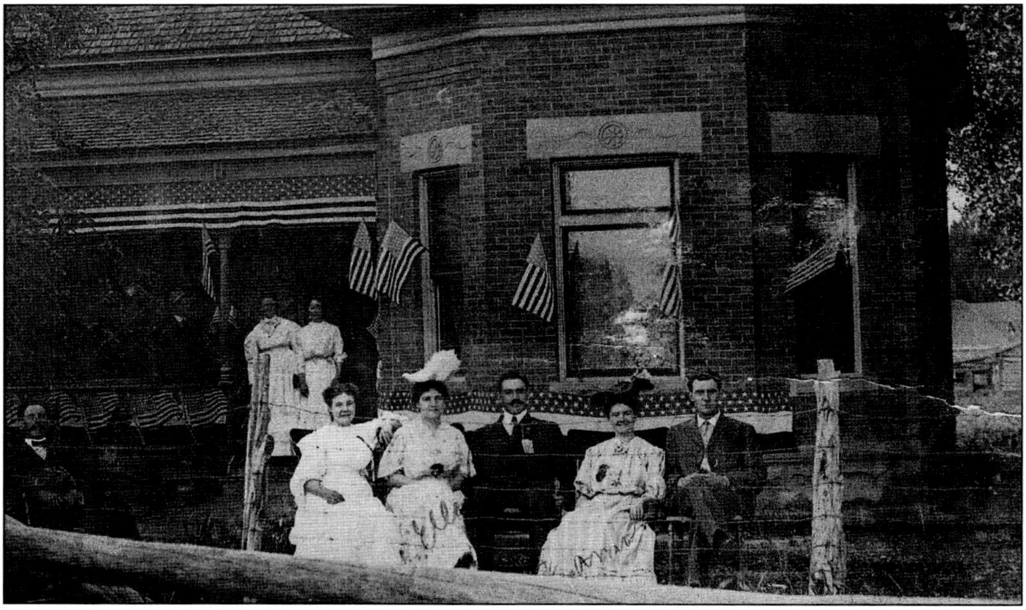

Jane Rich, along with her sons, built the Cottage Hotel. It was situated across the street from the Uintah Railway station and stage stop on Vernal Avenue; this made it convenient for visitors traveling by stage line. The hotel was a combined hotel and boardinghouse. It had four rooms and a kitchen on the ground floor and five rooms upstairs. The oversized landing at the top of the stairs served as a living room where boarders and visitors sat around a potbellied stove and shared stories. With hand carved woodwork, the hotel was plush for its day. The property remained in the Rich family for six generations. It was demolished in 1977.

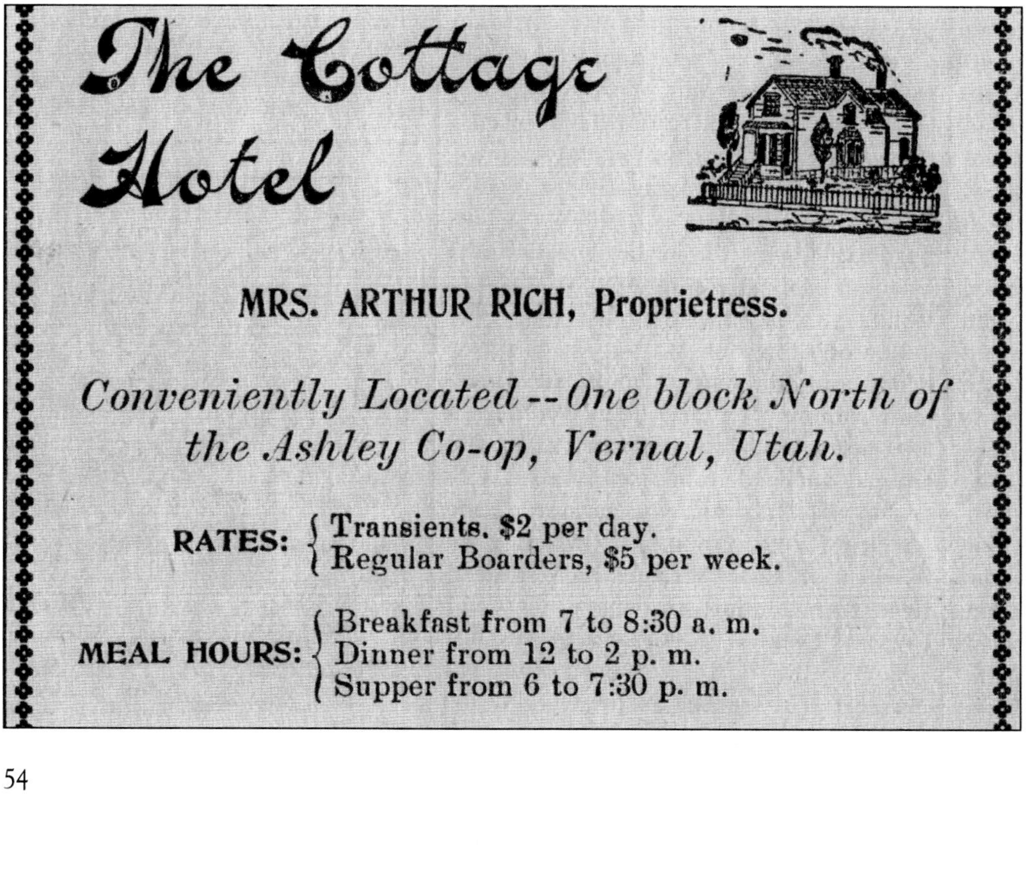

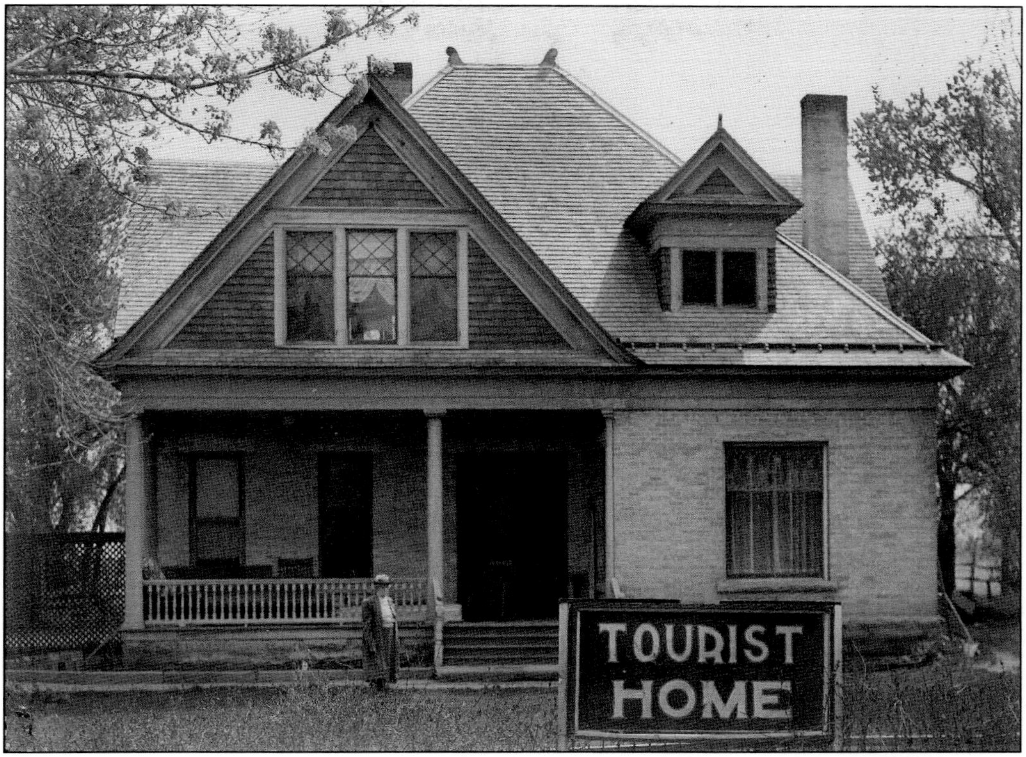

The Enos Bennion home was located at 842 East Main Street and was used as a tourist home. In 1937, rooms were rented out weekly or monthly. Enos and Jane Bennion were prominent folks in the valley. The woman standing in front is possibly Jane Bennion.

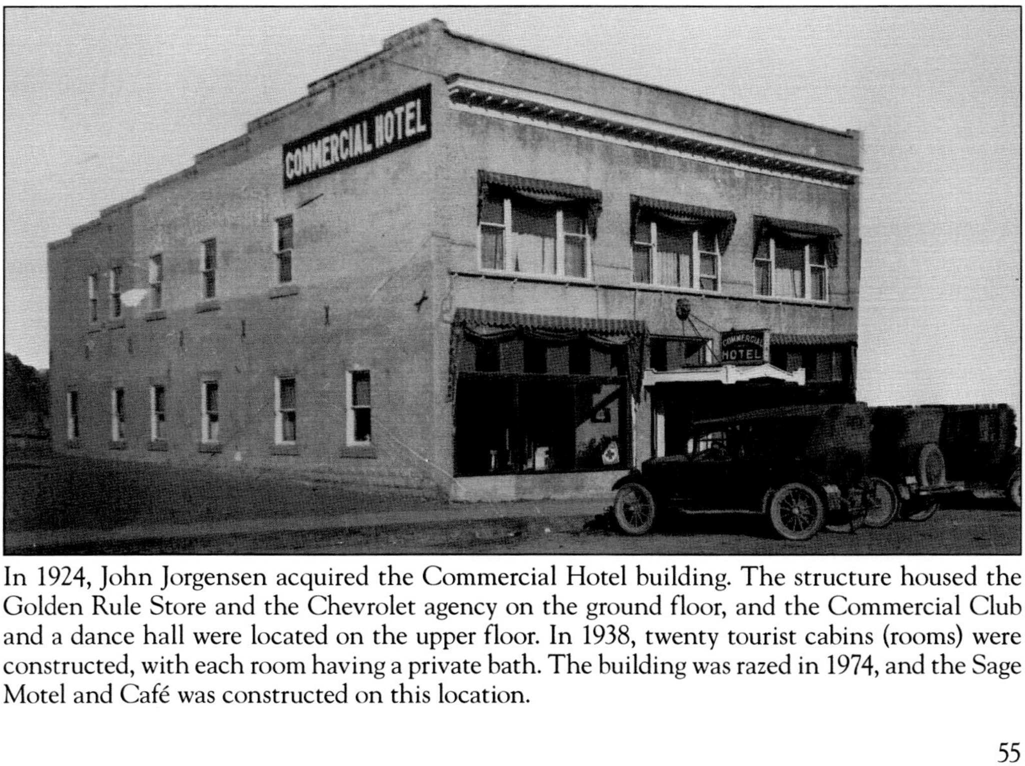

In 1924, John Jorgensen acquired the Commercial Hotel building. The structure housed the Golden Rule Store and the Chevrolet agency on the ground floor, and the Commercial Club and a dance hall were located on the upper floor. In 1938, twenty tourist cabins (rooms) were constructed, with each room having a private bath. The building was razed in 1974, and the Sage Motel and Café was constructed on this location.

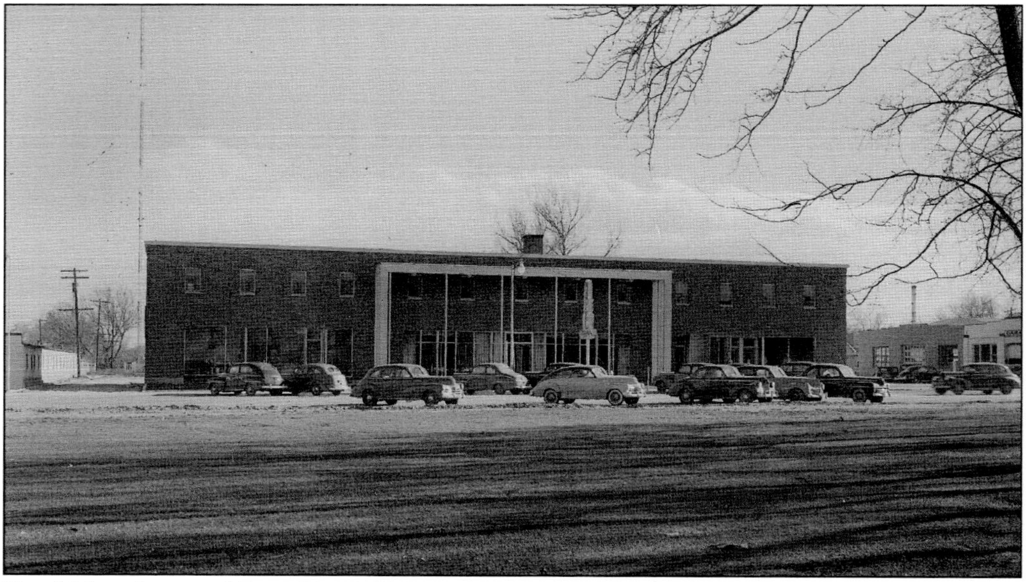

Hotel Vernal opened June 28, 1947. It was constructed for $350,000 and financed by a group of stockholders. The new hotel had 60 guest rooms and included a barbershop, beauty shop, haberdashery, fountain, coffee shop, and a restaurant. Vernal's first radio station, KJAM, was housed in the basement. When Hotel Vernal opened, it was said to be the finest small hotel in the United States.

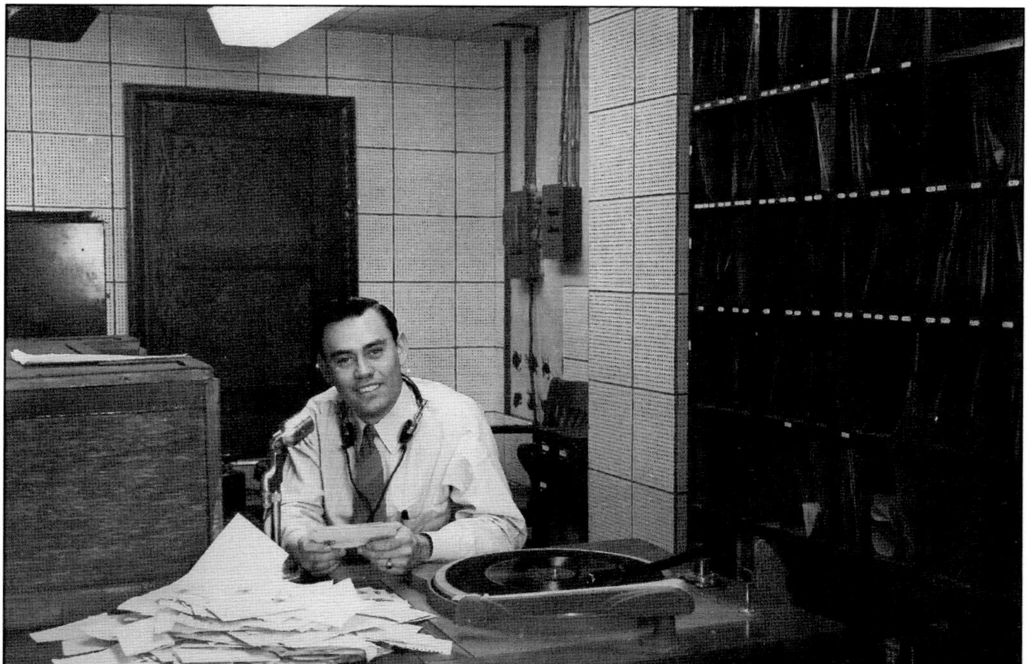

The first radio station in the Uinta Basin began broadcasting on January 19, 1947, in the basement of Hotel Vernal. With KJAM for its call letters, it was known as the "Voice of the Uinta Basin." Lee Walker helped bring entertainment over the radio waves into local homes. The station later became KVEL and is still in operation on North Vernal Avenue.

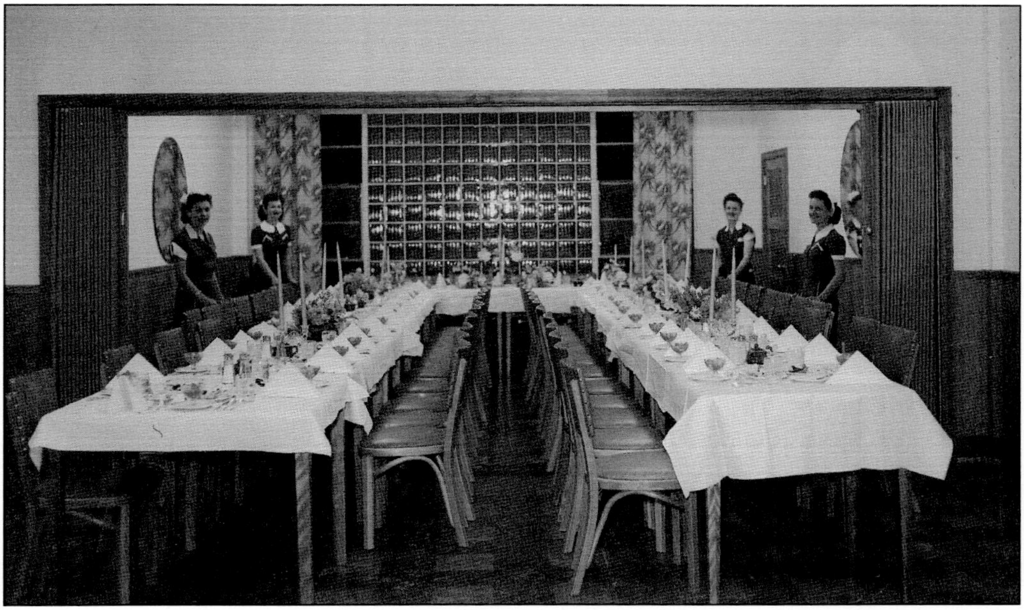

A banquet for Hotel Vernal was held for the stockholders and distinguished guests during the hotel's opening. Here, servers wait to serve their distinguished guests in the dining room. Many formal dinners and banquets were held in the Hotel Vernal dining room.

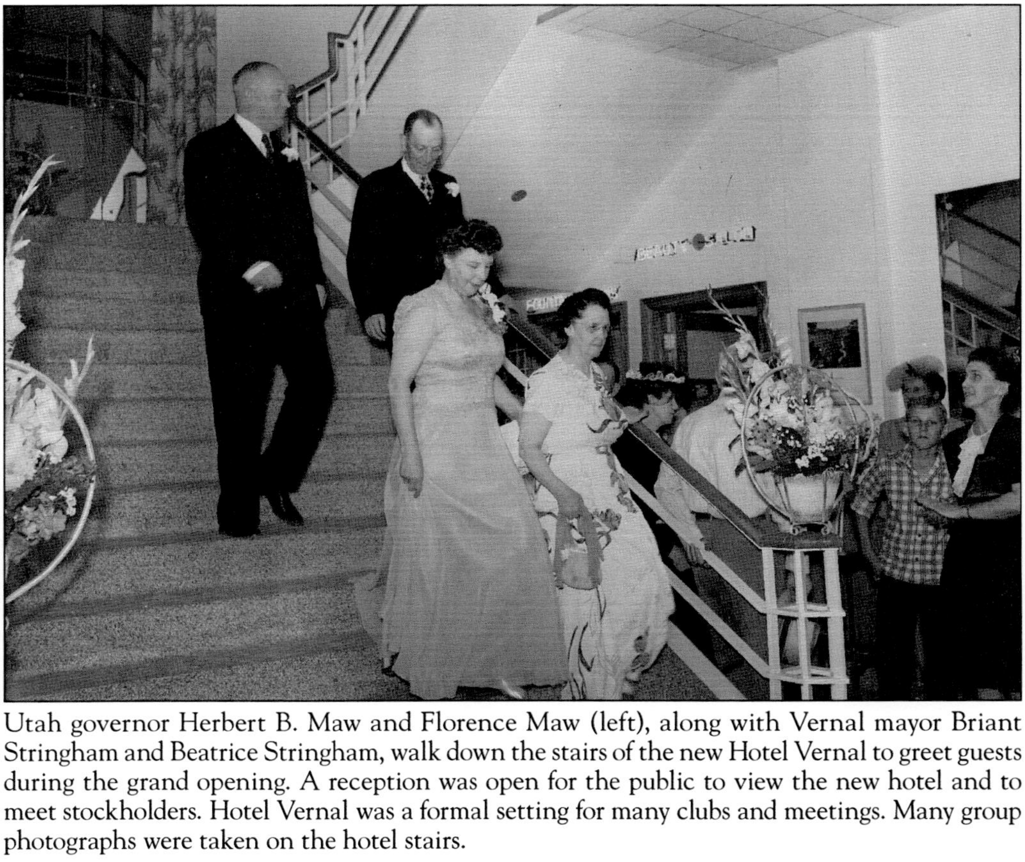

Utah governor Herbert B. Maw and Florence Maw (left), along with Vernal mayor Briant Stringham and Beatrice Stringham, walk down the stairs of the new Hotel Vernal to greet guests during the grand opening. A reception was open for the public to view the new hotel and to meet stockholders. Hotel Vernal was a formal setting for many clubs and meetings. Many group photographs were taken on the hotel stairs.

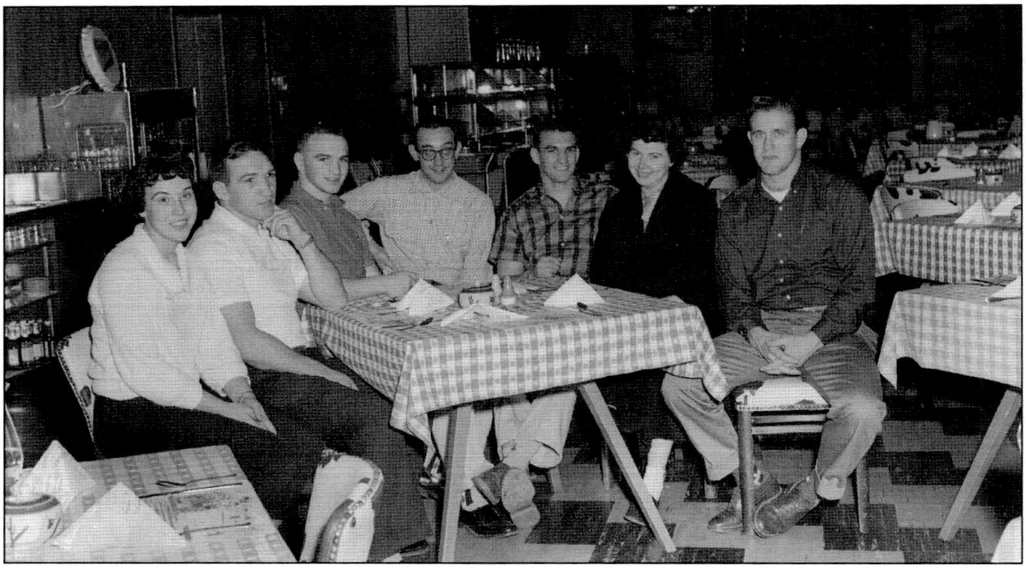

Warren and Daisy Belcher operated their restaurant as the Grub Box Diner during the 1930s and 1940s. They extended the back, installed a counter, and added table and chairs. In 1949, they built a new building near the Grub Box Diner. The new café was named 7-11 Ranch Café. It sported four dice on its marquee because Warren loved to gamble and shoot craps. It was said that the Belchers wanted 11 children but only had seven. The café became known for its Saturday-night Chuck Wagon Buffet and always had a packed house. Some well-known boxers dined at 7-11 Café prior to a boxing exhibition in Vernal in 1959. In the photograph above are, from left to right, Nedra Fullmer, Gene Fullmer, Don Fullmer, Paul Armstrong, Jay Fullmer, Marilyn Fullmer, and LaMar Clark. The 7-11 Café is still a popular place to eat in the valley.

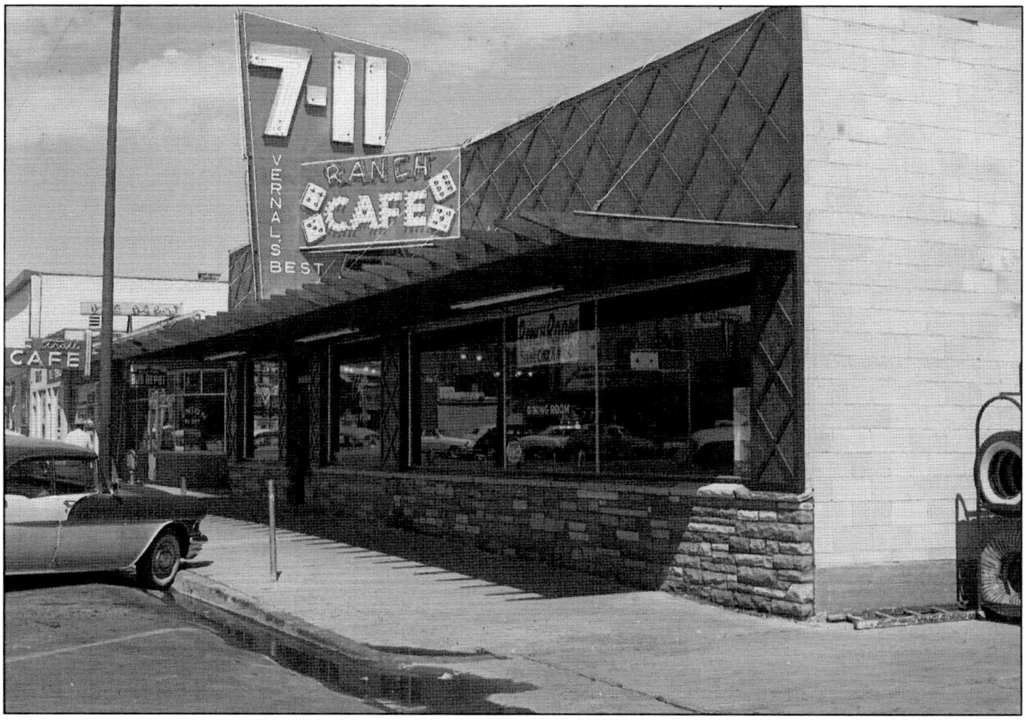

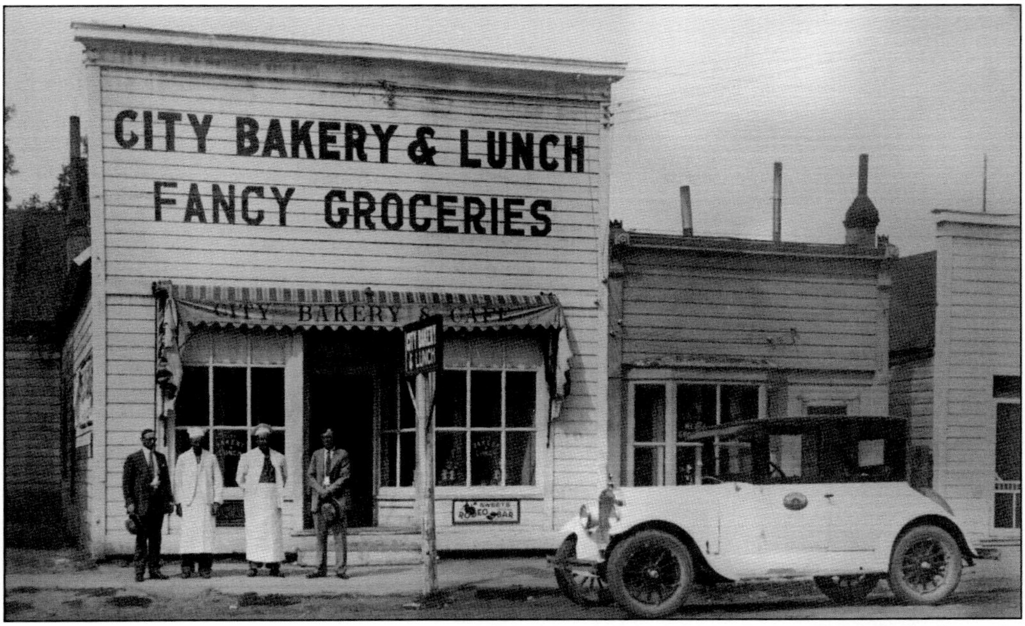

The City Bakery was opened to serve the community with fine foods and fresh baked goods. The bakery began business in the early 1900s and was located on South Vernal Avenue. The business went through several owners, with the last one being in February 1960. The building burned down two months later.

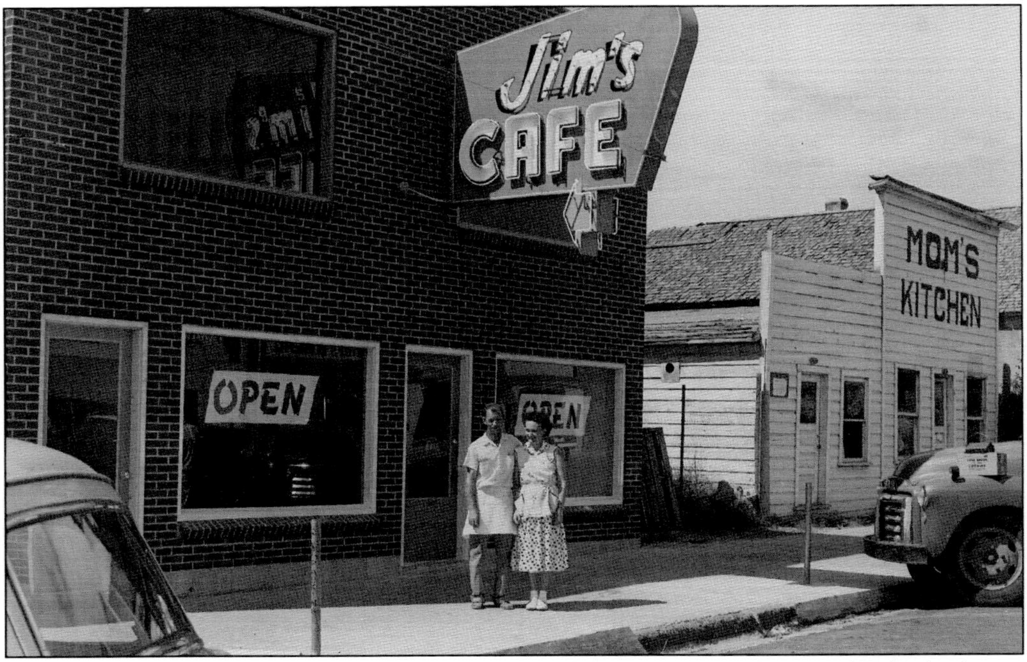

Jim Anderson opened Jim's Café in the building west of the Gipson Hotel. Jim and Ruby Anderson are pictured outside the café. They did most of the cooking and kept the place open 24 hours a day; the couple lived in an apartment above. Jim's Café was located here from 1945 to 1957. A few years later, he bought the lot east of the building and built a new café. Mom's Kitchen, another local eatery, can be seen next to Jim's Café.

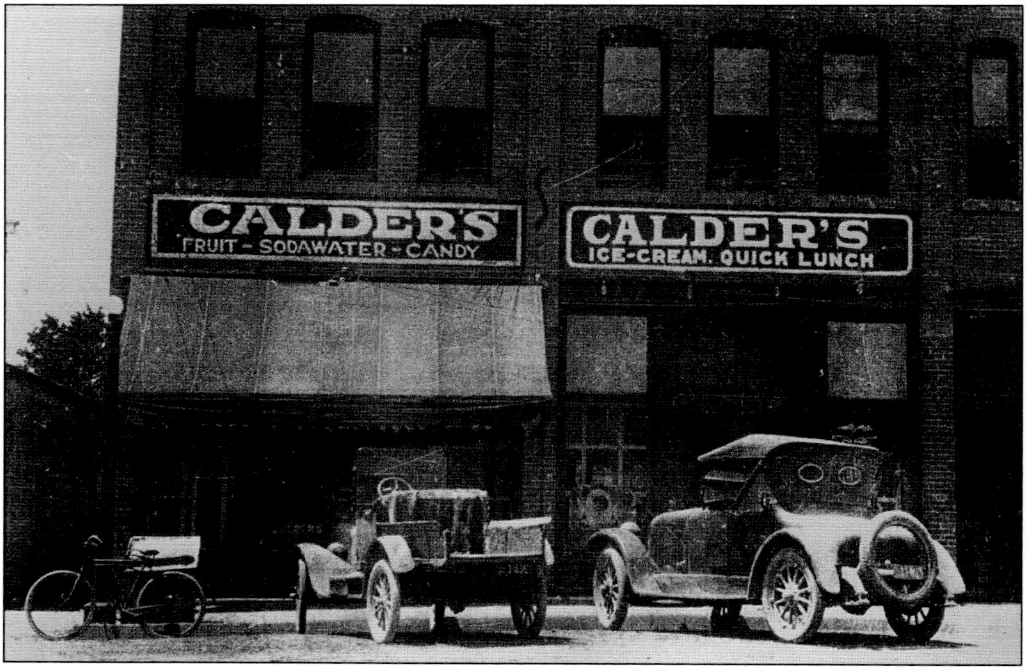

Calder's Confectionary was a candy store, soda fountain, and a restaurant. It was located between the Bank of Vernal and the Shamrock Saloon, and the Stockman's Club was upstairs. The first owners of the confectionery were the Calder family. Bill Taylor bought it from the Calders. While Bill ran the business, Vilate Jensen worked for him, and a Mr. Daily made the candy. Bill played the phonograph player in the candy store, which was an annoyance to the club upstairs. Some of the men from the Stockman's Club sneaked downstairs and put coyote scent in the phonograph. They never got the smell out and were no longer able to use the phonograph.

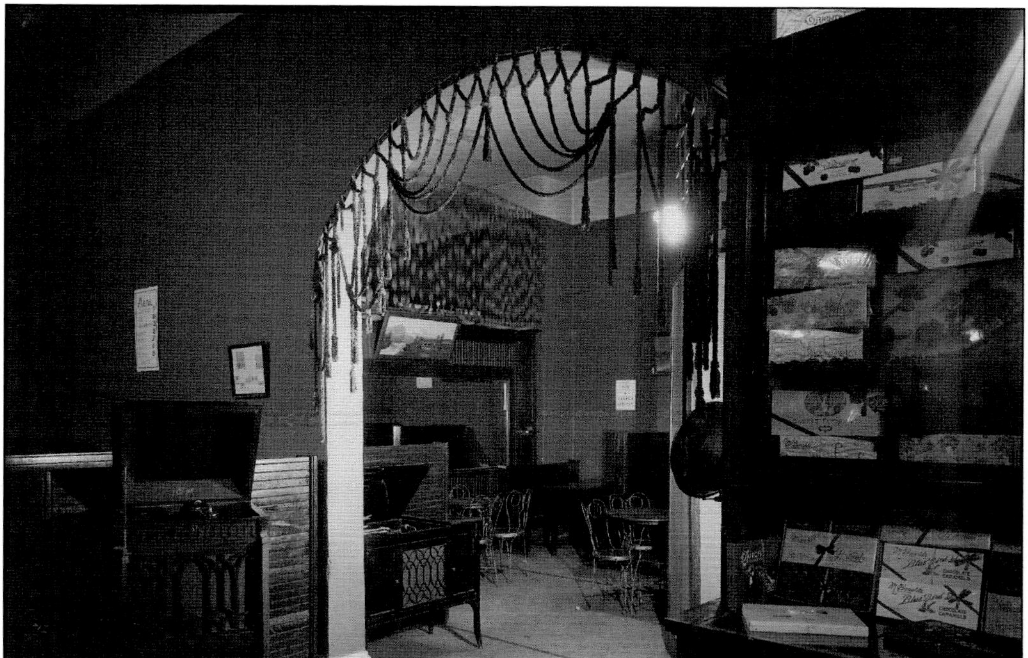

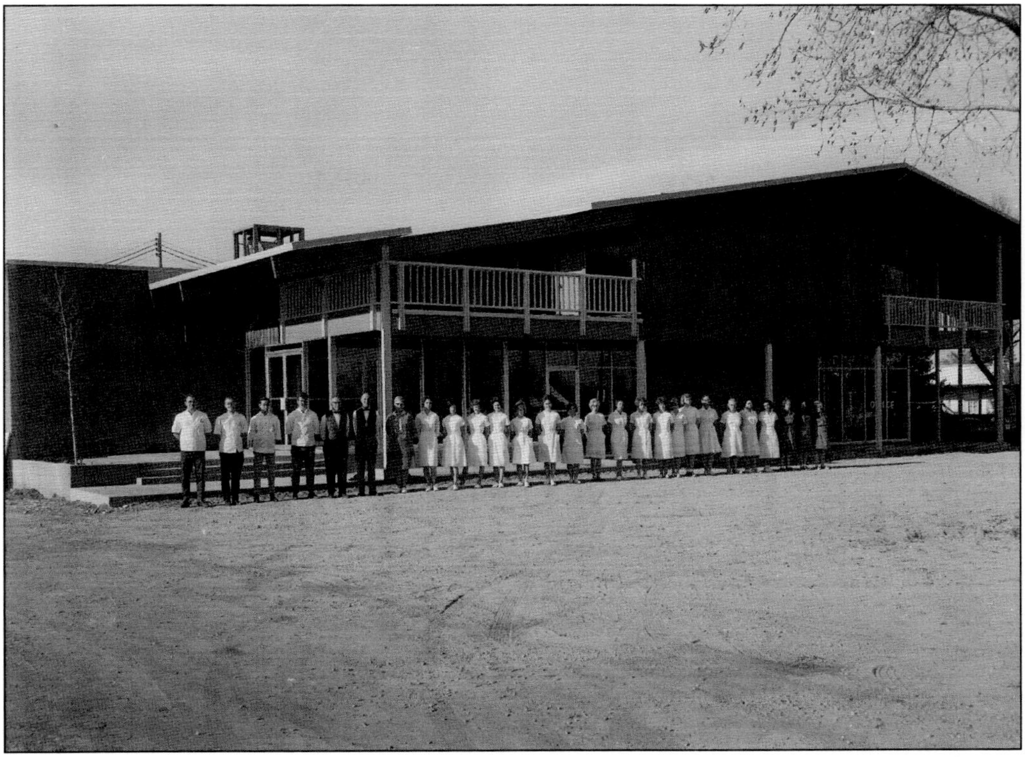

The staff of the Skillet East stands in front of the restaurant located at 251 East Main. In February 1961, Don Millecam was the owner. The large dining room was called Car 19.

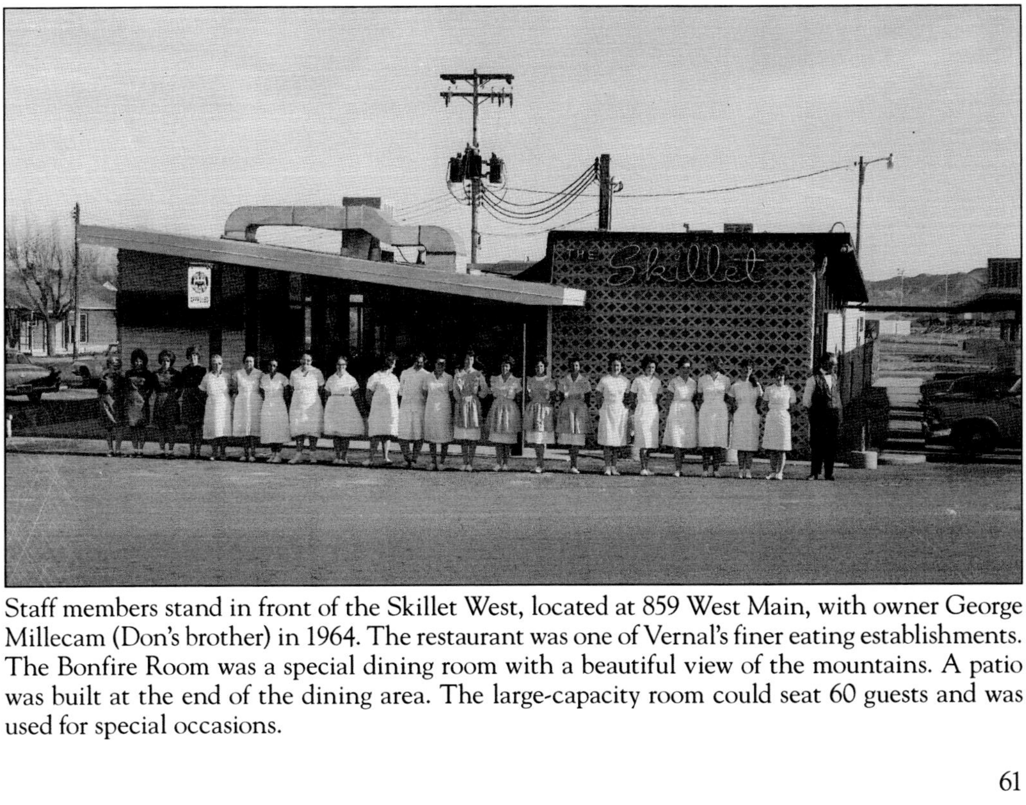

Staff members stand in front of the Skillet West, located at 859 West Main, with owner George Millecam (Don's brother) in 1964. The restaurant was one of Vernal's finer eating establishments. The Bonfire Room was a special dining room with a beautiful view of the mountains. A patio was built at the end of the dining area. The large-capacity room could seat 60 guests and was used for special occasions.

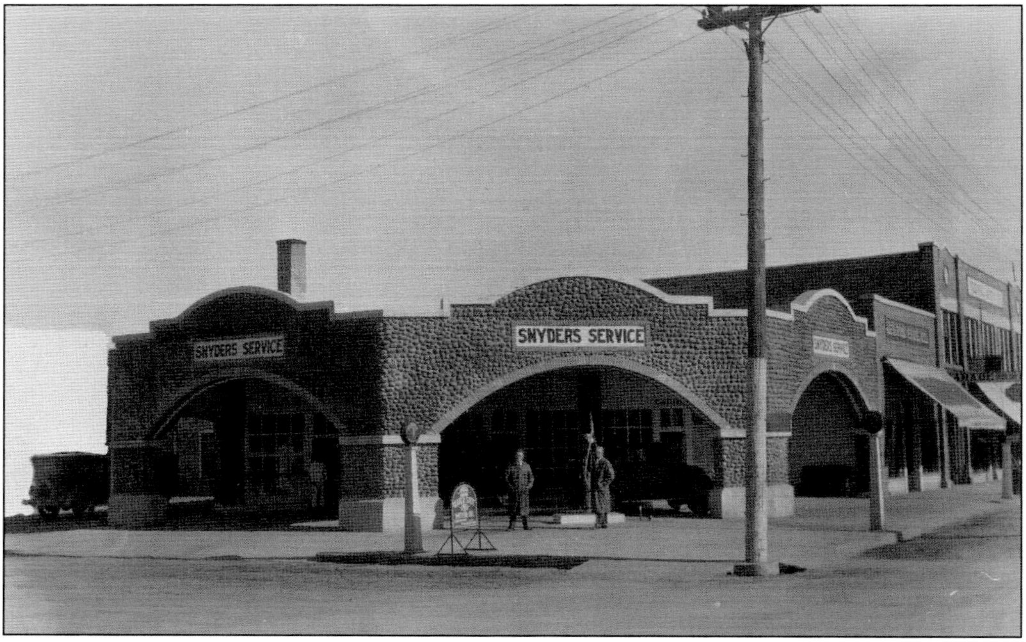

The Cobble Rock Station was built in 1925 as part of the Vernal Auto Company. The station had three beautiful arches that were constructed of cobble rocks hauled from the Ashley Creek. It was a state-of-the-art service station with access from Main Street and Vernal Avenue. The corner station changed ownership several times as it became Snyder's Service, Ashton's Service, and lastly, Conoco Service. In 1970, it was demolished to make room for extra parking space downtown. In 2002, a replica was built, and it is now the Cobble Rock Park.

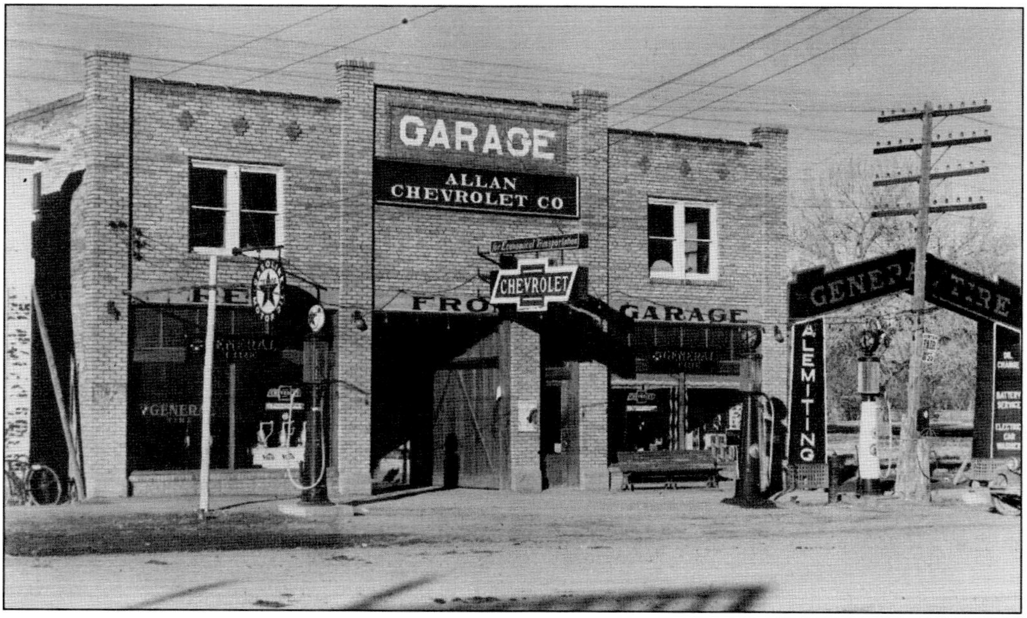

Charles F. Tucker, manager of the Red Front Garage, constructed a new two-story building right over his existing garage. The new structure was a modern, steam-heated garage with full automobile service, including tire repair and fueling pumps. The Allan Chevrolet Company and later Basin Chevrolet occupied space in the modern new garage.

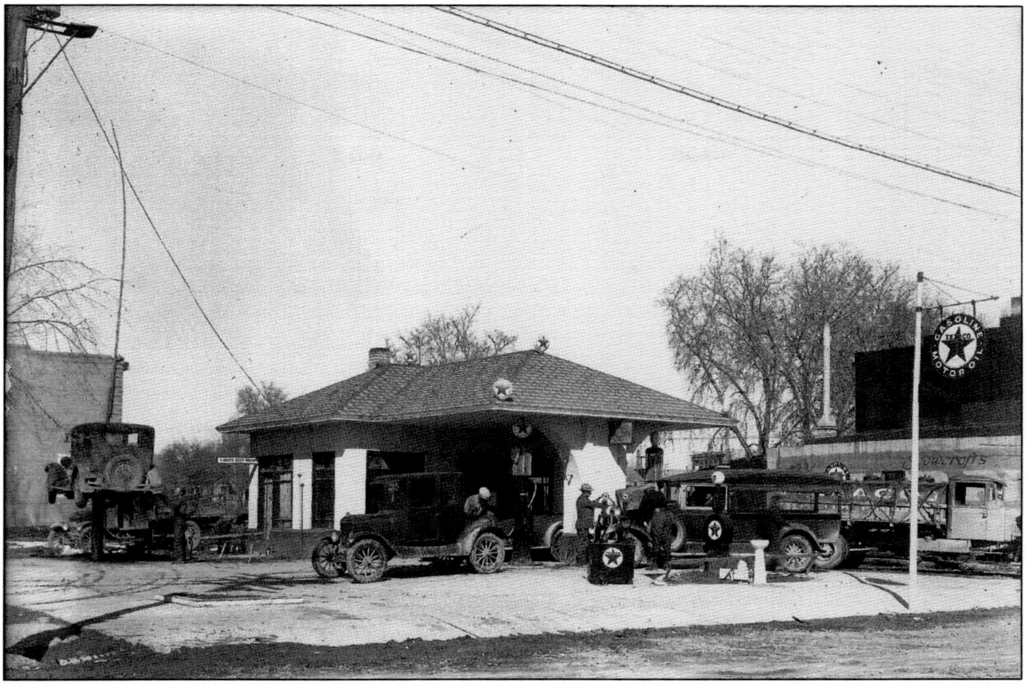

Calder's Texaco Station was built in 1928 and owned by Zelph Calder. The full-service station offered residents and travelers Texaco gasoline, oil changes, auto accessories, a ladies' restroom, drinking fountains, and tourist information.

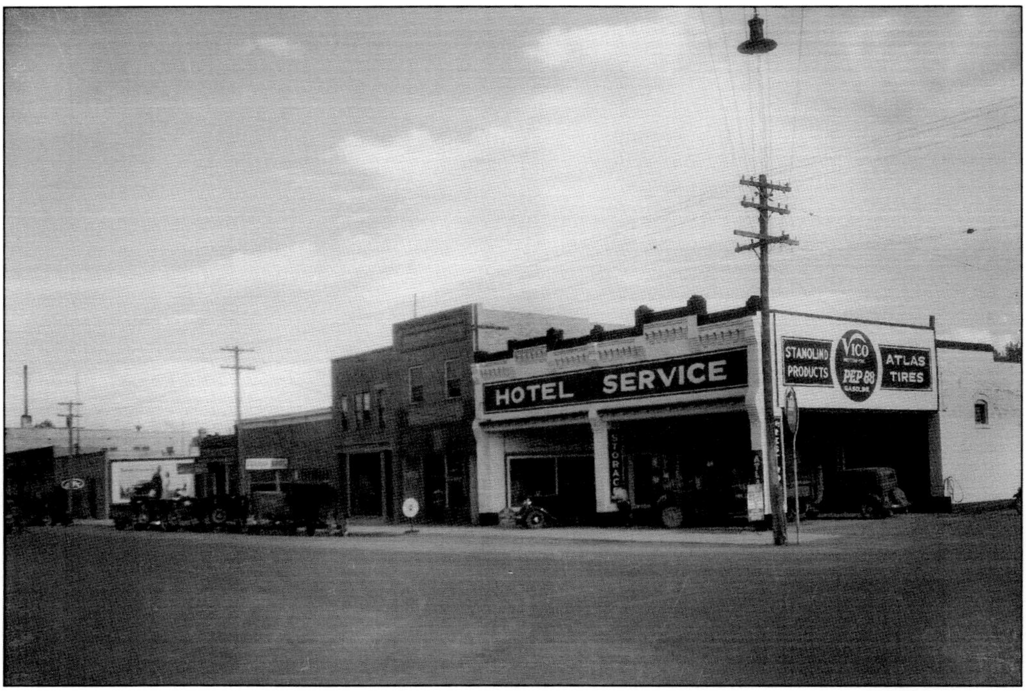

In June 1933, a new service station began business on the south side of 100 West Main Street. The business was named Hotel Service Station because it was located midway between the Commercial Hotel and the Gibson Hotel, two leading lodgings in Vernal. In 1944, a body and fender shop was added.

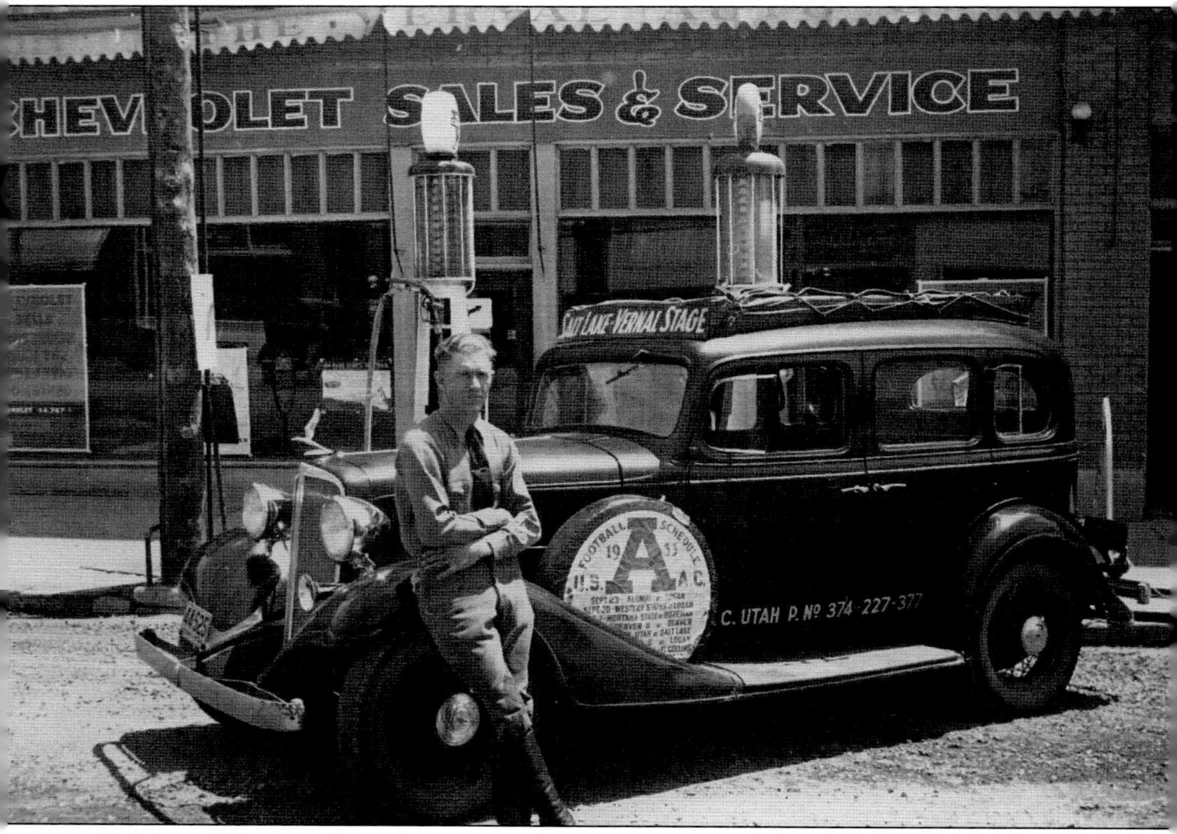

Ralph and George Alexander owned Salt Lake to Vernal Stage Line. The operation provided transportation by automobile from Vernal to Salt Lake City and back. Passengers met at the Basin Chevrolet Sales and Service located in the Red Front Garage. Here, the cars were fueled and made ready for travel over the scenic highway. The stage line provided a convenient schedule that would allow passengers three extra hours in Salt Lake City before their return back to Vernal, making it a one-day trip. In 1935, Denver-Colorado Springs-Pueblo Inc., a large bus line company, bought out the Salt Lake to Vernal Stage Line.

Six

Gold Mine of Resources

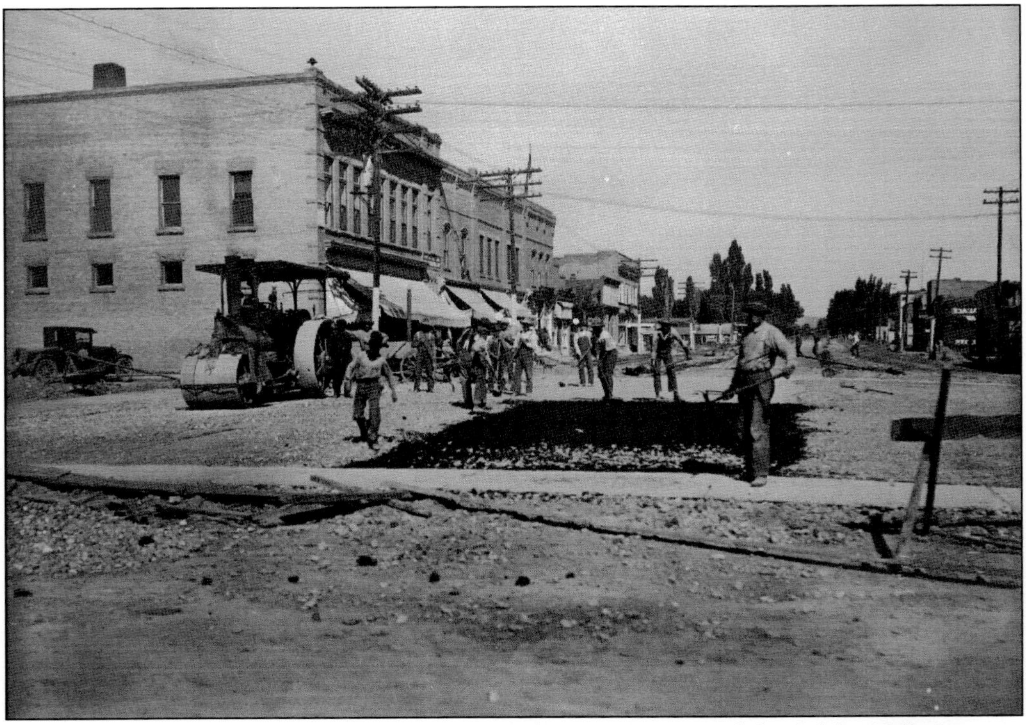

In 1923, the federal government and the state road commission tested the Ashley Valley's native asphalt for paving roads. This local asphalt was found to be the cheapest when mined, and when laid with proper machinery and methods, it proved to be the greatest paving material to be found in the United States. In this photograph, men use the native asphalt to pave the intersection of Main Street and Vernal Avenue.

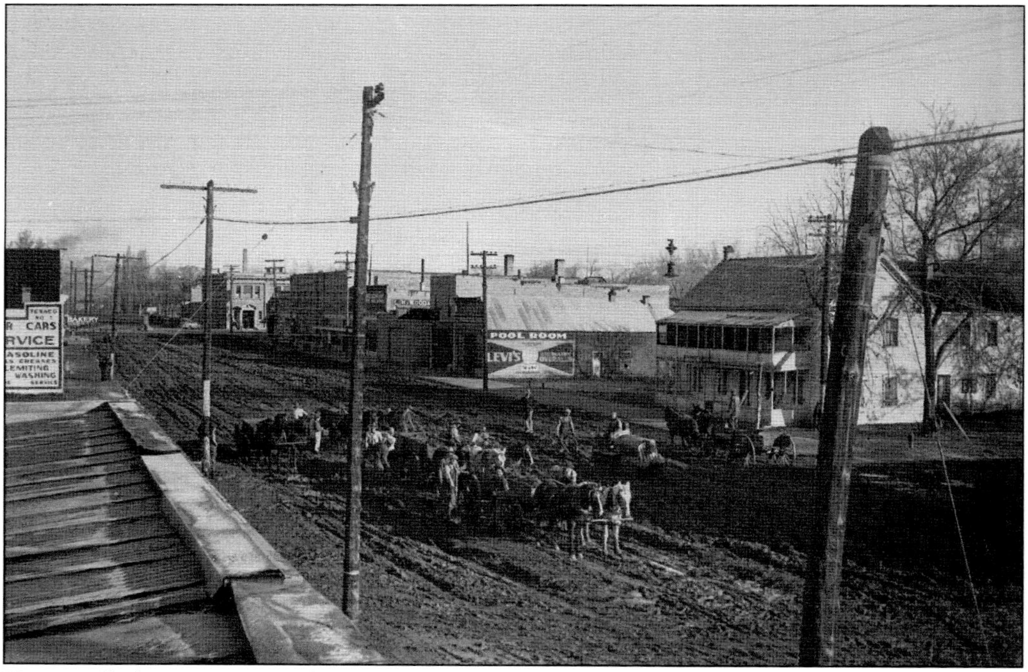

Horse-pulled scrapers smooth out the muddy ruts on South Vernal Avenue. Main roads were laid with native asphalt in 1934. Businesses shown on the east side of Vernal Avenue are Vernal Hotel, Vernal Pool Room, L.H. Woodard, and Uintah State Bank.

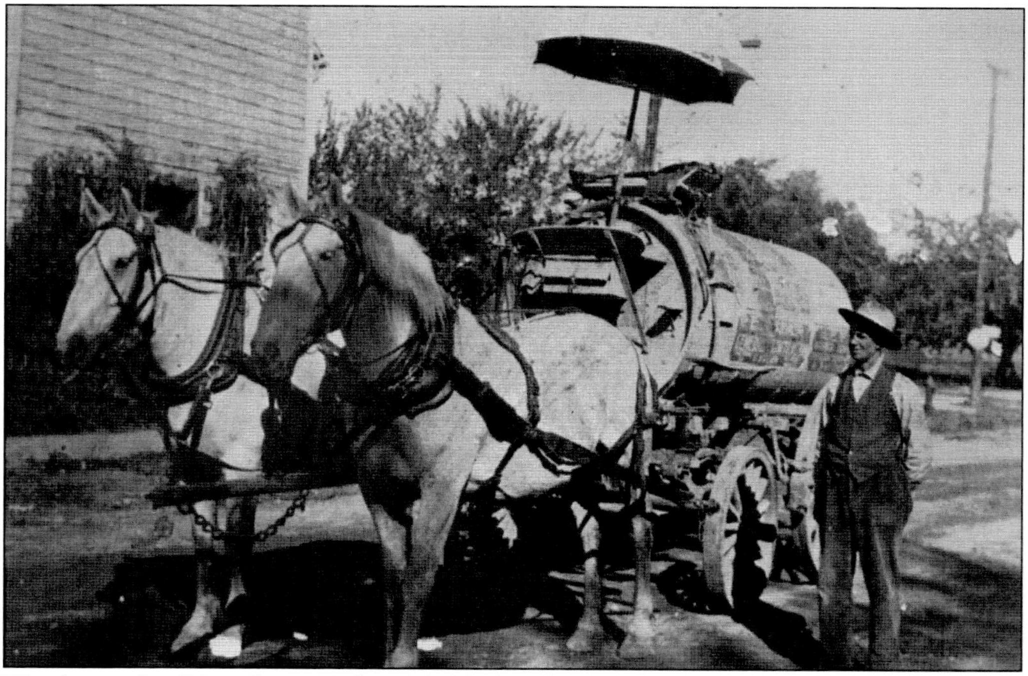

The dirt roads of Vernal were well traveled by horses, wagons, and early automobiles. To combat the dust caused by this heavy traffic, Vernal City purchased a sprinkling wagon. This horse-pulled water tank was contracted out annually. John Corless won the contract to sprinkle the roads in 1921 and did so for 10 years.

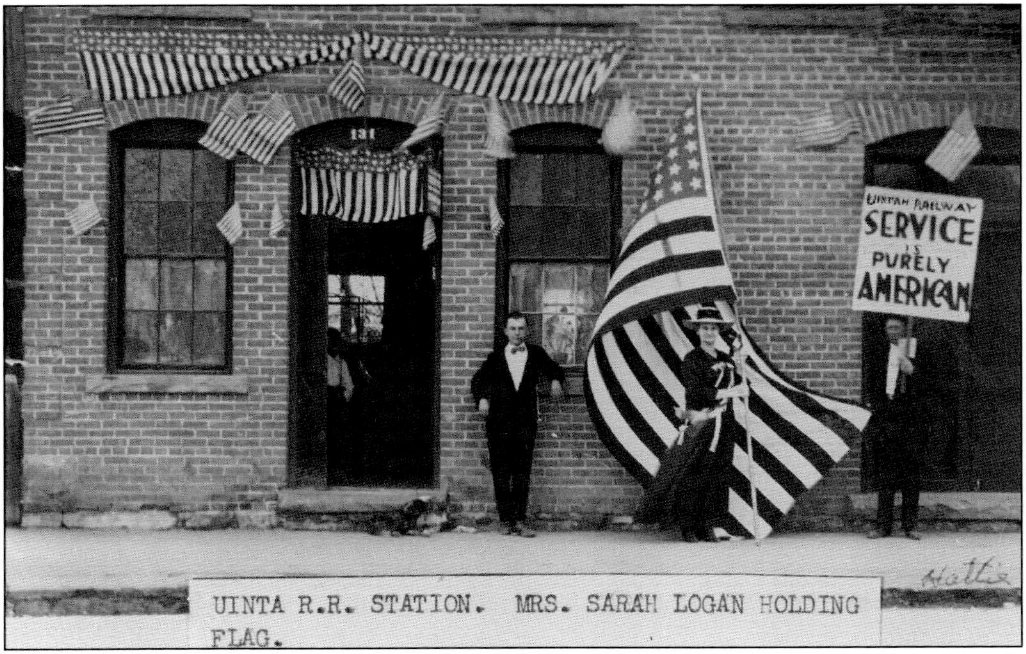

UINTA R.R. STATION. MRS. SARAH LOGAN HOLDING FLAG.

A railroad station was built in 1905 at 80 North Vernal Avenue in anticipation that the Uintah Railway would extend its rails to Vernal. The intended railroad never made it to Vernal. Containing both freight house and passenger depot, the Uintah Railway Station had shipments every day of the week, both in and out of the Ashley Valley. In the upper floor of the Uintah Railway Station, the telegraph office connected Vernal to Dragon, Utah, and Mack, Colorado. John Q. and Sarah Logan, pictured in front of the building, were hired to manage and operate the telegraph line exchange. The man holding the sign is unidentified. The couple operated the Uintah Railway Depot until John's death in 1915, and Sarah in 1931. Shown is an example of a telegraph sent over the telegraph lines to the Ashley Valley. The old Railway Station building still stands today.

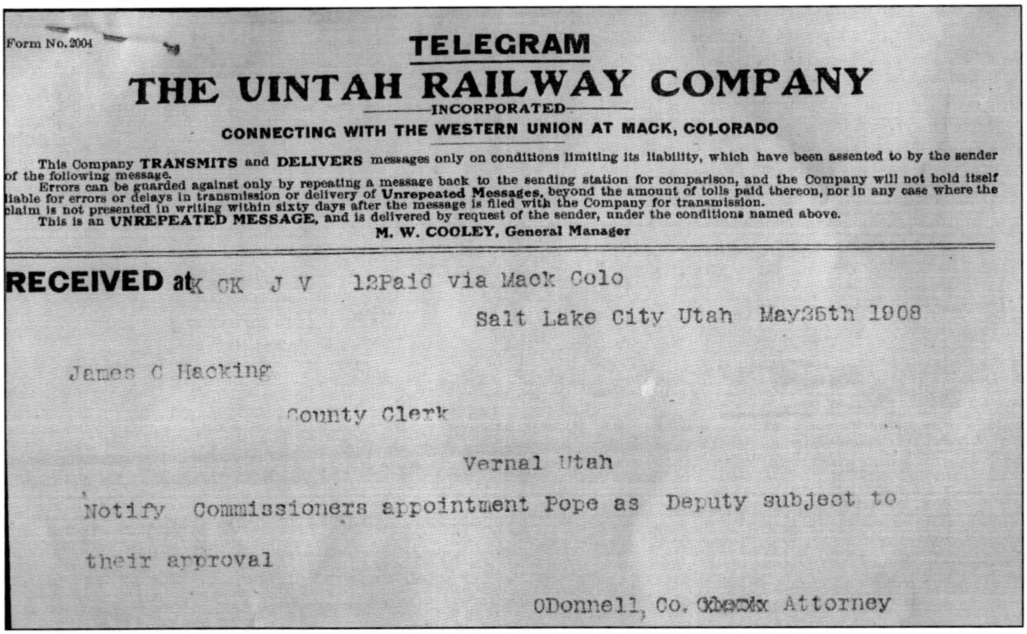

Form No. 2004

TELEGRAM

THE UINTAH RAILWAY COMPANY

INCORPORATED

CONNECTING WITH THE WESTERN UNION AT MACK, COLORADO

This Company **TRANSMITS** and **DELIVERS** messages only on conditions limiting its liability, which have been assented to by the sender of the following message.

Errors can be guarded against only by repeating a message back to the sending station for comparison, and the Company will not hold itself liable for errors or delays in transmission or delivery of **Unrepeated Messages,** beyond the amount of tolls paid thereon, nor in any case where the claim is not presented in writing within sixty days after the message is filed with the Company for transmission.

This is an **UNREPEATED MESSAGE,** and is delivered by request of the sender, under the conditions named above.

M. W. COOLEY, General Manager

RECEIVED at K CK J V 12Paid via Mack Colo

Salt Lake City Utah May25th 1908

James C Hacking

County Clerk

Vernal Utah

Notify Commissioners appointment Pope as Deputy subject to

their approval

ODonnell, Co. ~~Clerk~~ Attorney

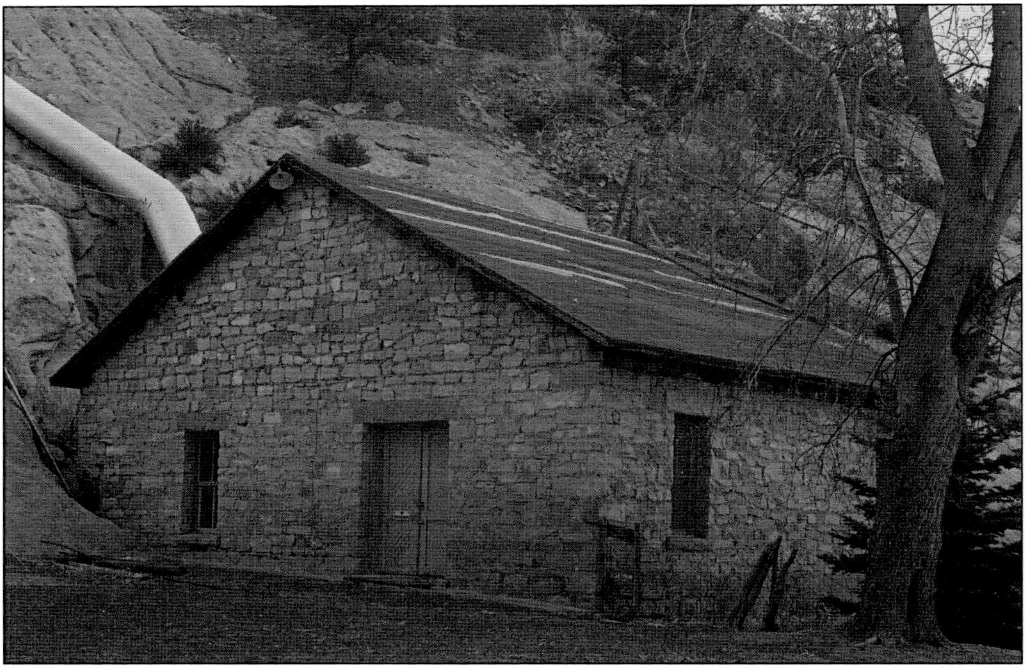

On March 10, 1903, Vernal City Council met with officials from Salt Lake City to take action on an electric-light franchise. They visited the Ashley Canyon to determine a power site location. Residents looked forward to having electricity to replace their coal oil lights. The sum of money estimated to bring the plant into running order was $35,000; this included the mill building, foundation, excavations, and poles from the power site.

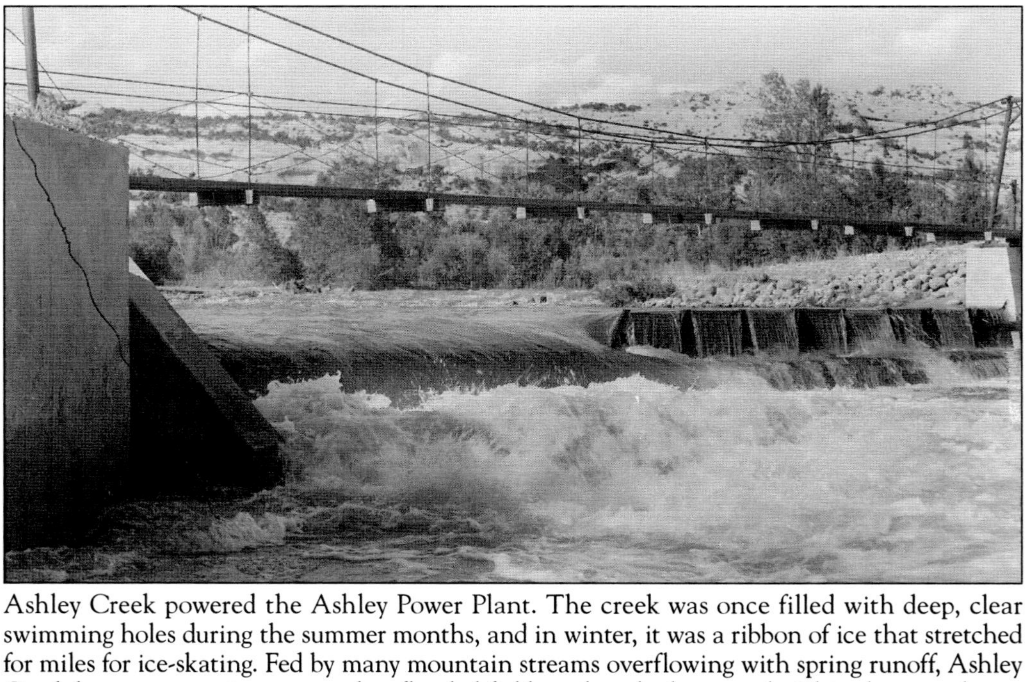

Ashley Creek powered the Ashley Power Plant. The creek was once filled with deep, clear swimming holes during the summer months, and in winter, it was a ribbon of ice that stretched for miles for ice-skating. Fed by many mountain streams overflowing with spring runoff, Ashley Creek became a roaring stream that flooded fields and washed out roads. This photograph was taken during the 1958 spring runoff.

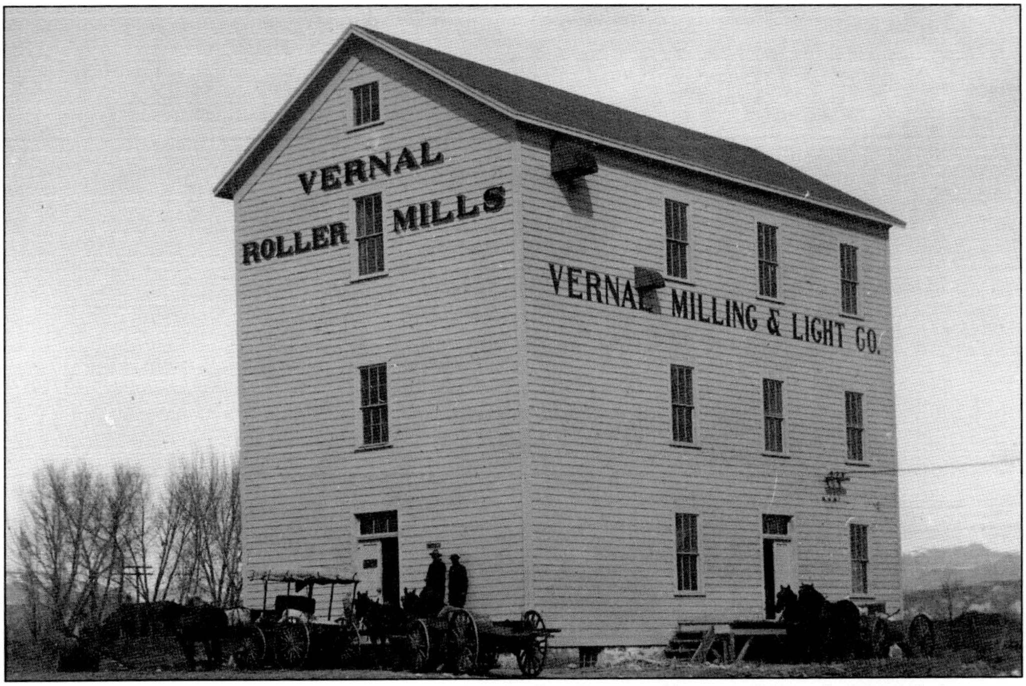

The Vernal Milling and Light Company erected a flour mill on 445 North Vernal Avenue. Ashley Valley farmers used the mill as a depository for their fall grain, drawing out what flour was needed for the winter. Utah Power and Light purchased the utility portion of the mill in 1925. The mill operated until 1946, when E.H. Peterson purchased it. It was destroyed by fire on January 25, 1952.

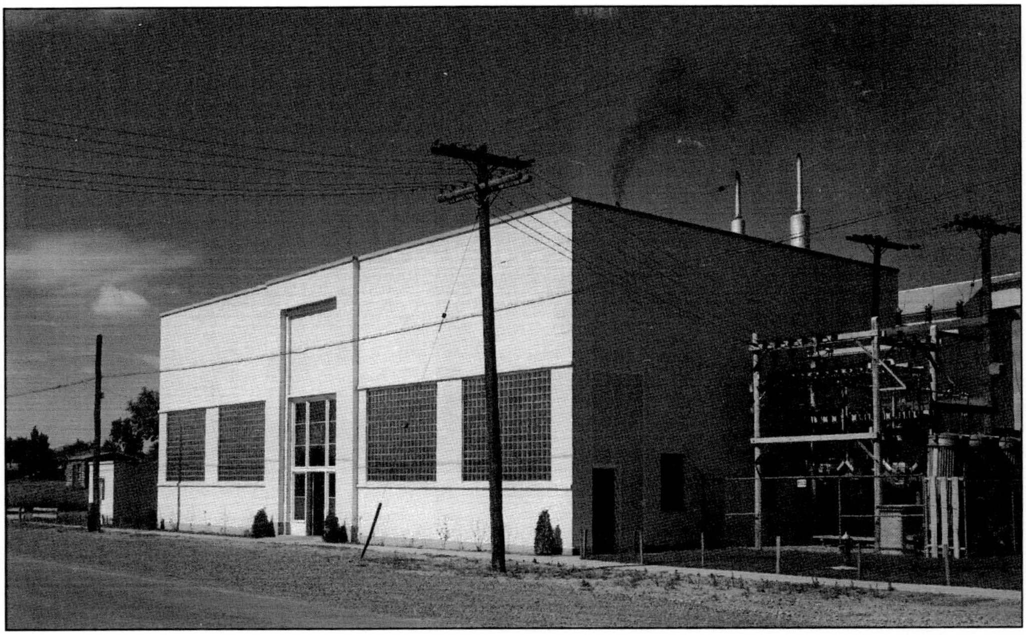

By 1938, the valley needed more power. The Utah Power and Light auxiliary generating plant was established on Vernal Avenue at 500 North. Power was generated by a diesel generator, which provided the valley's electricity until the mid-1960s.

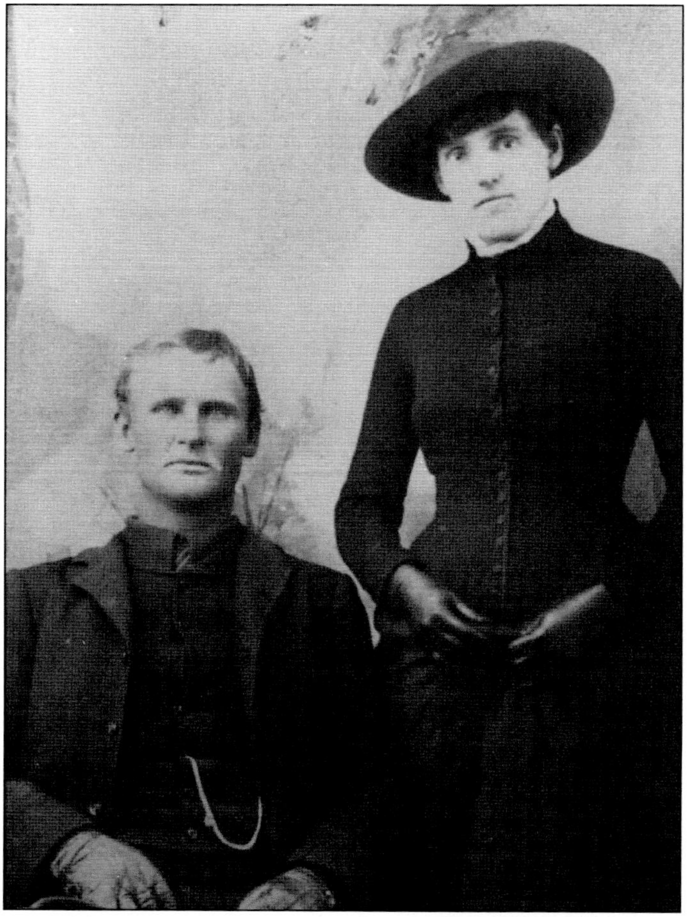

The first newspaper in Ashley Valley was called the *Uintah Papoose*. It was owned and operated by Kate Jean Boan, pictured at left with her husband, Frank, who was the paper's first editor. She purchased her printing press from a mail-order house. The first issue of the paper was four pages long, with three columns per page. After one year of operation, Boan sold the paper to James Baker. He was a bachelor who did not like being teased about his papoose, so he renamed the newspaper *Vernal Express*. For most of its years, the paper was located at 54 North Vernal Avenue and was run by four generations of the Wallis family.

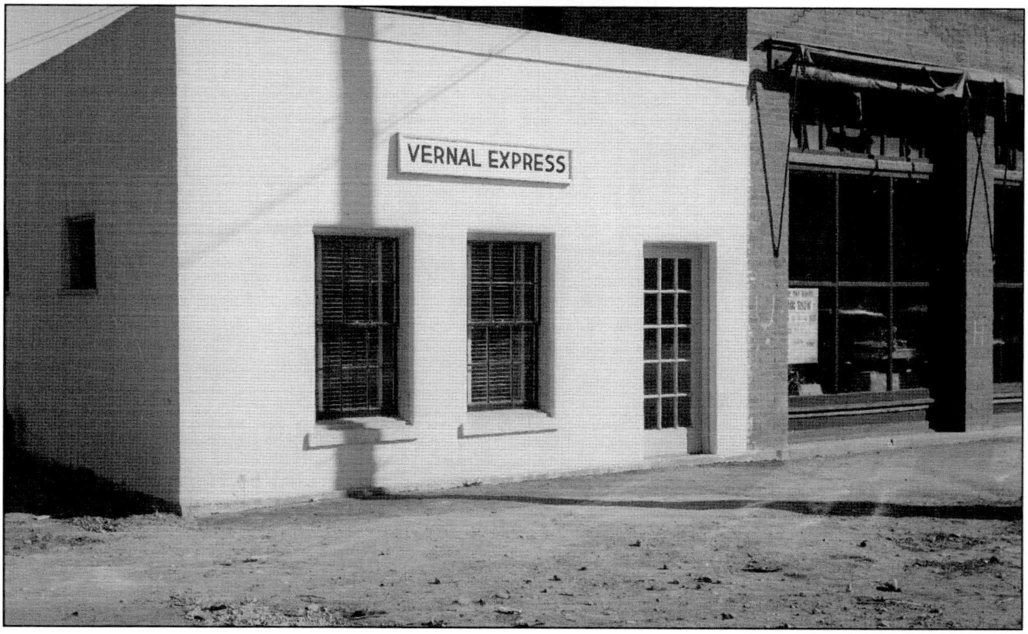

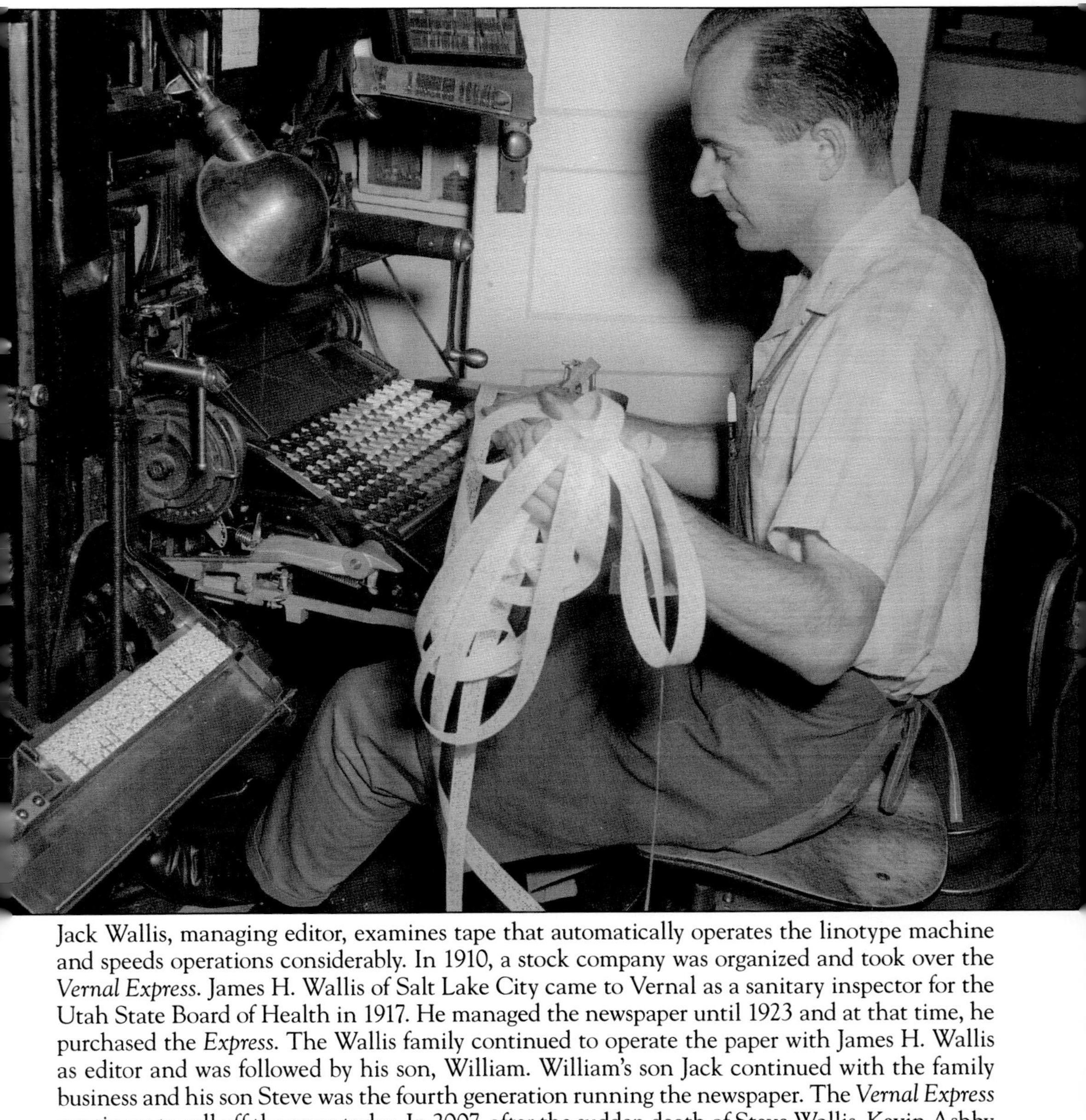

Jack Wallis, managing editor, examines tape that automatically operates the linotype machine and speeds operations considerably. In 1910, a stock company was organized and took over the *Vernal Express*. James H. Wallis of Salt Lake City came to Vernal as a sanitary inspector for the Utah State Board of Health in 1917. He managed the newspaper until 1923 and at that time, he purchased the *Express*. The Wallis family continued to operate the paper with James H. Wallis as editor and was followed by his son, William. William's son Jack continued with the family business and his son Steve was the fourth generation running the newspaper. The *Vernal Express* continues to roll off the press today. In 2007, after the sudden death of Steve Wallis, Kevin Ashby purchased the newspaper. It is now located at 100 North.

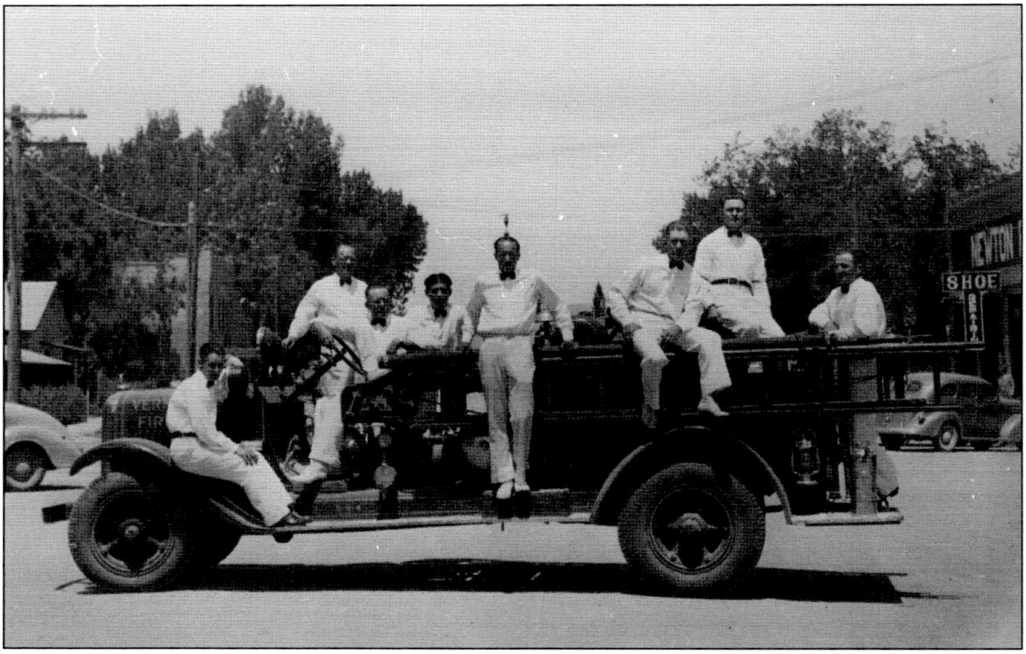

In 1911, the city council appointed George Adams as fire chief and instructed him to begin a volunteer fire department. The volunteer firemen pose on the fire truck in 1940. They are, from left to right, Joe Milburn, Henry Millecam, Wendell Pope, Ace York, Ken Richardson, Ralph Alexander, Henry Schaefermeyer, and Mick Batty.

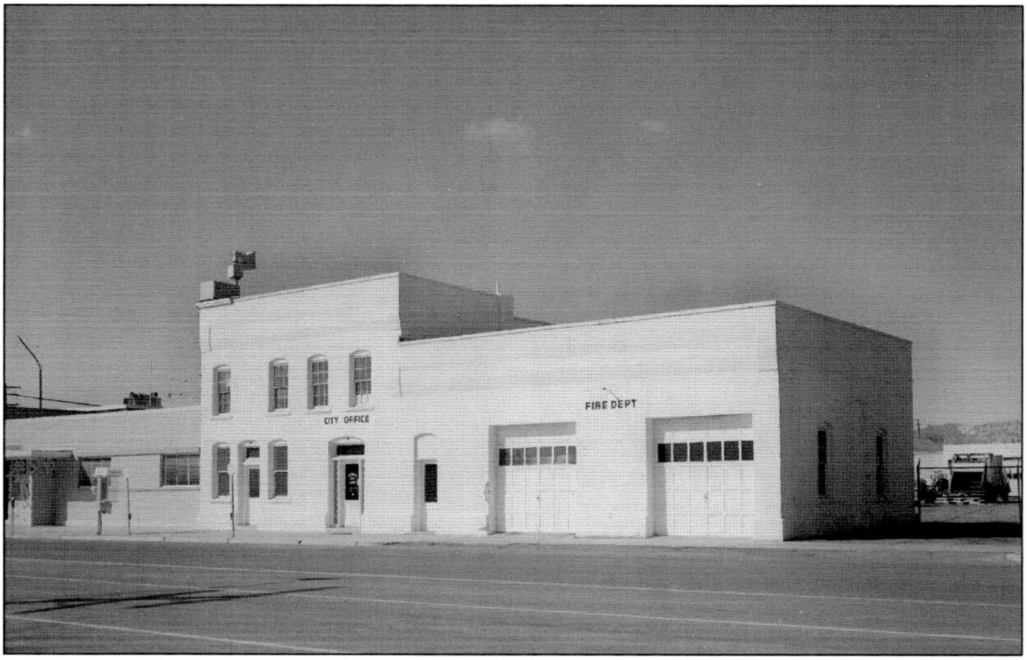

In 1946, Vernal City moved its offices, along with the volunteer fire department, to the old Uintah Railway Building. The civil defense siren was placed on top of the building. It could be heard all over the valley when there was a fire or emergency. By 1973, Vernal City relocated again to 500 East Main Street.

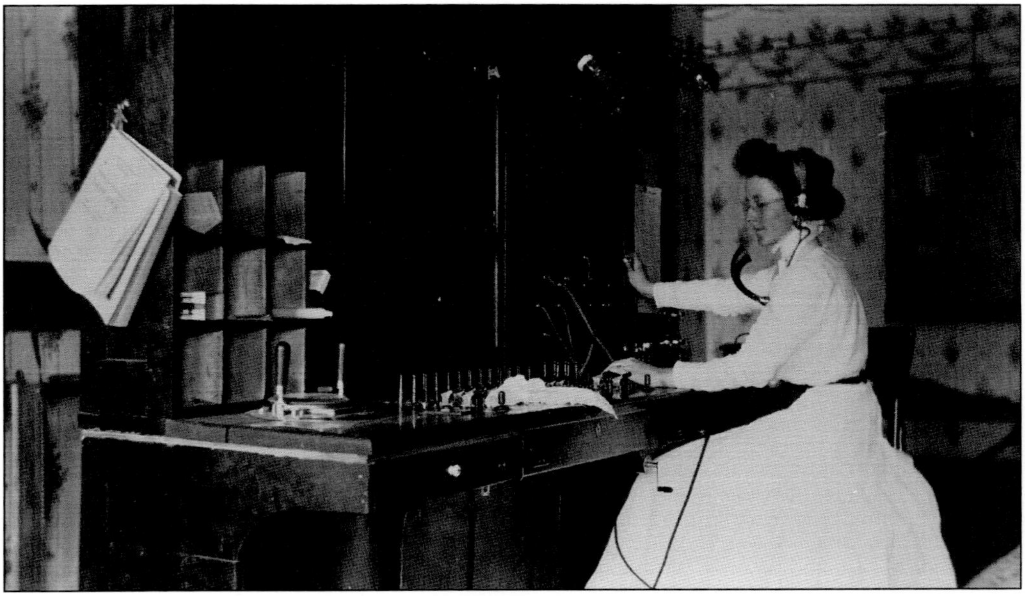

In 1907, C.J. Neal developed the Uintah Telephone Company. The first telephone office was run out of the Neal home. Essie Neal trained operators, making the telephone service available 24 hours a day. Then, it was located on the upper floor in the Ashley Co-op building. At the switchboard in this 1911 photograph, Louie Atwood asks in her sweet voice, "Number, please?"

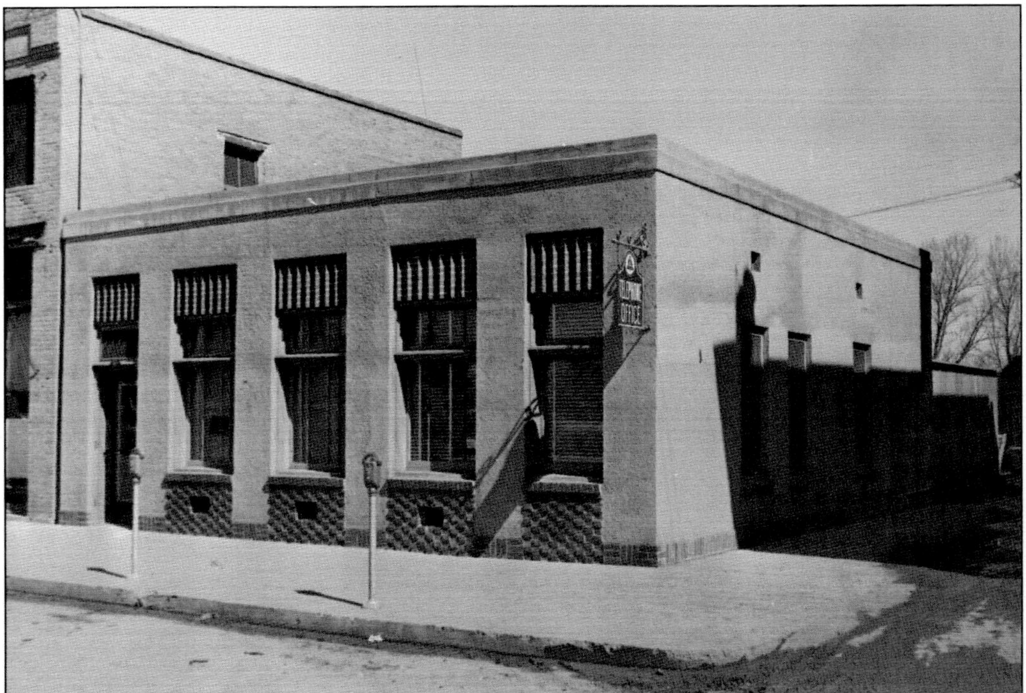

In 1928, the Uintah Telephone Company was sold to Mountain States Telephone and Telegraph. The company sought permission to construct lines to the Colorado border. The Mountain States Telephone office was located on the east side of North Vernal Avenue next to Uintah State Bank. Later, a telephone office was built on the west side of Vernal Avenue.

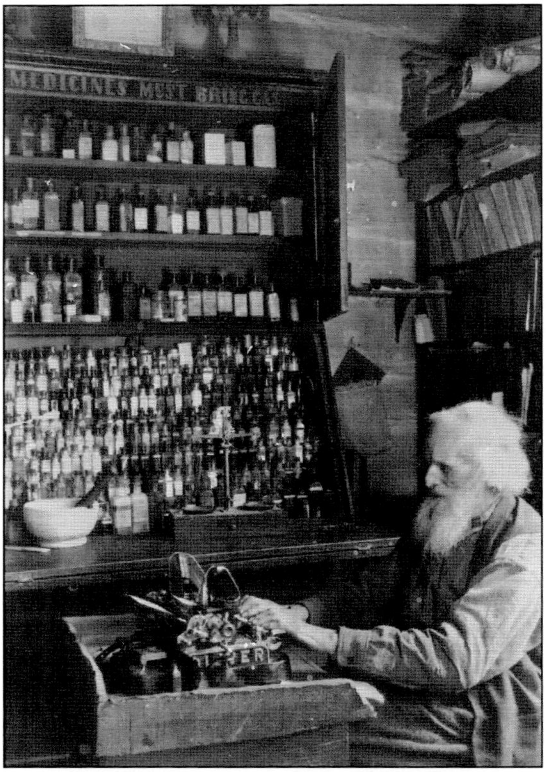

Dr. Harvey Coe Hullinger was born December 2, 1824. He began practicing medicine in 1852. He moved to the Ashley Valley in 1883, and was the first real practicing doctor there. Hullinger delivered over 1,000 babies while practicing medicine and achieved the distinction of being the oldest practicing physician in the United States. He practiced until 1925, when he was 101 years old. He died the following year, on January 29.

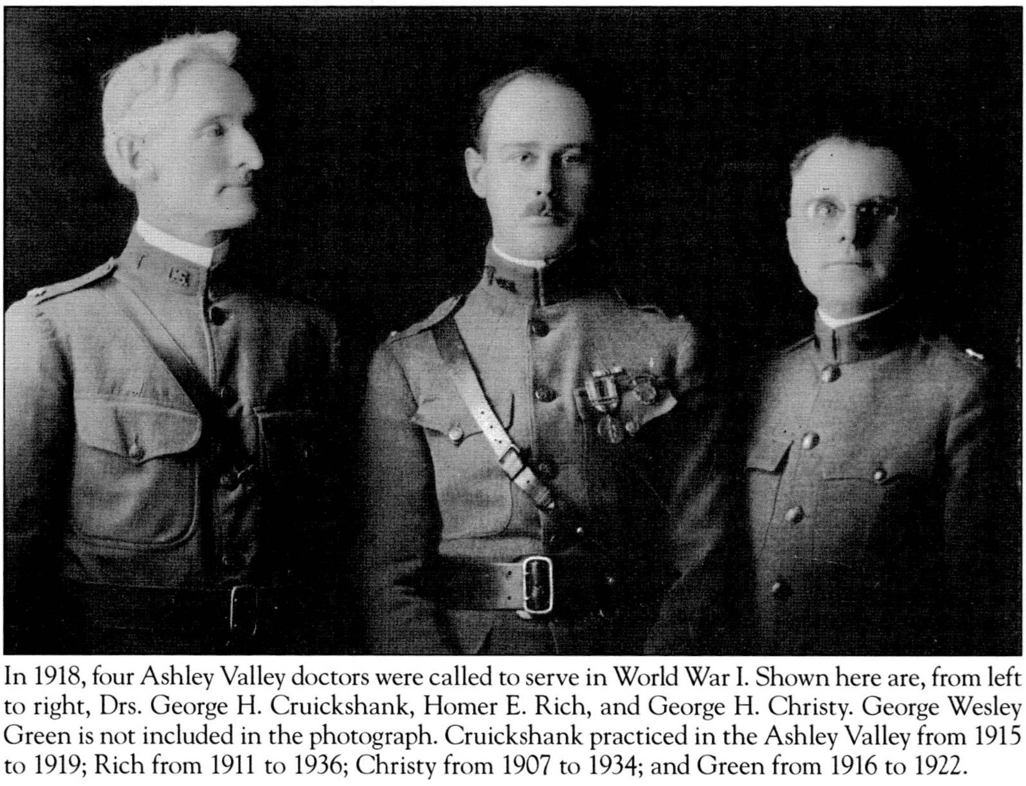

In 1918, four Ashley Valley doctors were called to serve in World War I. Shown here are, from left to right, Drs. George H. Cruickshank, Homer E. Rich, and George H. Christy. George Wesley Green is not included in the photograph. Cruickshank practiced in the Ashley Valley from 1915 to 1919; Rich from 1911 to 1936; Christy from 1907 to 1934; and Green from 1916 to 1922.

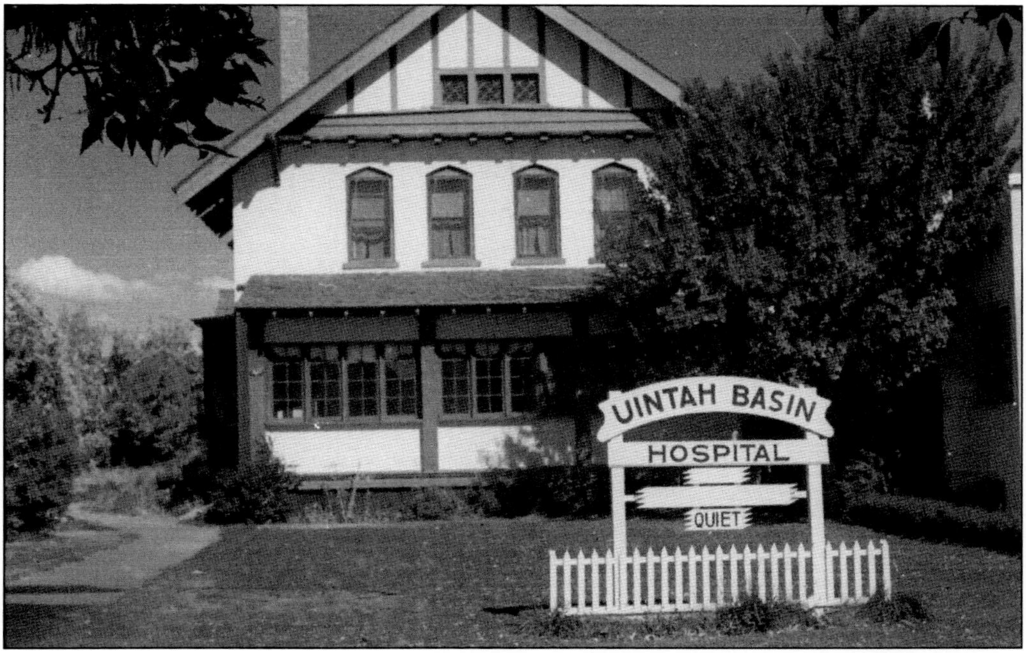

St. Paul's Episcopal Lodge was once used as a temporary hospital during the flu epidemic of 1918. Later, in the 1930s, the lodge was purchased by Dr. Farley Eskelson and was known as the Valley Hospital. It later became the Uintah Basin Hospital. When the county built a new hospital in 1949, the lodge was resold to the Episcopal Church.

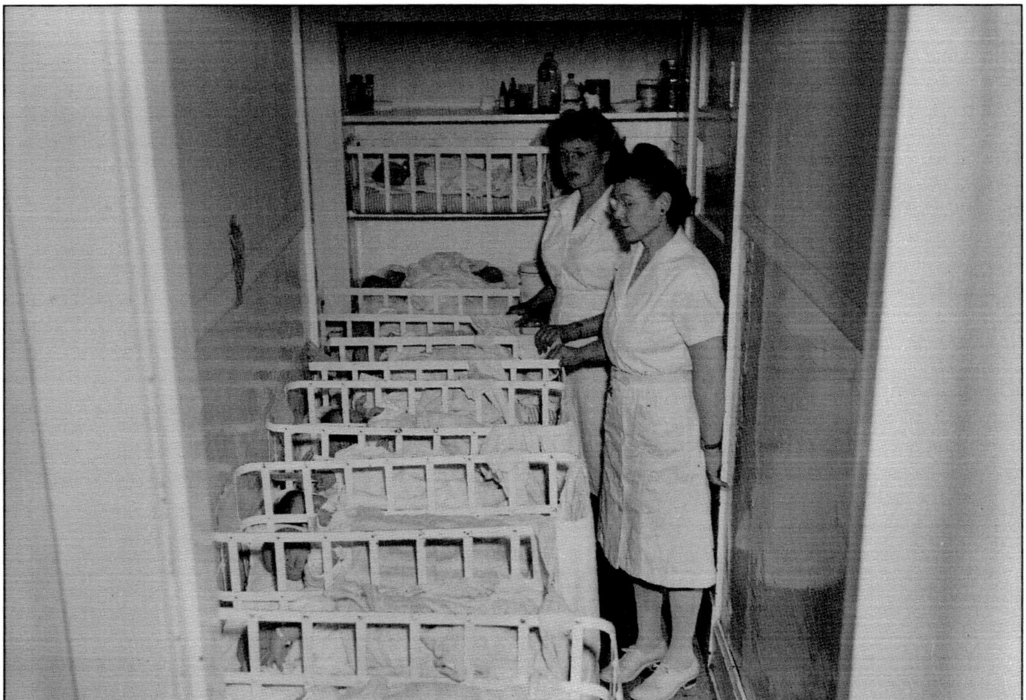

The nursery in the Uintah Basin Hospital was designed for six babies. On the week of December 19, 1946, the six-bed nursery was over flowing with 12 new babies.

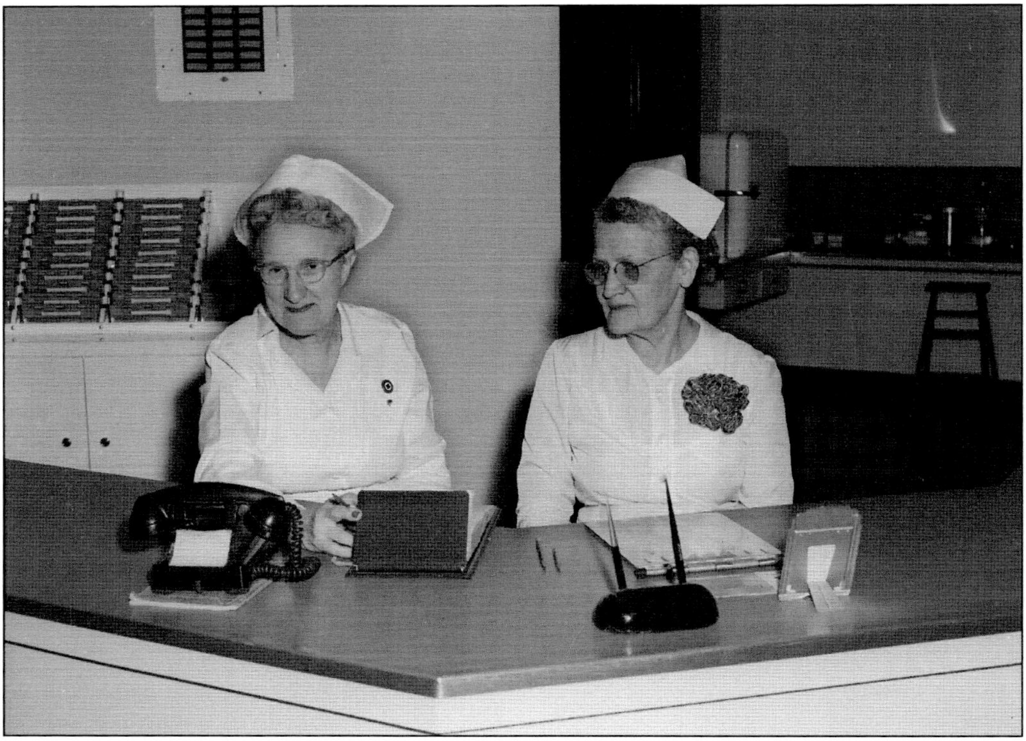

Constance Thorne (left) and Elsie Moffitt were honored in February 1955 for their years of service to the public. Under their care, thousands of patients benefitted from the two nurses' vast knowledge and comforting ways. Constance began nursing in 1914, and Elsie began in 1925. Together, the two nurses put in 70 years of service.

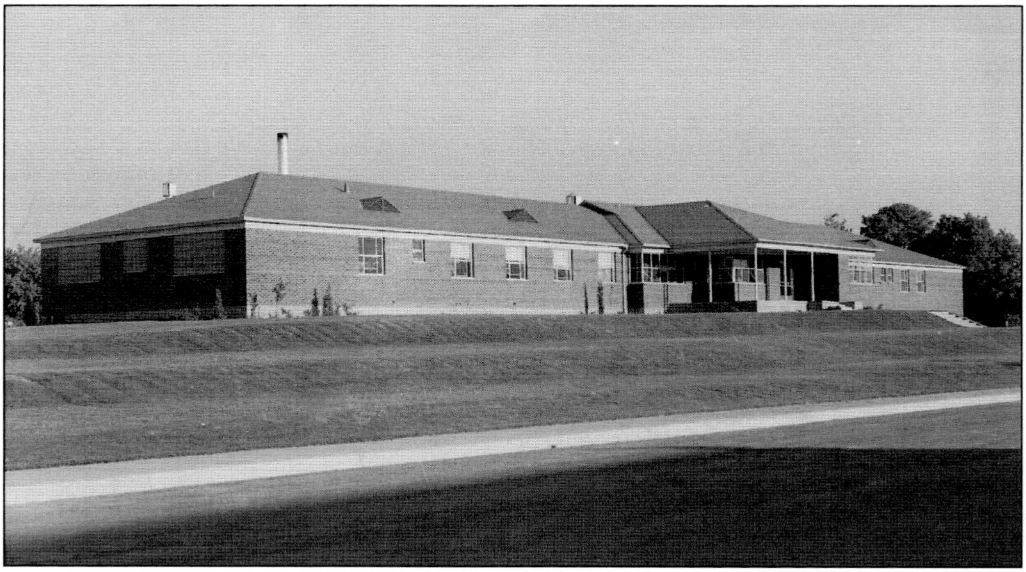

The 30-bed Uintah County Hospital was built in 1948. It is located on a large landscaped lot with sloping lawns at 175 West 100 North. Erland Preece was the administrator until 1973. In 1974, additions were made. The present hospital was built in 1980, west of the old structure. In 1984, the old building came down, and doctors offices were added to the new hospital.

Seven

Red, White, and Blue

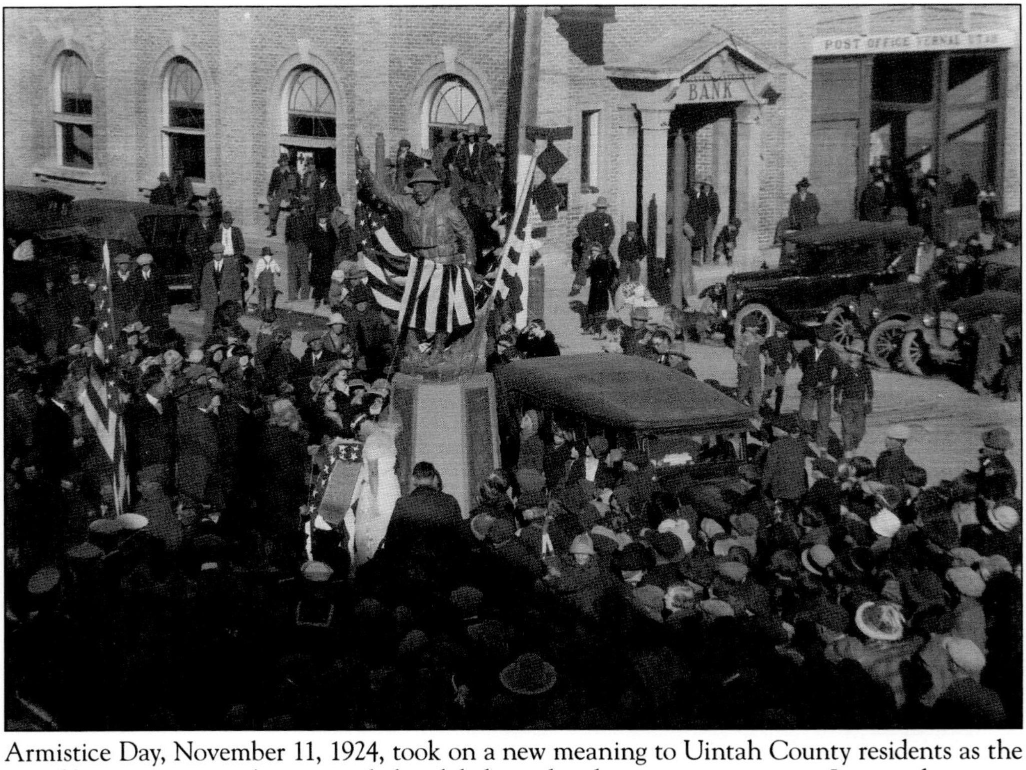

Armistice Day, November 11, 1924, took on a new meaning to Uintah County residents as the *Doughboy* war memorial was unveiled and dedicated with a patriotic program. In attendance was a crowd of 2,500 people, with 1,200 of those being school children. Dr. Harvey Coe Hullinger and Rev. D.H. Minick, Civil War veterans, pulled the strings that released two large flags that unveiled the bronze statue. Intense silence from the crowd showed their respect for this special occasion.

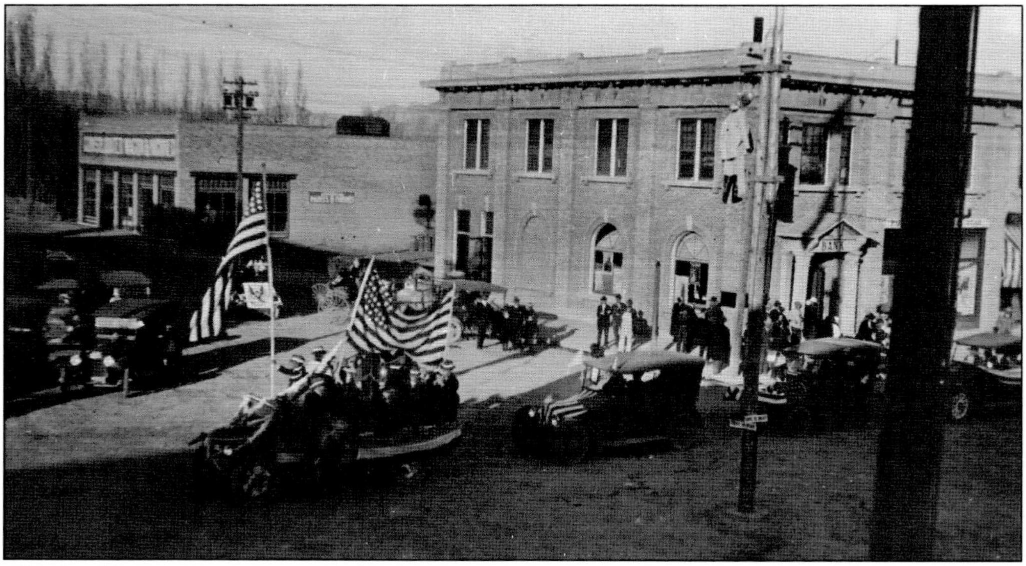

The World War I Peace Day Parade was a grand event. On November 15, 1918, local communities and dignitaries formed a procession celebrating the signing of the armistice with Germany. Families of soldiers and others traveled in automobiles along Main Street. Representing patriotism, freedom, and victory for the United States of America, the American flag was held proudly and draped across automobiles.

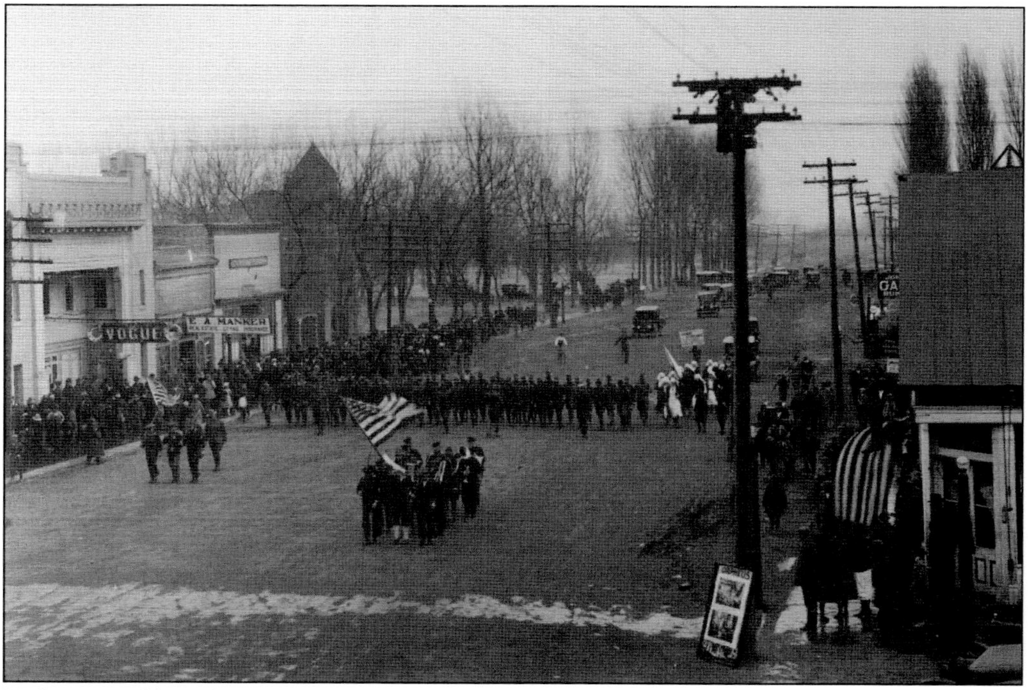

Unhampered by a heavy downpour, Uintah County welcomed home its soldiers, sailors, and marines on Friday, March 21, 1919. A military parade and drill took place on Main Street in Vernal in front of a spirited crowd. A military band led the procession under the leadership of Pat Merkley. The military review was under the direction of Lts. George Wesley Green and Leon Pack. Nellie Smith led the Red Cross section.

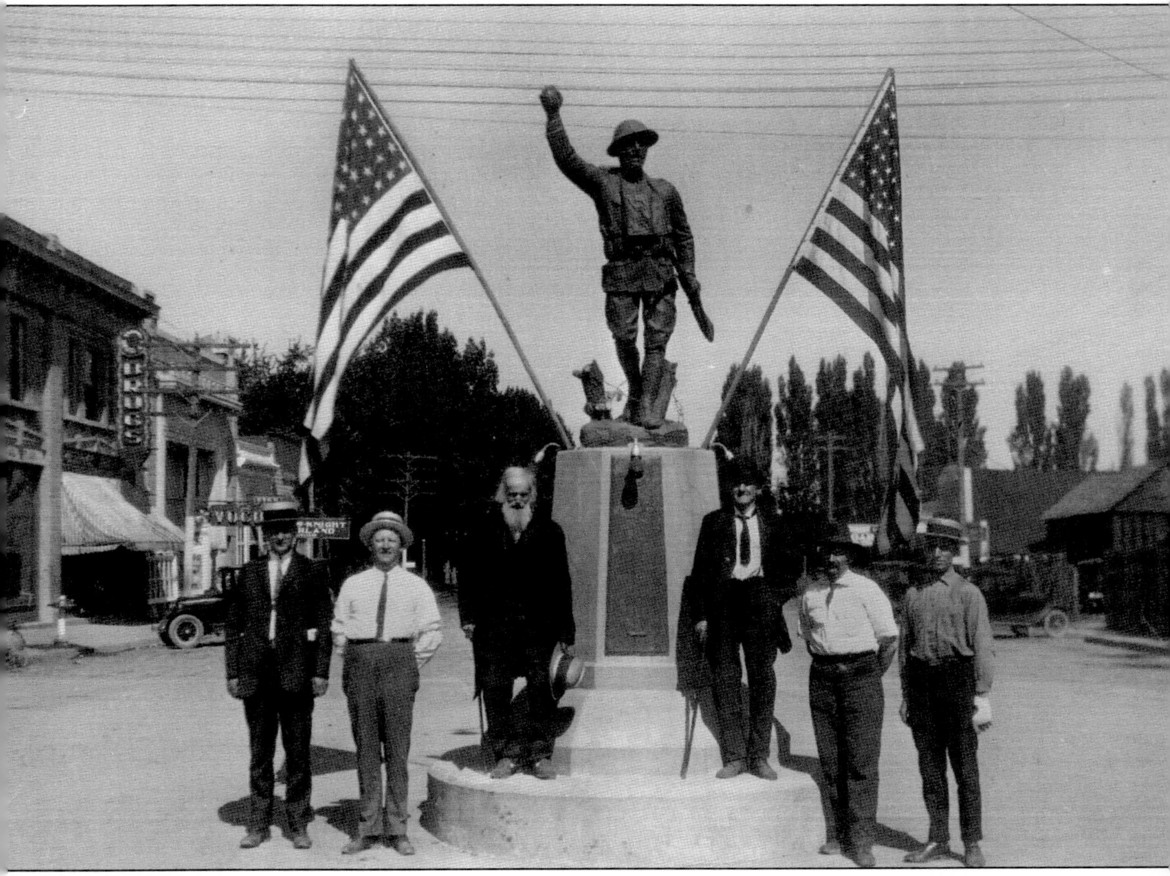

Veterans from various wars stand next to the *Doughboy* in the center of town. The statue was placed in the intersection of Vernal Avenue and Main Street in 1924. It was the first war memorial of its kind to be erected in Utah. In this photograph are veterans of different wars who served their country. They are, from left to right, Isabrand Sanders, World War I; Thomas W. O'Donnell, "Teddy's Rough Riders," Spanish-American War; Dr. Harvey Coe Hulllinger, member of Capt. Lot Smith's troop, Civil War; Daniel H. Minick, Pennsylvania Volunteer Infantry, Civil War; Charles W. Hanna, Spanish-American War; and George R. Goodrich, World War I.

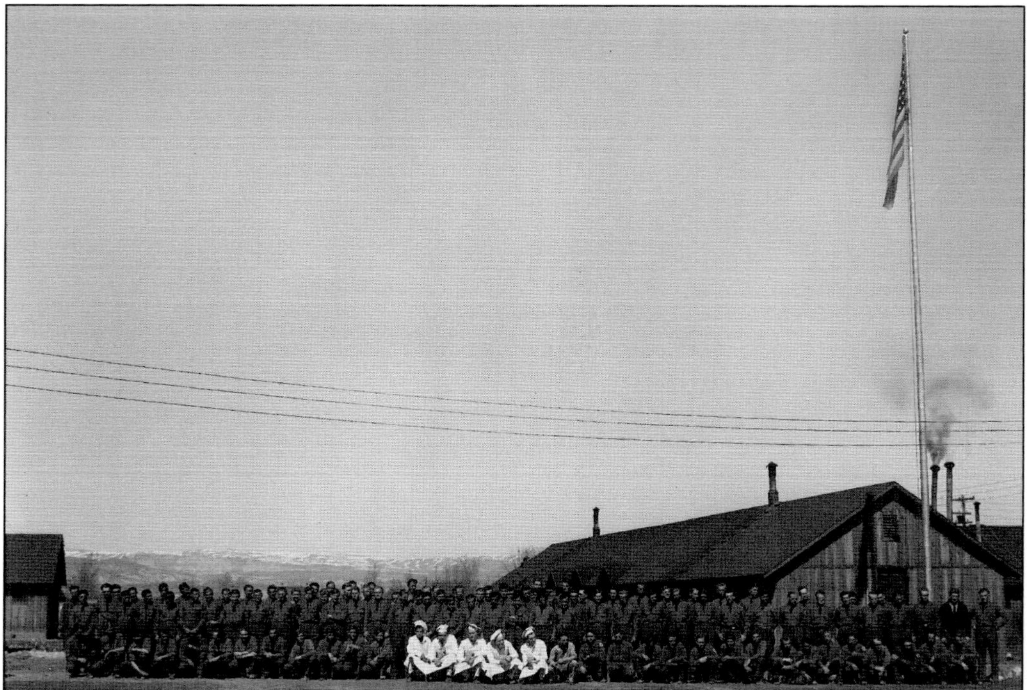

Camp Vernal, DG-31, Company 1507, Civilian Conservation Corps (CCC), was located at approximately 330 East 200 South. The CCC was created to help the country stimulate economic recovery by providing jobs for unemployed young men. Due to its efforts, all sections of the public domain in Uintah County could be reached by improved roads. Reservoirs were built for the benefit of sheep and cattle. The CCC was also responsible for helping to build the grandstand at the fairgrounds. Another phase of the program included rodent control as well as destroying 200 bushels of crickets to save feed for stock. In 1938, all members of the camp posed for a picture (above) for their fifth anniversary.

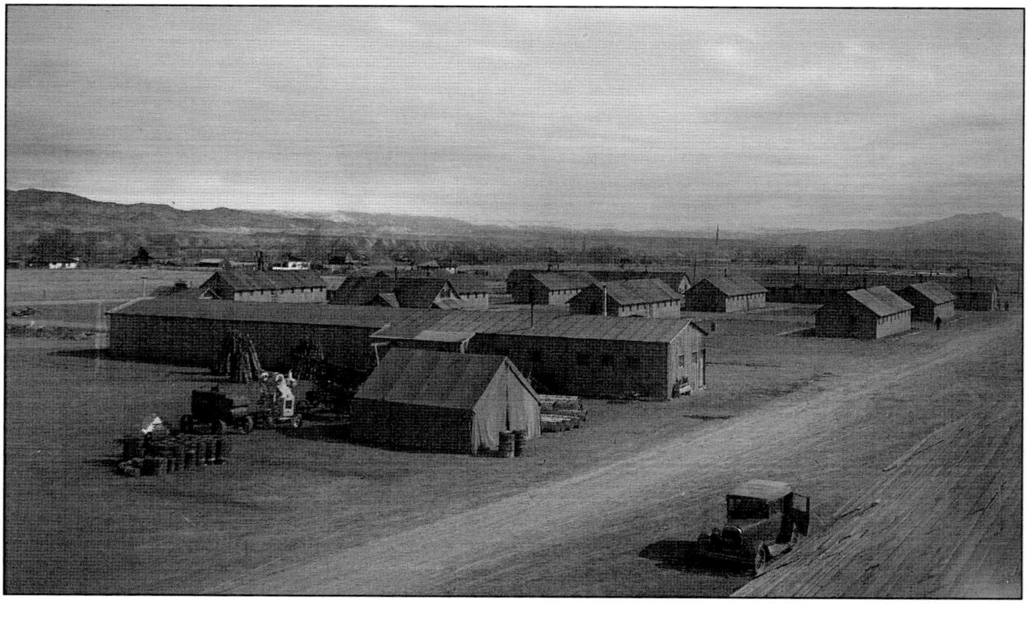

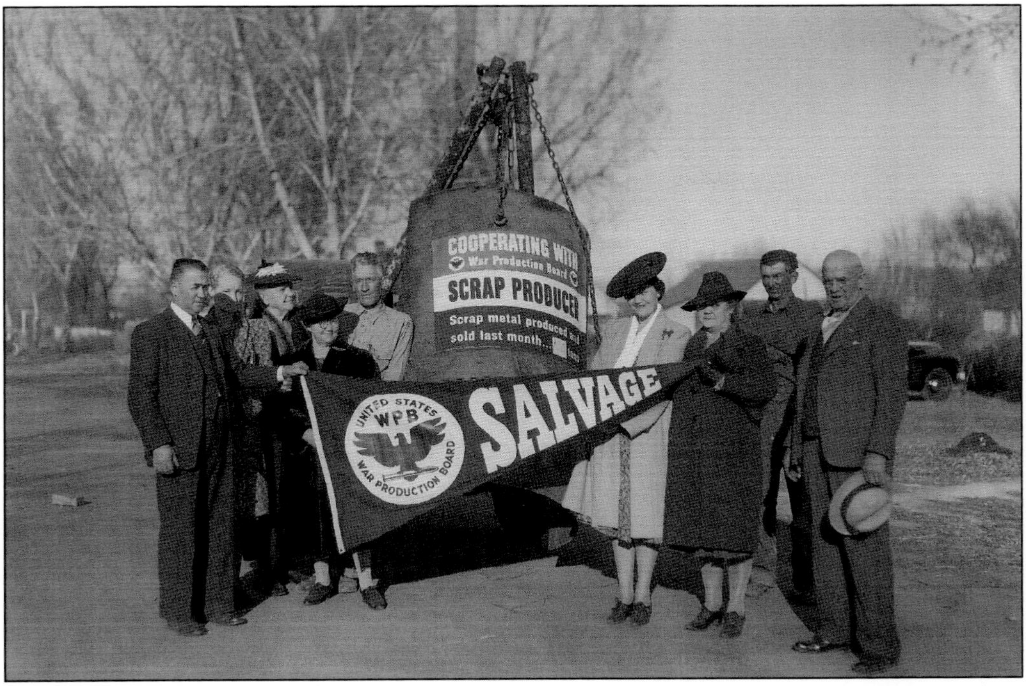

Many organizations and residents rallied to support the war effort by collecting scrap metal. In 1942, the Uintah Chapter of the Red Cross was one of many organizations involved in helping the war effort. Dorothy McCarrell, local Red Cross chairman, is holding the right end of the flag.

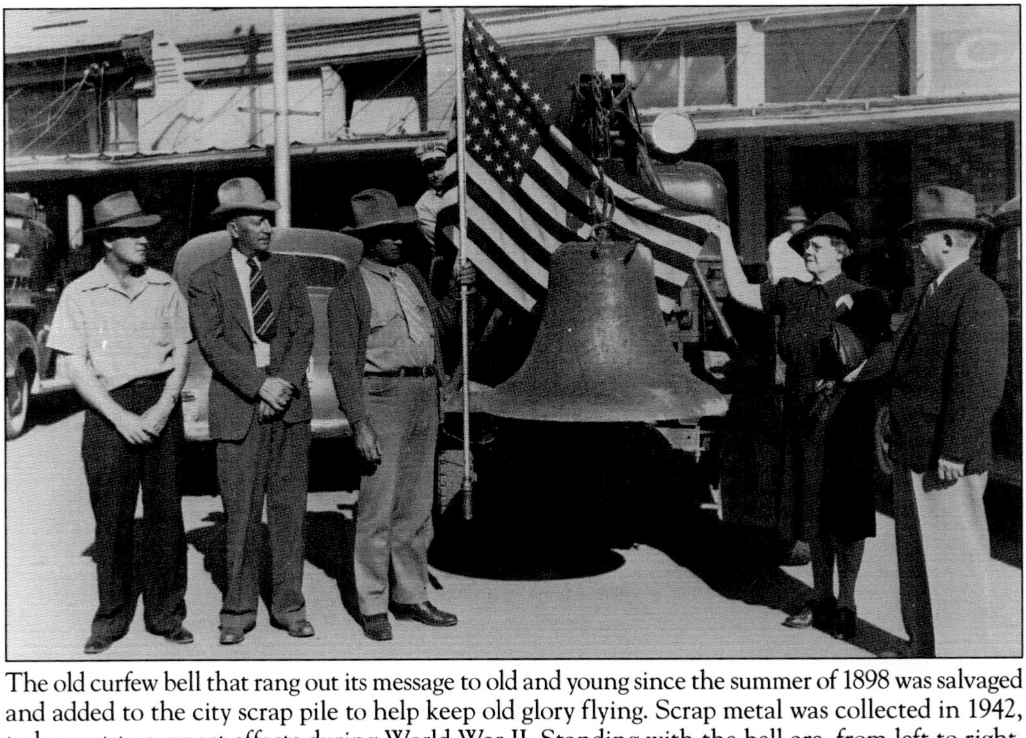

The old curfew bell that rang out its message to old and young since the summer of 1898 was salvaged and added to the city scrap pile to help keep old glory flying. Scrap metal was collected in 1942, to be sent to support efforts during World War II. Standing with the bell are, from left to right, Fran Feltch, Bry Stringham, Russell Montgomery, LaVern Pope Adams, and Harold Lundell.

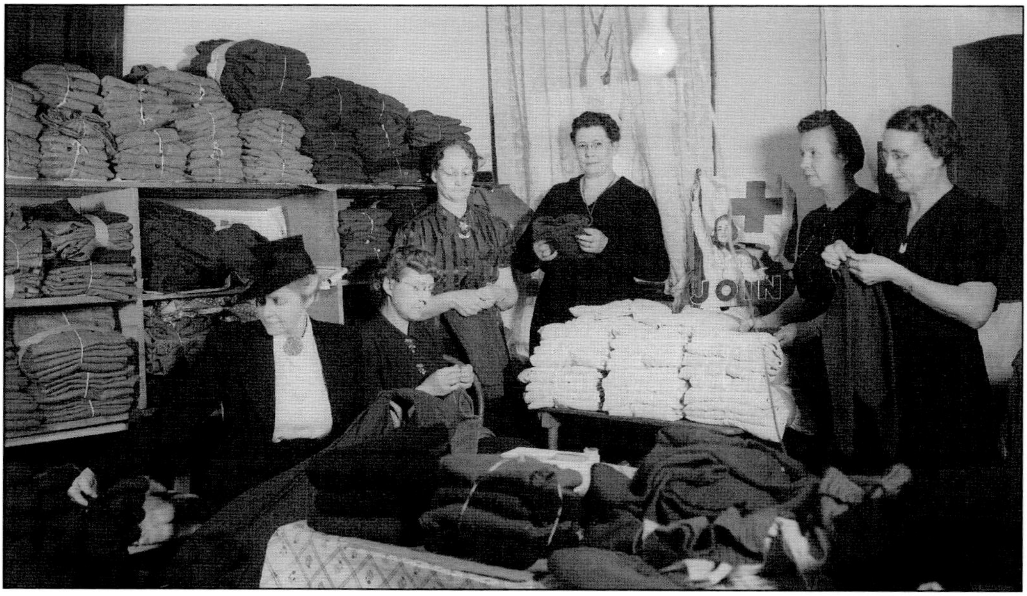

In 1942, the Uintah Chapter of the Red Cross organized and collected clothing for war victims. Workers in the Ashley Valley made clothing and took ready-cut materials to their homes to sew at their convenience. In December 1941, 349 articles representing 2,060 hours of sewing and 185 knitted articles requiring 3,700 hours of knitting were sent. The women are, from left to right, Dorothy McCarrell, Margaret Lambert, Alice Owen, Hattie Johnson, Effie Hall, and Mabel Stagg.

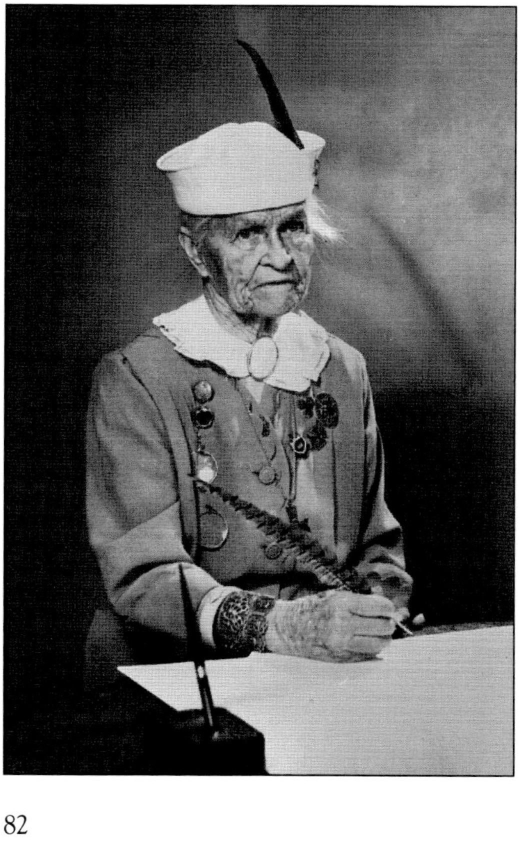

Kate Adams, fondly known as Mother Adams, was a favorite to many in the valley, especially young children. On Saturdays, she gathered youngsters and treated them to a matinee, picnic, or party. Mother Adams was very generous with her wealth, such as helping boys and girls gain an education. She supported servicemen by sending letters and gifts, and she presented a building to the American Legion for its meetings. Many remembered her for the sailor cap that she always wore.

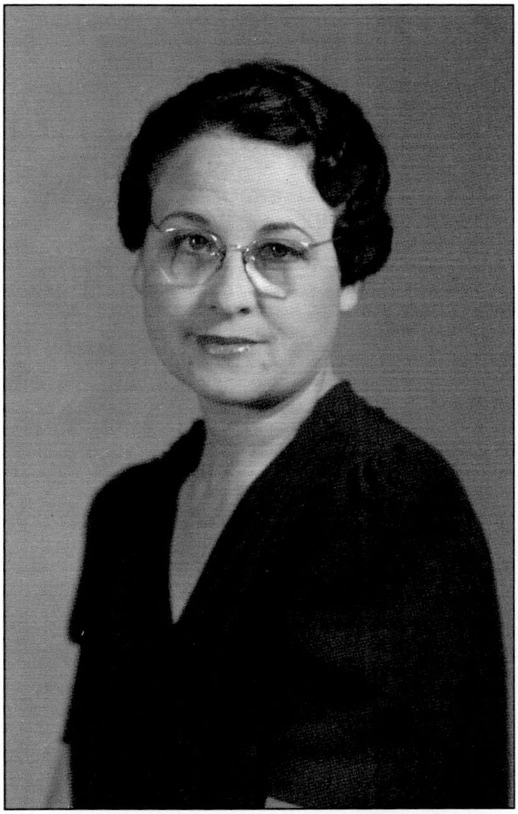

Eve (Eva) Stewart Ashton was born May 7, 1898, in Jensen, Utah. She married Rae Ashton and had two sons, Stewart and Ralph. She was a nationally known civic and educational leader and spoke to groups around the country. She served as a state president for the American Legion Auxiliary and became the group's national president in 1952. Eve was named Outstanding Woman of the Year for Uintah County in 1953. After her husband died, she became president of the Ashton Brothers Store in Vernal. She also served on the board of trustees of Utah State University. She died on November 17, 1962. Below, Eve is photographed with her family. From left to right are Eve, Stewart, Ralph, and Rae Ashton.

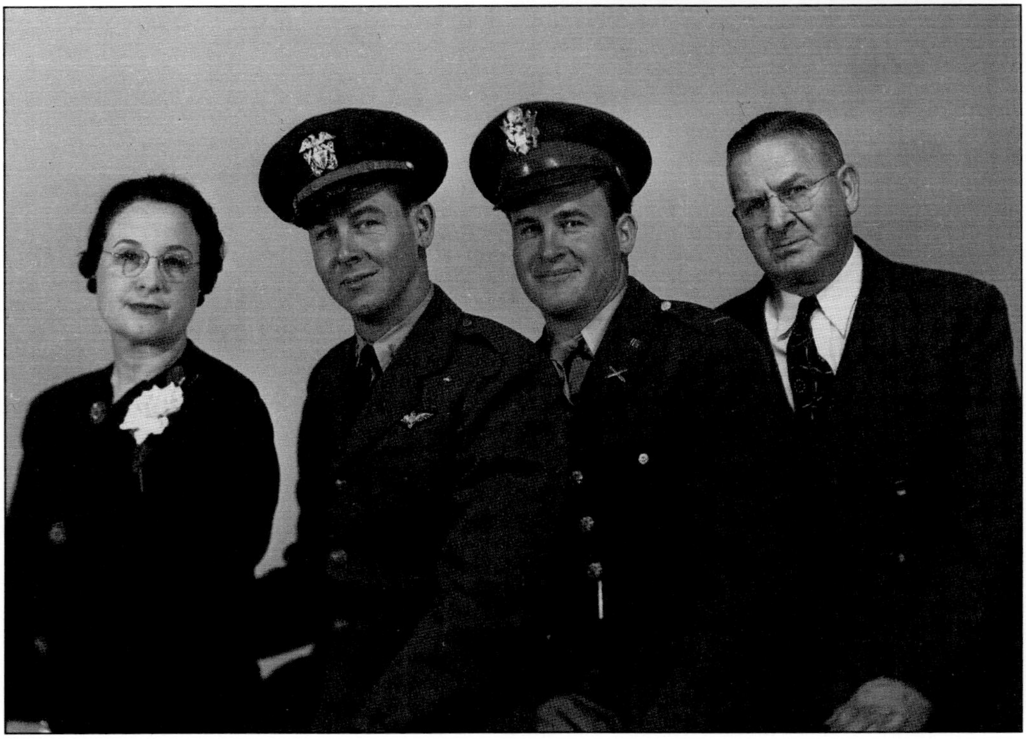

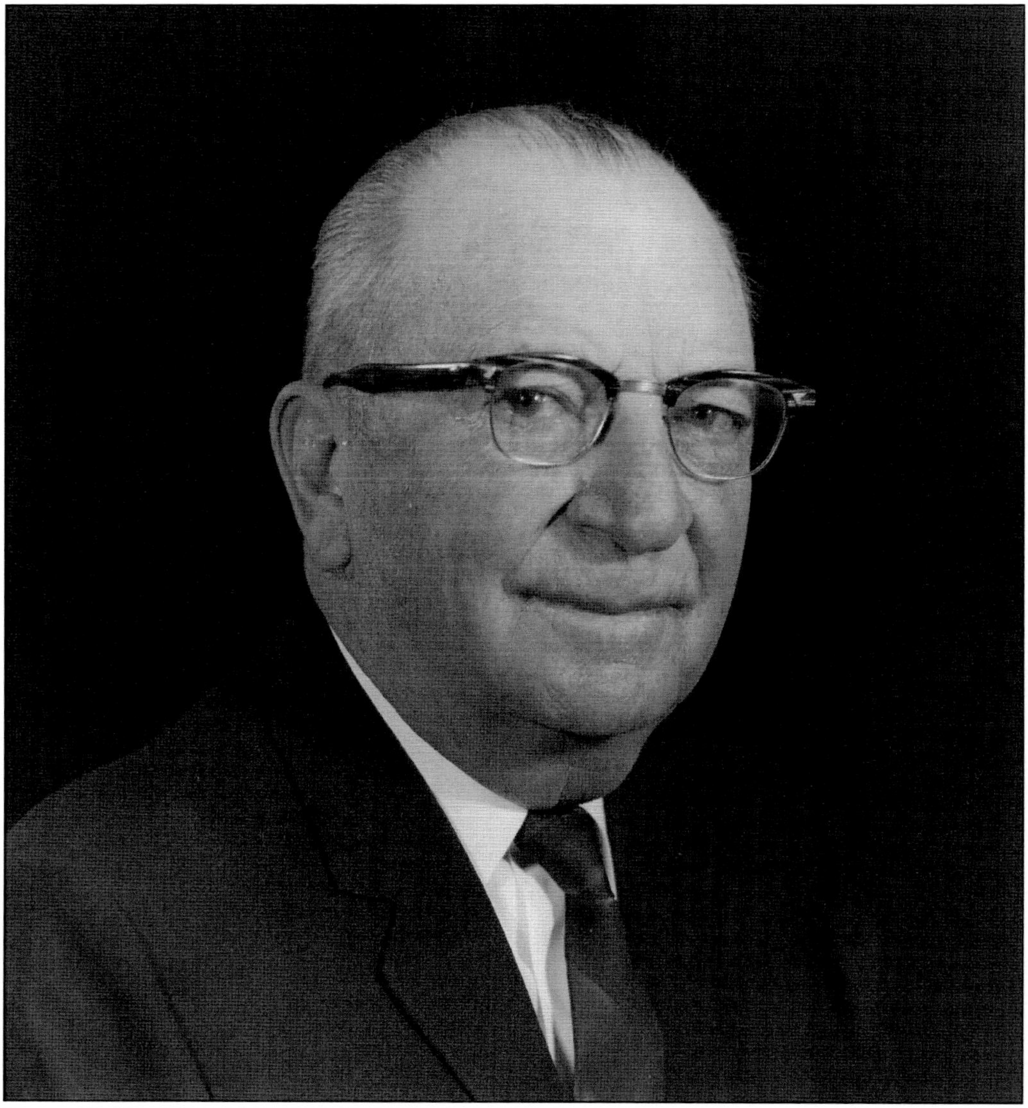

Briant H. "Bry" Stringham was born April 2, 1889. One day in 1939, while he was separating the sheep on Diamond Mountain, standing there in a cloud of dust and wearing an old pair of bib overalls, a fellow named George Roth came up to Stringham. The first thing Roth said to the dust-covered shepherd was, "Bry, we want you to run for mayor." After much debate, he made the decision to run because so many people supported him; however, he lost by a slim margin. Despite his unsuccessful political debut, he ran as a Republican candidate for the Utah House of Representatives. He was on his way to a 12-year career as a Utah lawmaker. Stringham had been in office less than a year when he was approached to run for mayor again. By 191 votes, Vernal had a new mayor, and the name Bry Stringham started attracting attention throughout the state. He served eight years as mayor, serving three years as both a state legislator and mayor.

Eight

Reading, Writing, and Worship

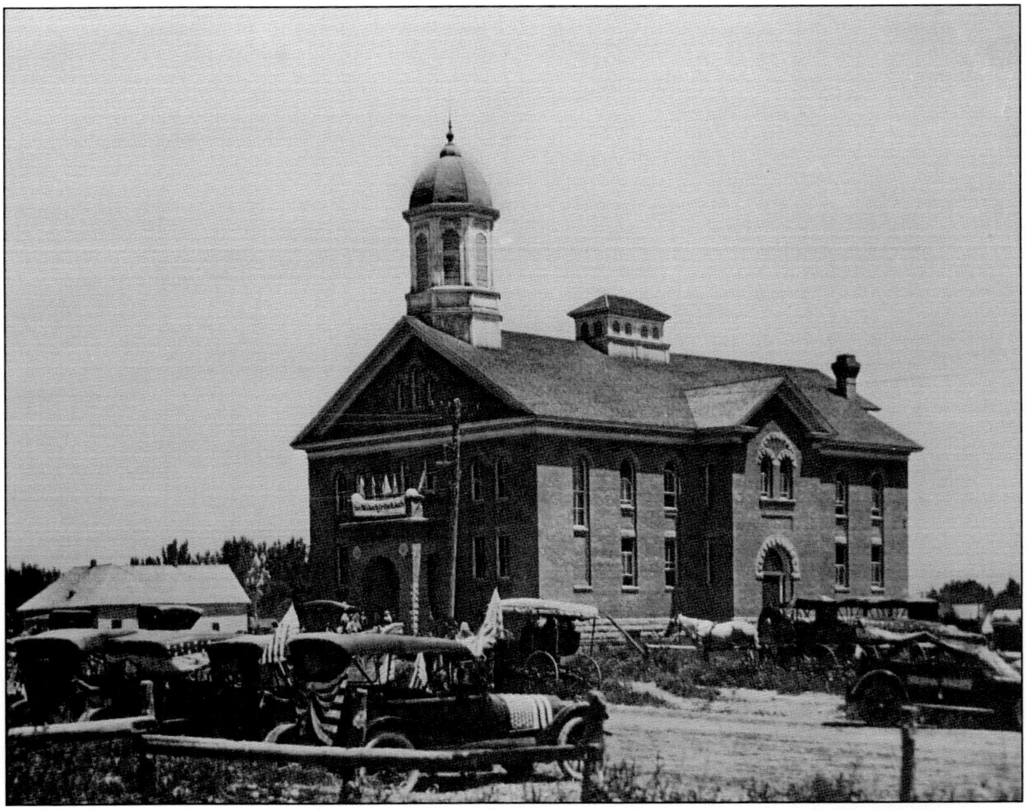

LDS stake president Samuel R. Bennion directed the majority of the Uintah Stake Tabernacle construction, beginning with site selection and architectural drawings in 1898. In 1900, a groundbreaking ceremony took place. Building the native sandstone and brick edifice occupied the next seven years. The tabernacle was dedicated in August 1907 by church president Joseph F. Smith. In 1994, the LDS Church announced the tabernacle would be renovated to become the Vernal Utah LDS Temple. On November 2, 1997, Mormon president Gordon B. Hinckley dedicated the temple.

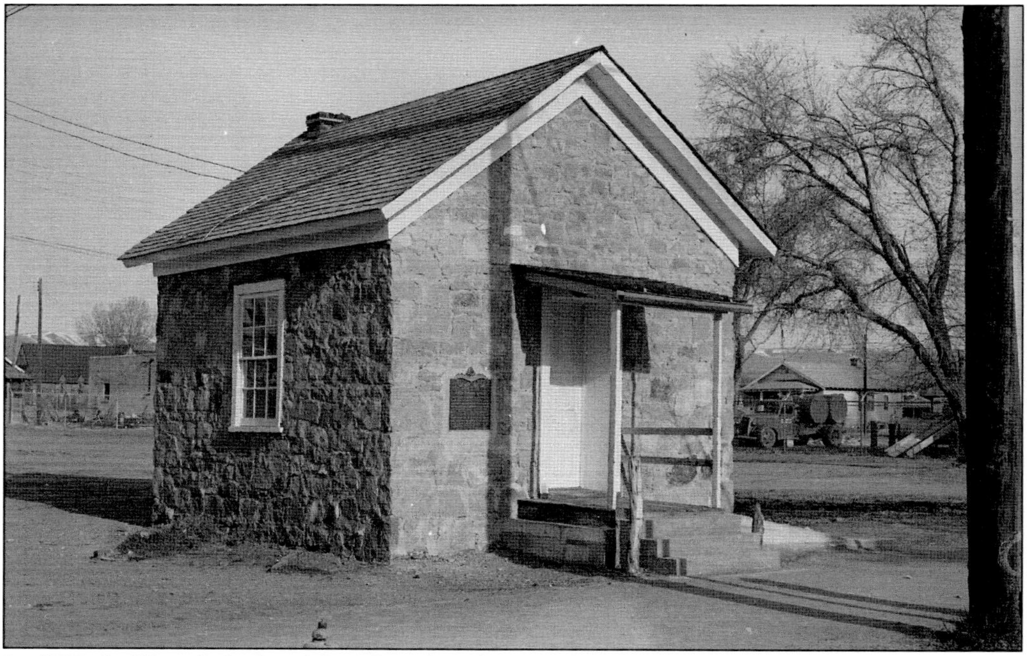

In 1887, the Uintah Stake of the LDS Church erected the Little Rock Tithing House on ground that was contributed by Jeremiah Hatch Sr. for $1. Men hauled rock from which experienced stonemasons Harley Mowery and John Jacob Slaugh constructed the tithing office, where the church members paid their tithing, which was one-tenth of their earnings in money or produce. The proceeds were used for general church purposes.

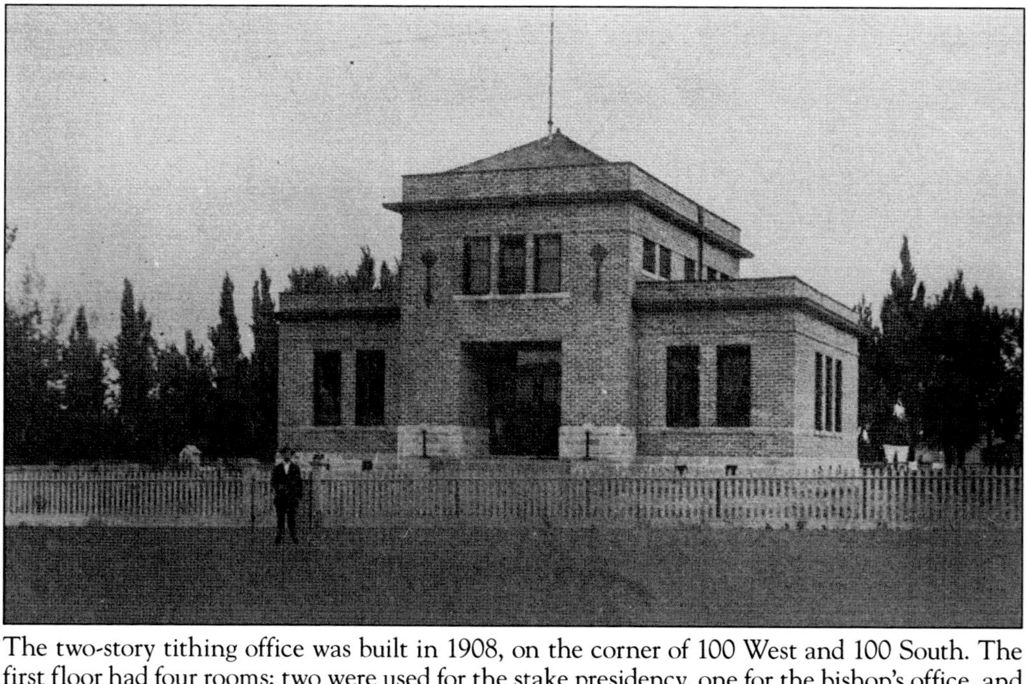

The two-story tithing office was built in 1908, on the corner of 100 West and 100 South. The first floor had four rooms; two were used for the stake presidency, one for the bishop's office, and one room for the tithing office. Church records were kept here in a fireproof vault. The second floor was divided into several small meeting rooms.

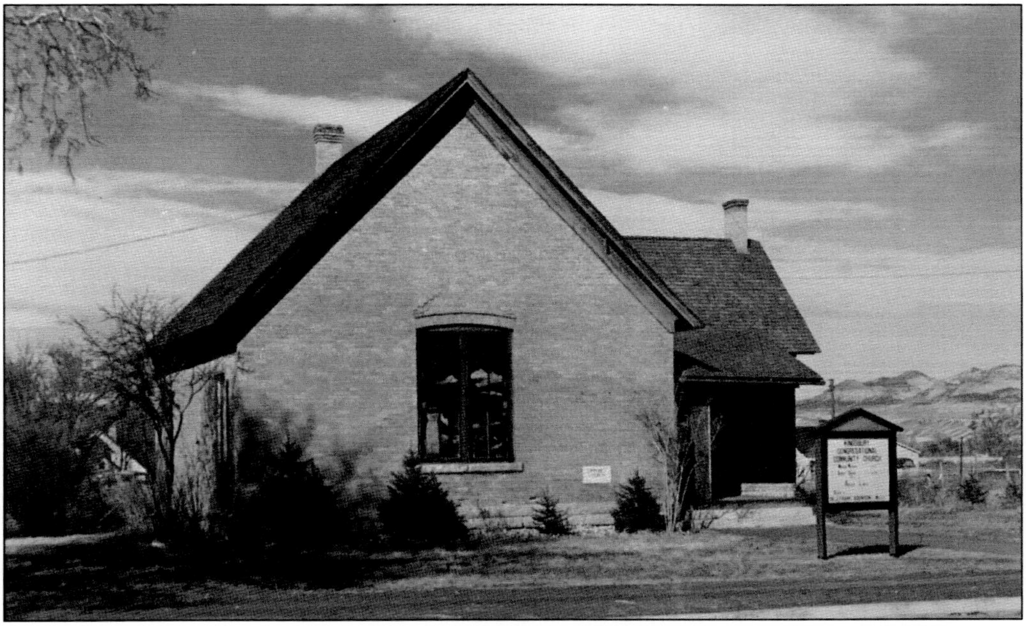

In 1901, the missionary program of the Congregational Church began in Vernal. The Kingsbury Congregational Church furnished a haven for a group who could not otherwise express the faith of their own background. It furnished a Sunday school for their children and activities for their young people. The church was located on the corner of 100 North and 100 East. It was used until 1961, when a new building was built.

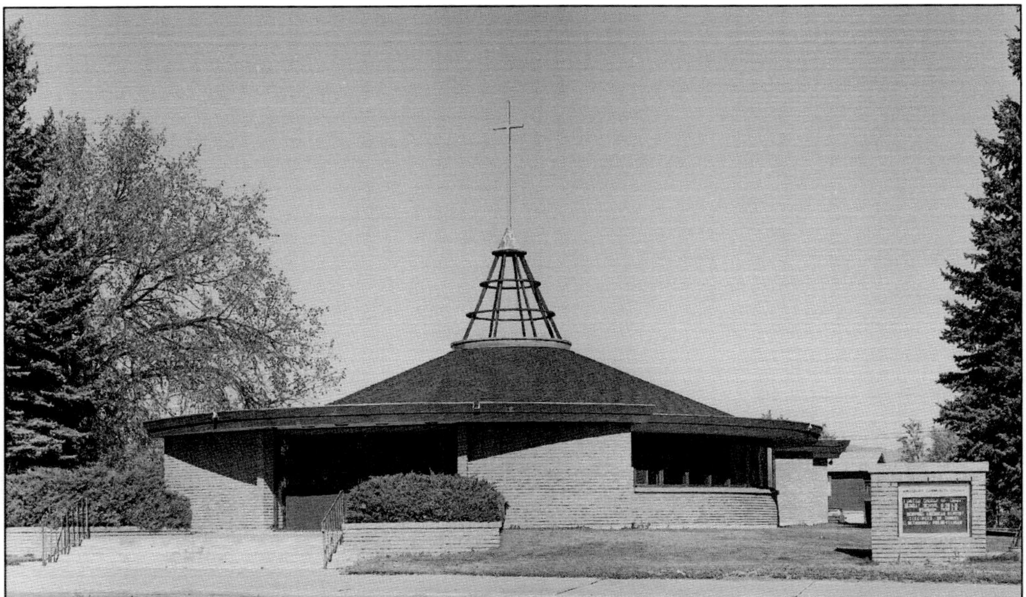

Members of the new Kingsbury Congregational Community Church were delighted with the beautiful new structure and pleasing arrangement of the interior of their new church. The impressive circular gold-colored brick building was erected with careful study and design. On top of an open steeple stands a tall cross that is illuminated by floodlights at night. The new church added to the fine facilities and culture of the community.

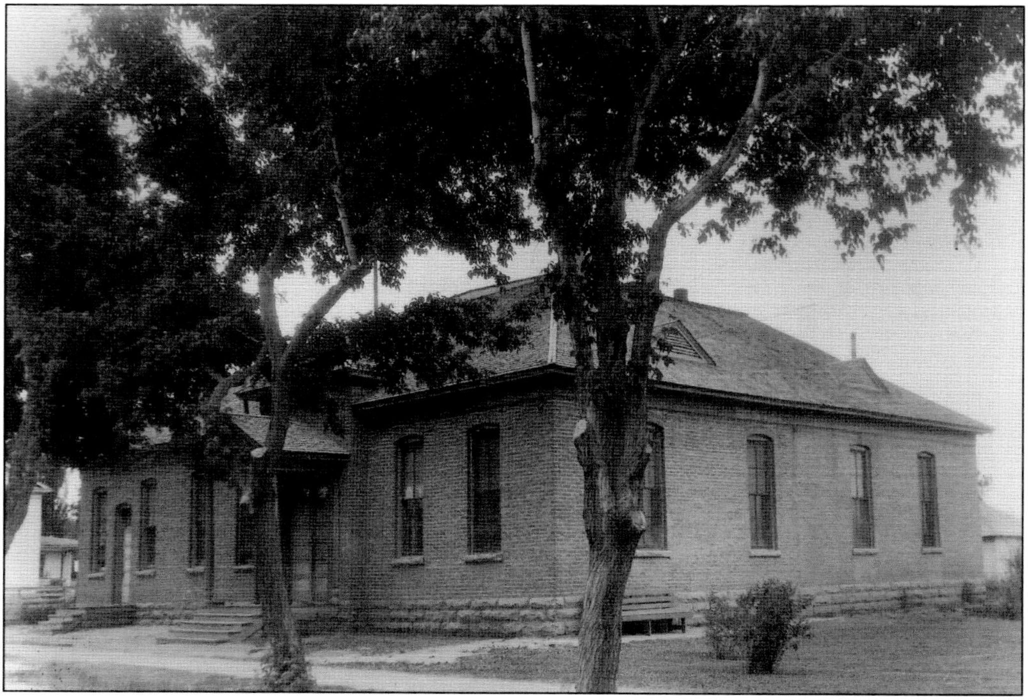

In 1903, the Congregational Education Society founded the Willcox School, which was held in a former saloon. There were 50 students and up to eight grades, with a Mrs. Chance being the first teacher. When school began in 1906, students attended the new Willcox School in a building next to the Congregational church. Two rooms in the church were also utilized for school classes. In 1910, the school took the name Willcox Academy; it was the first school in the Uinta Basin to offer a four-year academic course preparatory for college. The academy closed in 1922. Below is an undated image of unidentified students and teachers at the school.

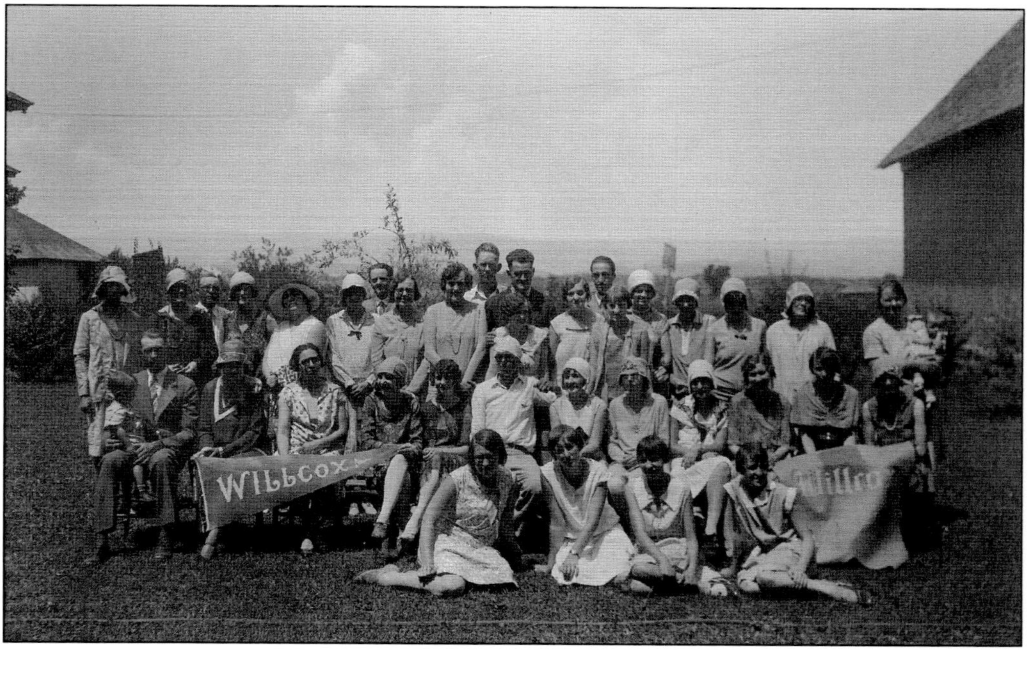

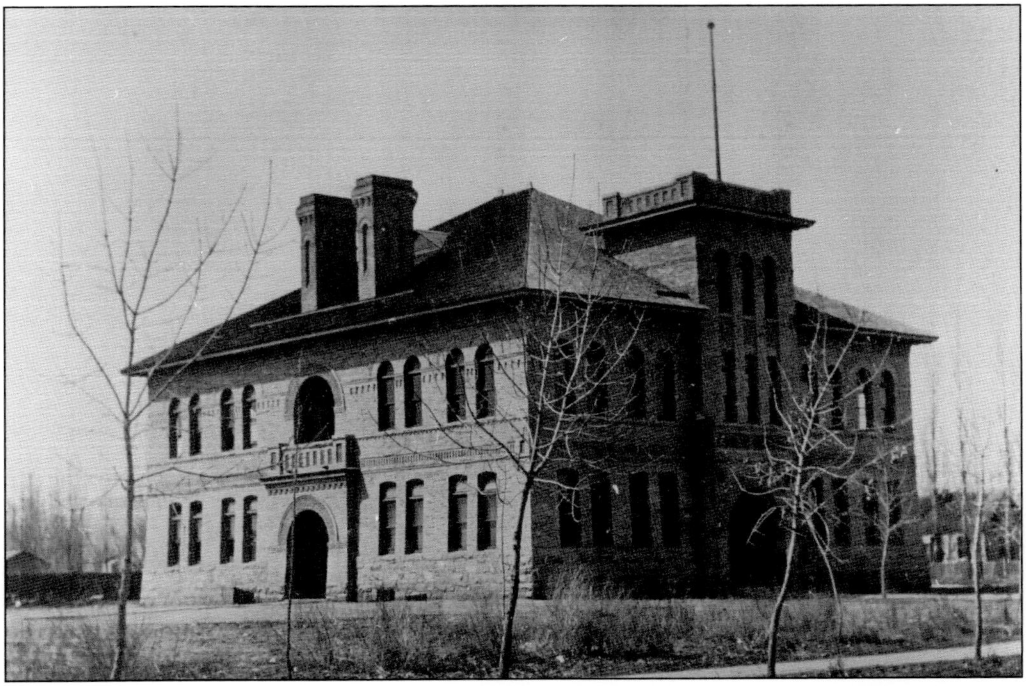

By early 1900, the Central School was in an overcrowded condition. In the fall of that same year, construction began on a new school. In 1902, 323 students were enrolled, and there were eight teachers. The second Central School was torn down in the 1960s.

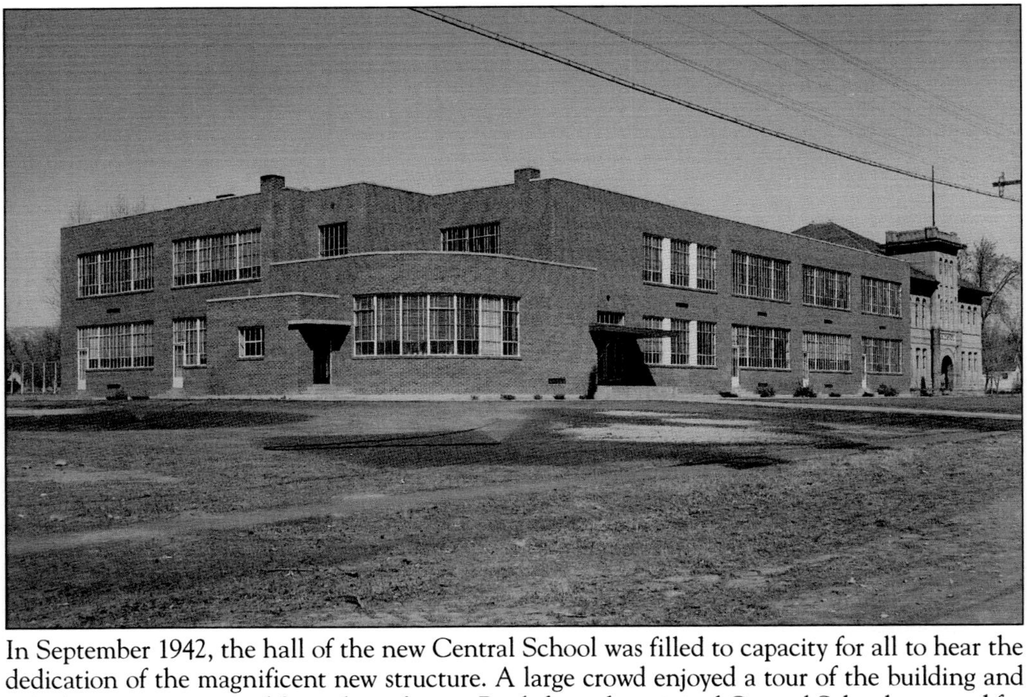

In September 1942, the hall of the new Central School was filled to capacity for all to hear the dedication of the magnificent new structure. A large crowd enjoyed a tour of the building and refreshments were served from the cafeteria. Brick from the original Central School was used for the walls of the new structure. The second Central School can be seen next to the new building. The newer school became an alternative high school in the 1990s.

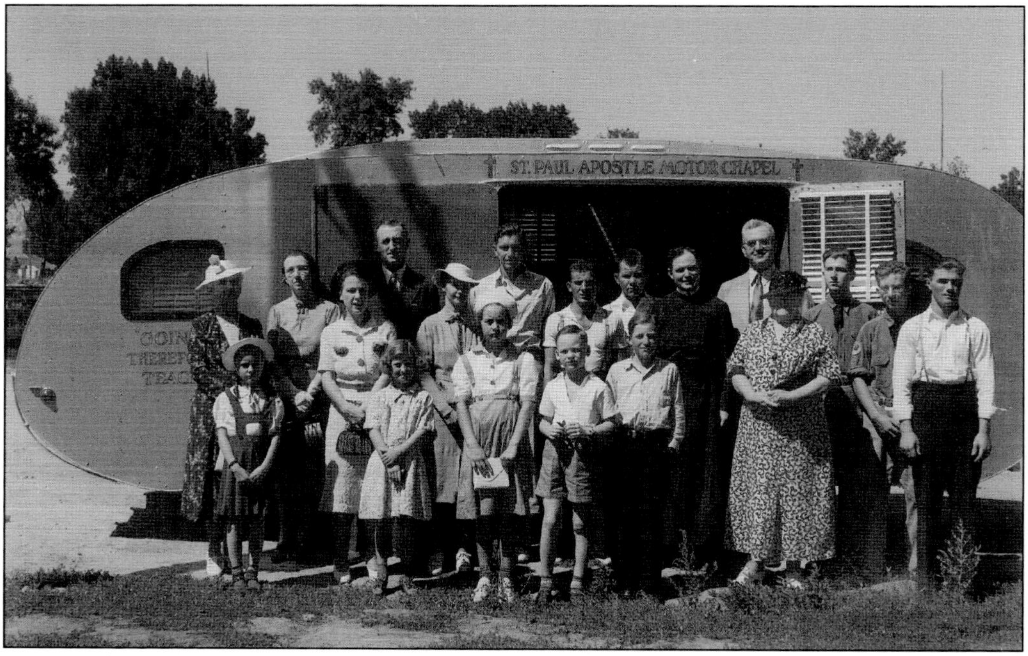

In 1938, the Catholic Church used a trailer, or motor chapel, in which the missionaries slept, ate, studied, and held Mass. Loretta Young, an actress in New Jersey, donated the motor chapel; it was then assigned to the Uinta Basin. Residents of Vernal, including M.J. Meagher (second row, far right), stand in front of the St. Paul Apostle Motor Chapel.

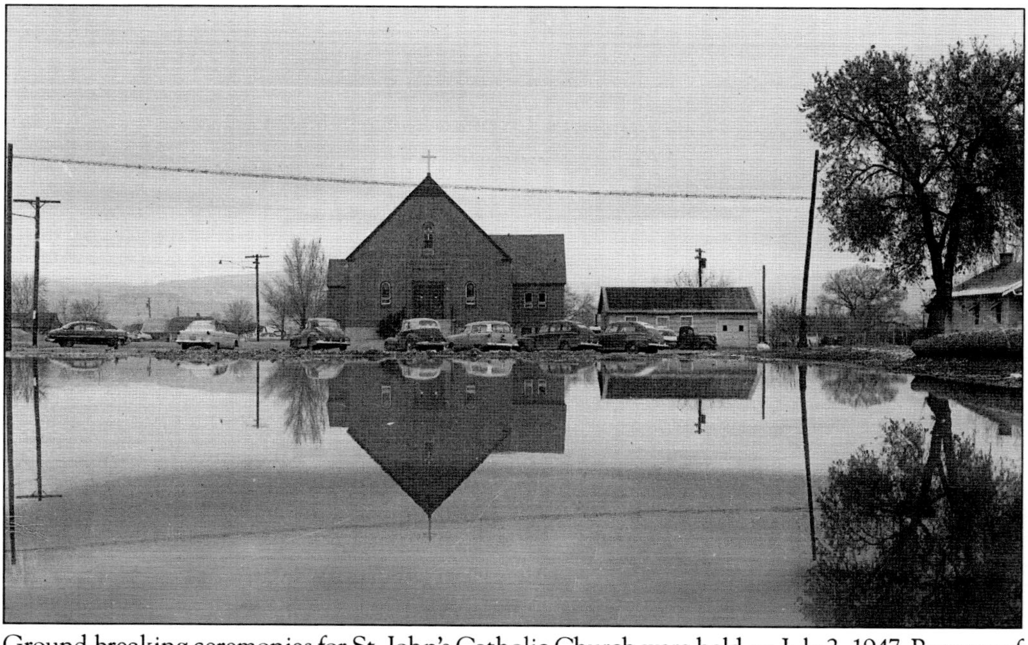

Ground-breaking ceremonies for St. John's Catholic Church were held on July 2, 1947. Because of delays in construction, the building was not dedicated until May 25, 1950. The new structure had a seating capacity of 200, and it later became St. James Catholic Church. South of the church, a large parking lot was flooded and allowed to freeze, turning it into an ice-skating pond that was enjoyed by the young people of the town.

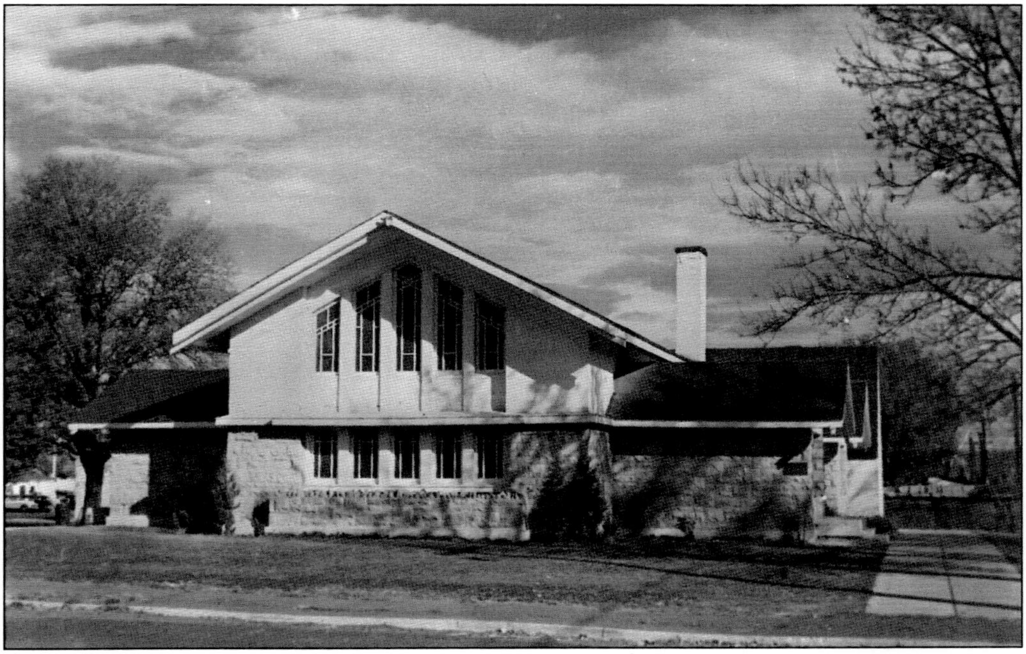

Vernal Second Ward had a carnival fundraiser in 1916 to begin construction of the new chapel. Because of World War I, the expense of material and labor made the cost nearly twice the original figure. The timber was milled on the mountain near Vernal and the stone quarried from Steinaker Draw. The ward moved into the building on April 6, 1919, but it was not dedicated until January 1920.

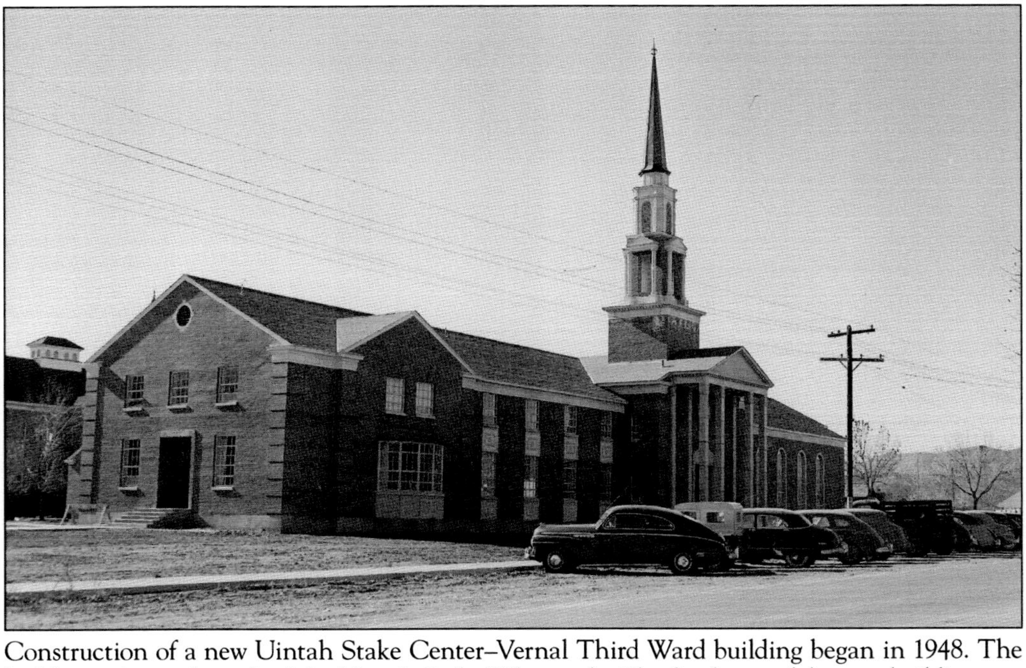

Construction of a new Uintah Stake Center–Vernal Third Ward building began in 1948. The building is located north of the Uintah Stake Tabernacle. The final cost of the new building was $263,000. The beautiful new chapel had a seating capacity of 400. The Uintah Stake Center–Vernal Third Ward was dedicated in July 1949, by Apostle David O. McKay.

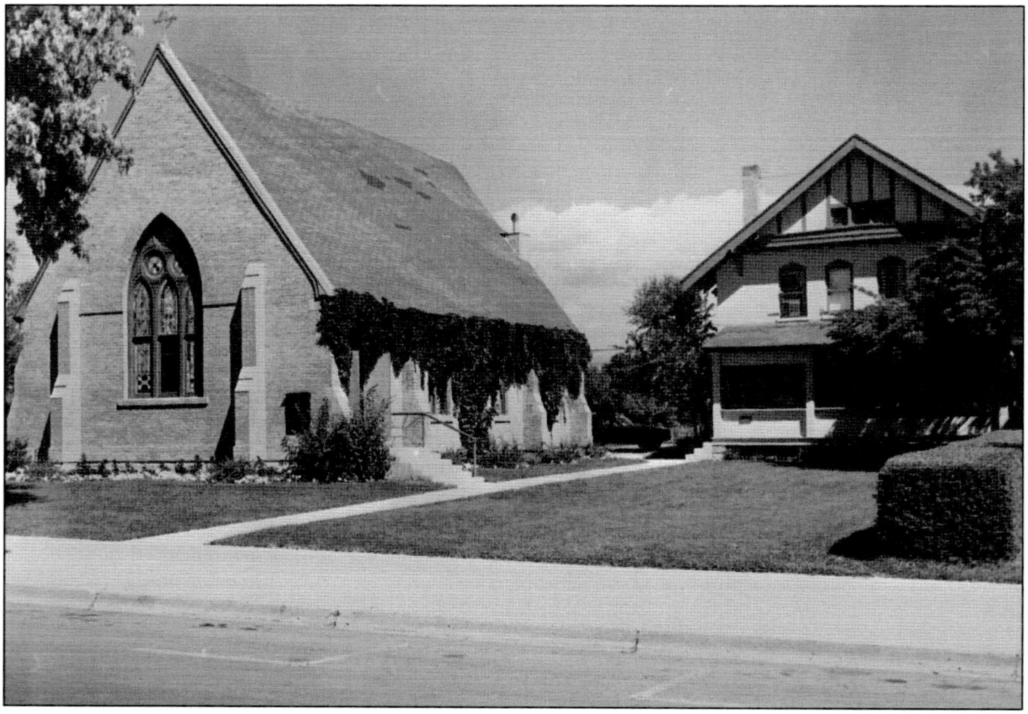

St. Paul's Episcopal Church was built in 1901, under the leadership of Rev. O. E. Ostenson. In 1909, a lodge was built to the east of the church by the Episcopal Church to serve as housing for girls from outlying areas who sought education. The lodge was once purchased and used as a hospital, but it was later resold back to the Episcopal Church.

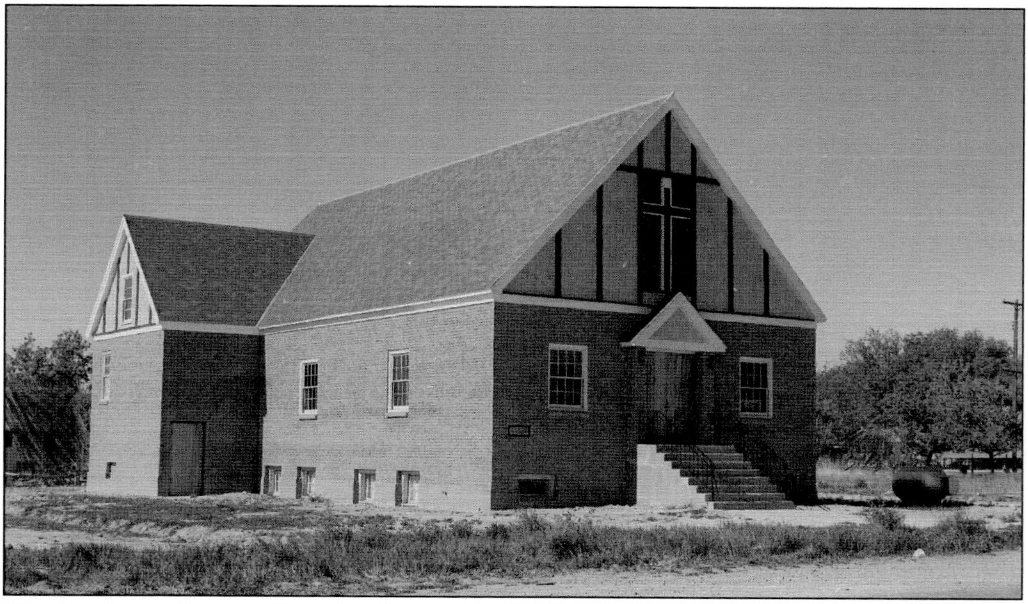

The Landmark Baptist Church is located at 288 East 100 South. In 1946, its members held meetings in a tent, and a basement was built in 1948. In 1953, the superstructure of frame and brick was built over the basement to make a nice church. The Baptist church was dedicated in April 1953.

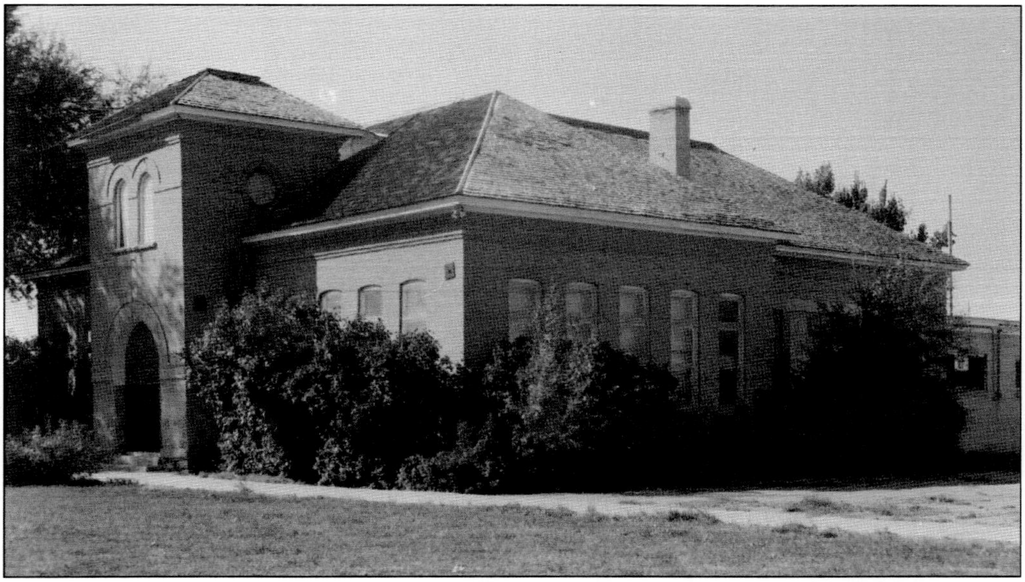

In 1902, the Jensen School was built on Highway 40. The school consisted of two large rooms with a hall between them. In 1907, two more ample rooms were added to the north end of the building. Samuel Haslem planted large trees around the grounds.

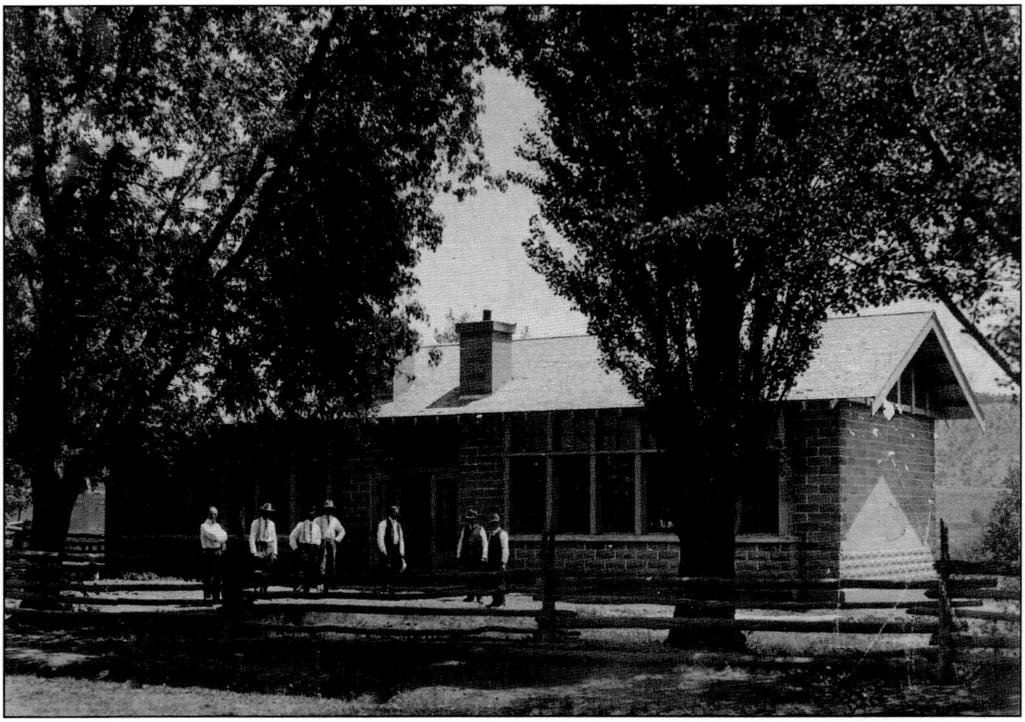

In 1917, Elisha Campbell built a two-room cinder-block school in Dry Fork; students had previously been attending a one-room log schoolhouse. In this picture, school district officers make an inspection of the new building. In 1927, children from Dry Fork were bused to Maeser School.

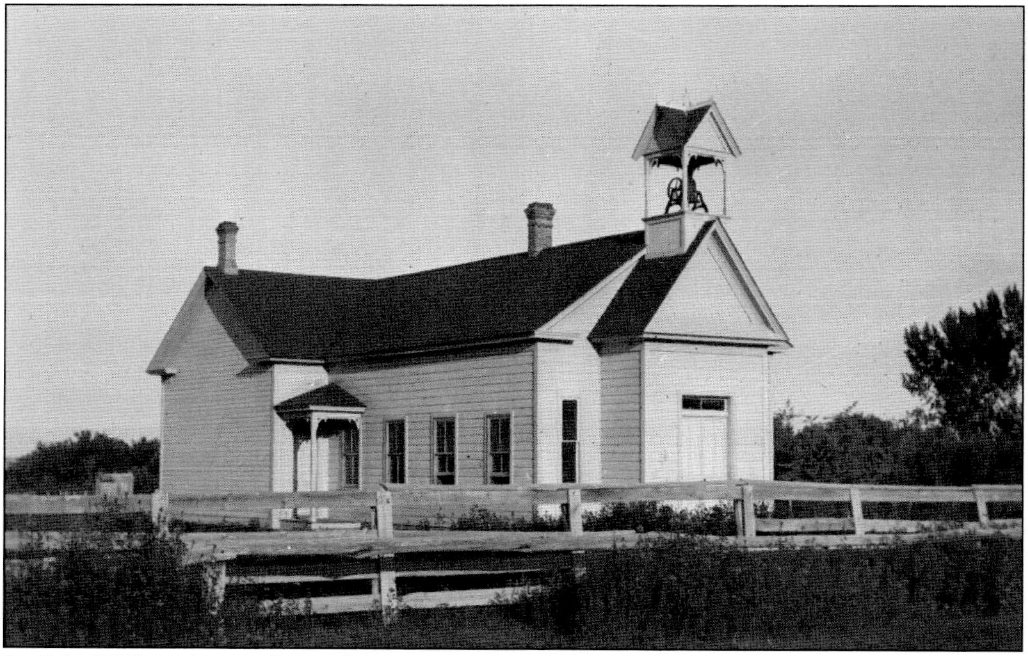

In 1905, William Preece donated ground at 2020 North 250 West for a new, larger school. Ashley White School replaced the log school building. Ashley School District was divided, and Union, a duplicate school, was built a couple years later on the Walter Anderson property at 1295 East 1500 North. These schools operated until 1917.

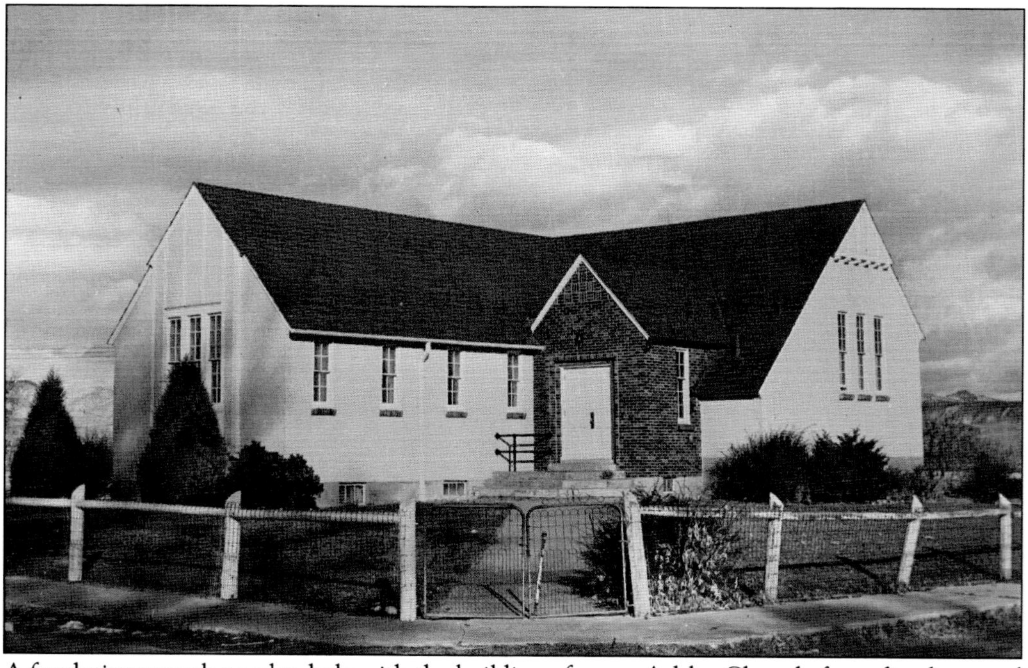

A fundraiser was planned to help with the building of a new Ashley Chapel after a fire destroyed the old one. A chicken dinner was served, a matinee was shown at the Vogue Theater, roller-skating was held at the Imperial Hall, and a dance finished off the daylong fundraiser. The new and larger chapel was built at 2000 North 500 East. It is now a private home.

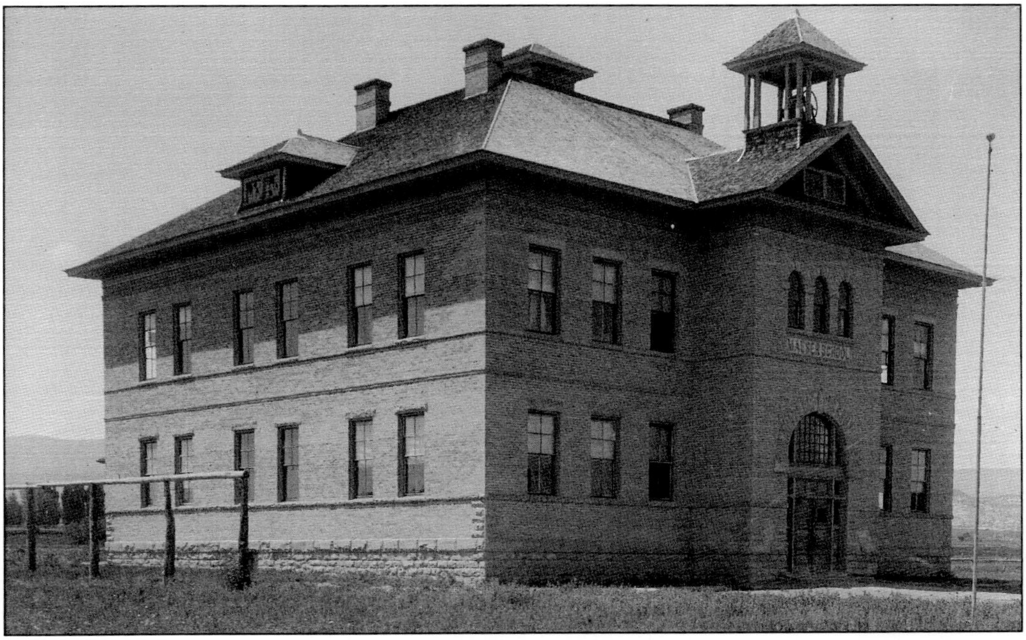

B.O. Colton met with the Utah State Board of School Buildings in June 1909 to present plans for the construction of the Maeser School. By August, building had begun, and the foundation had been completed. Lime for construction was burned on Taylor Mountain. By 1925, the attendance at Maeser had increased, making it necessary for another teacher to be added to the staff.

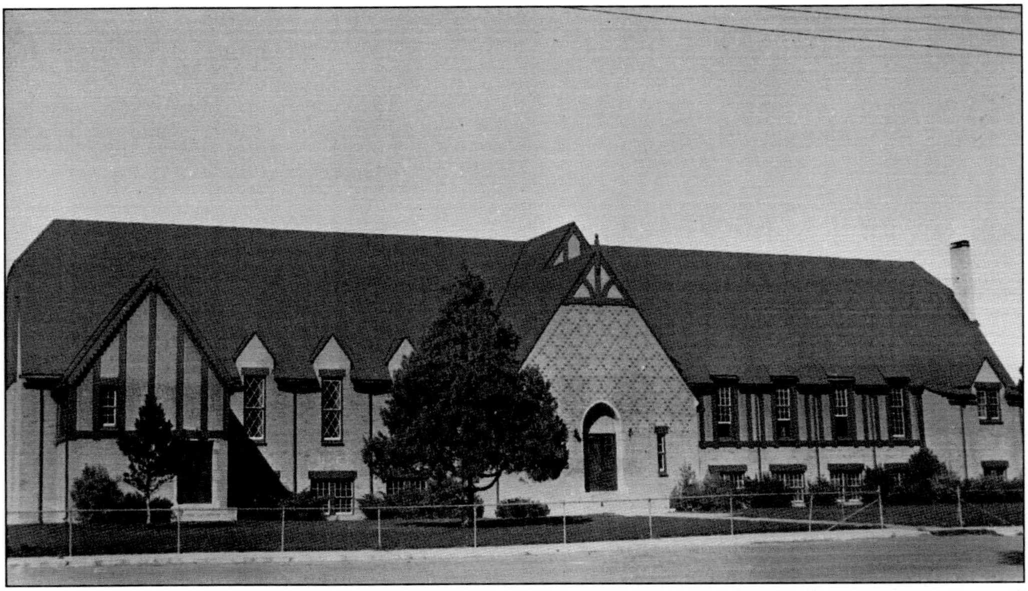

Carl R. Richens became bishop in 1927. His motto was, "I would rather be bishop one year and accomplish something than serve years and do nothing." Soon, a site for a new Maeser chapel was chosen south of the school. A kiln was built, and brick was fired for the structure. The old Relief Society Building and the Omaha Saloon were demolished, and the bricks were salvaged and used in the design. On May 7, 1929, ground was broken, and the chapel was dedicated in December of that same year.

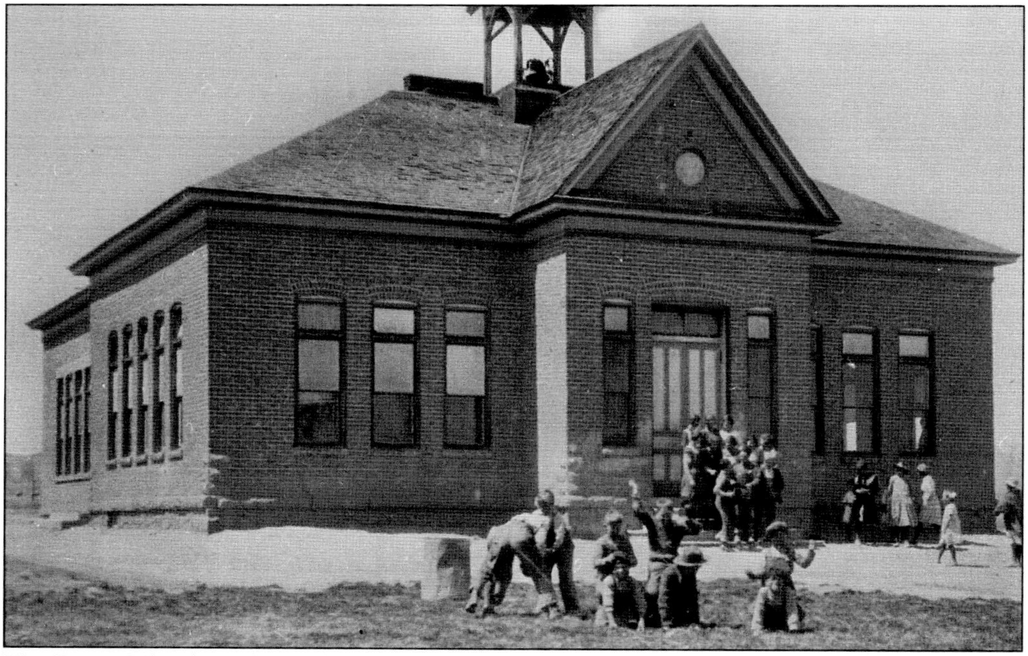

The Davis School was located on 4000 South 1500 East in the Davis area. In 1912, an addition was made to the school. Teacher Sterling Haws stands with the fifth- and sixth-grade students to the left. Hannah Richards is at the doorway. Seventh- and eighth-grade students are standing on the right.

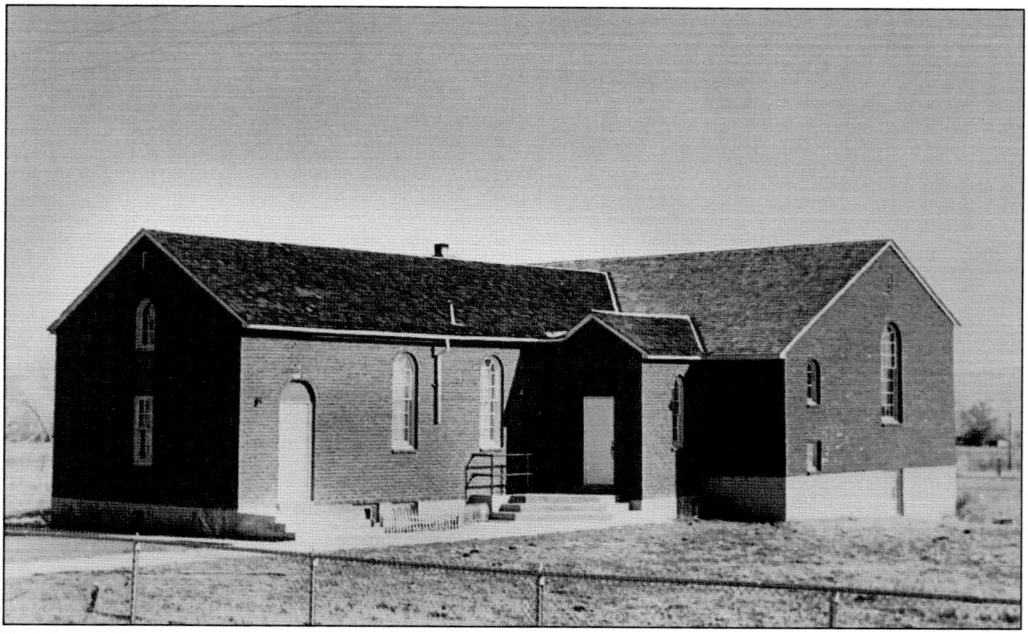

By November 1933, the pouring of cement for the basement of the new Davis Ward Church had commenced. The cement basement extended several feet above the ground and included eight classrooms, a relief society room, and a Boy Scout room. The upper floor housed the chapel, recreation hall, and bishop's office. The outside was finished with pressed brick veneer and gave a pleasing appearance. The church was dedicated in November 1937.

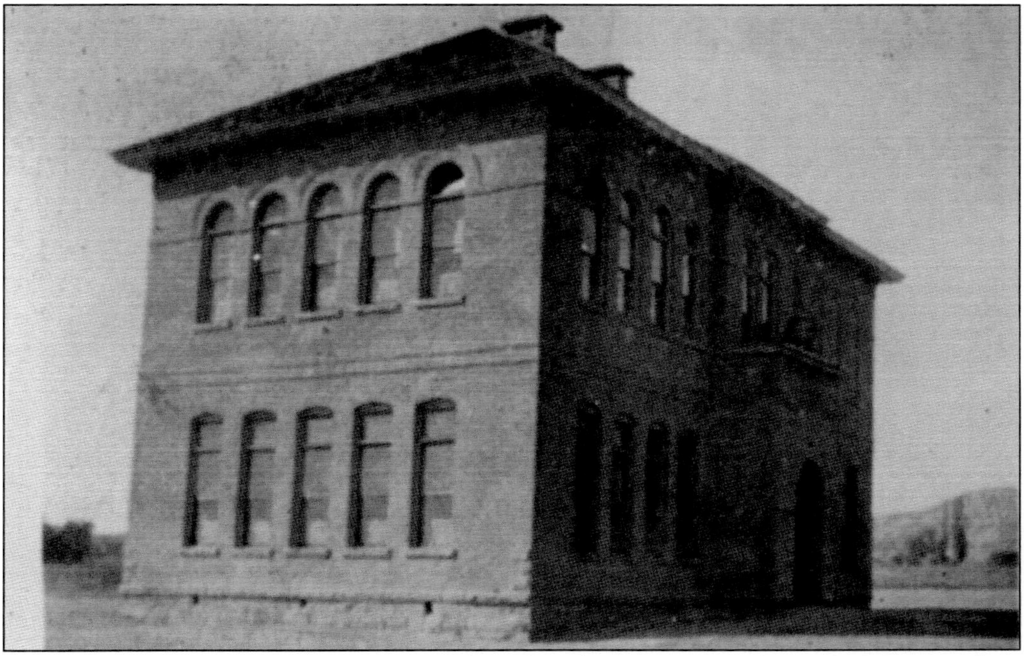

In 1902, a two-story redbrick school was built in the Glines area. It was located approximately at 1700 West 1000 South and contained four classrooms, two halls, and a library. Each room had a big potbellied stove right in the center and a large bucket with water and a dipping ladle for drinking. In 1934, the children were transported to the Maeser School, and the Glines School was torn down.

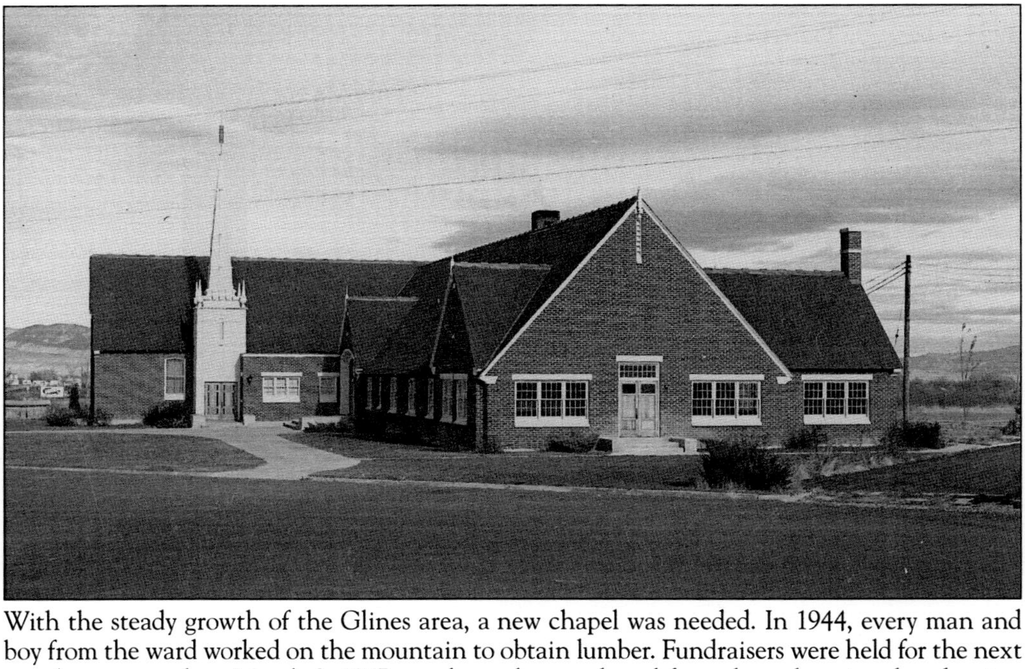

With the steady growth of the Glines area, a new chapel was needed. In 1944, every man and boy from the ward worked on the mountain to obtain lumber. Fundraisers were held for the next couple years, and on March 3, 1947, ward members gathered for a short devotional and razing of the old building that had served their purpose for 50 years. The new structure was dedicated on July 24, 1949.

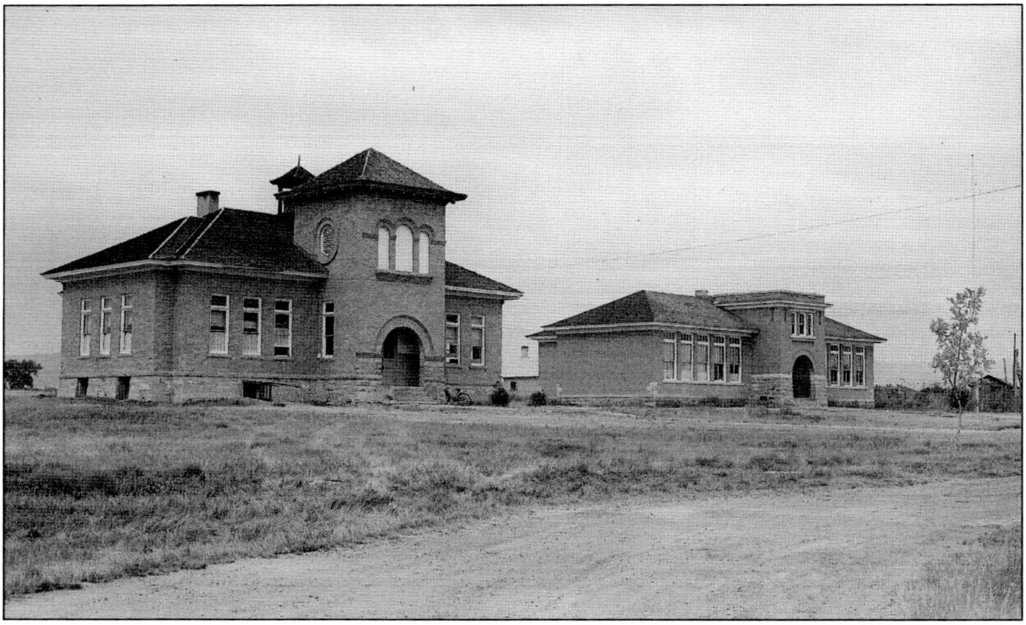

N.G. Sowards was principal of the Naples School when it opened for classes in the fall of 1900. School board members felt that the three large rooms would be sufficient for all children who would ever attend the Naples School. Six years later, a second building was constructed to the north to accommodate increasing numbers of schoolchildren. The schools were in use until 1960, when a larger modern facility was built.

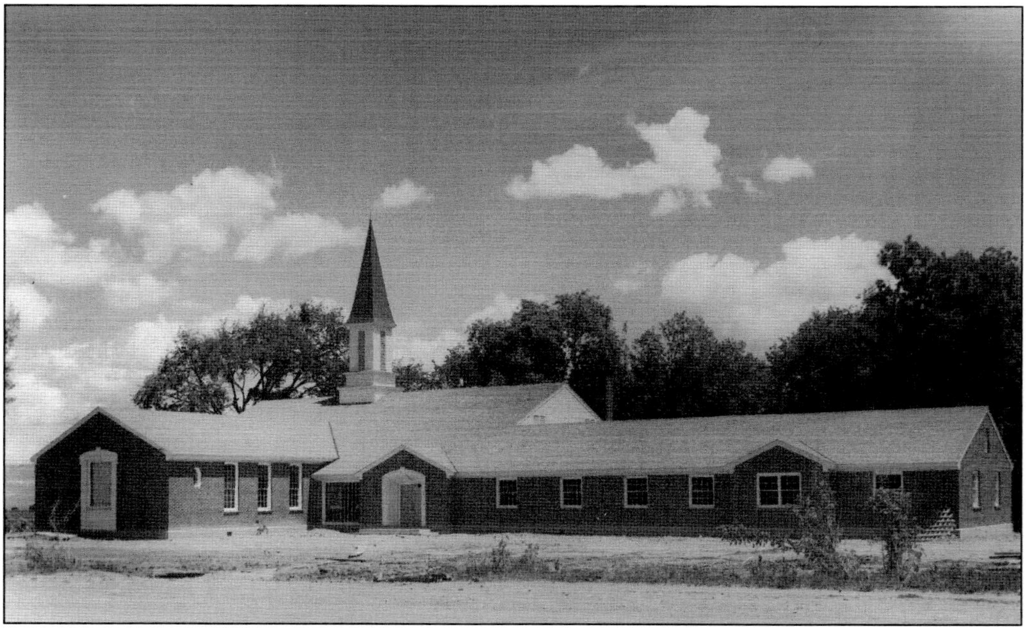

Growth in the Naples area forced Bishop Ross Merrell and his councilors to file an application for a new chapel. Each family in the ward was asked to donate $300 and 30 days of labor; many went to the mountain to cut timber. The old building was demolished, and materials were salvaged for the new church. Anyone who could use a hammer helped in the construction of the new church. The Naples chapel was dedicated on July 24, 1949.

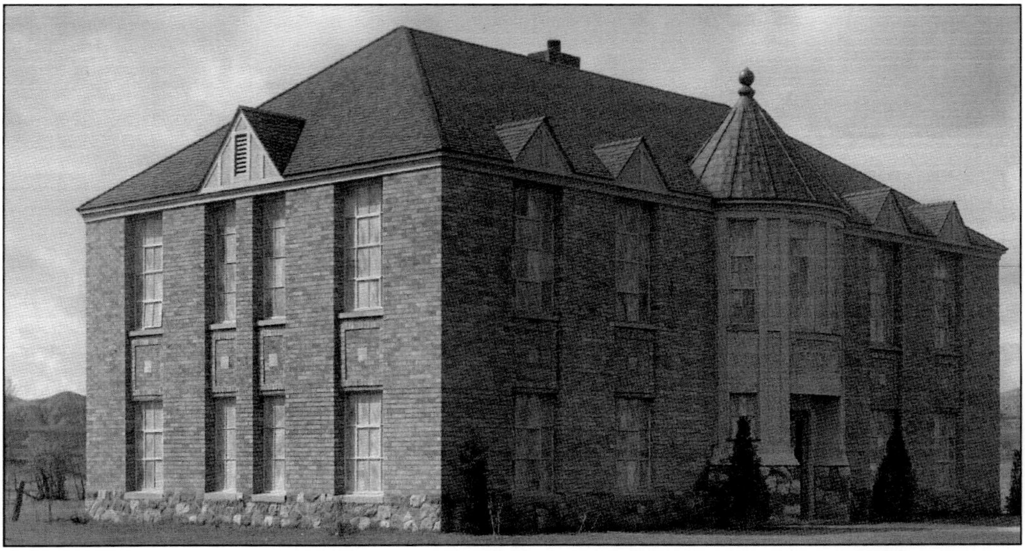

The Vernal Seminary building of French colonial architecture is a two-story design of colored stone masonry with brick veneer finish. The upper floor has two classrooms, an office, and a foyer. The lower floor has one classroom, a library, an office, cloakrooms, and restrooms. The building was completed in 1937 and is located south of the Uintah Academy.

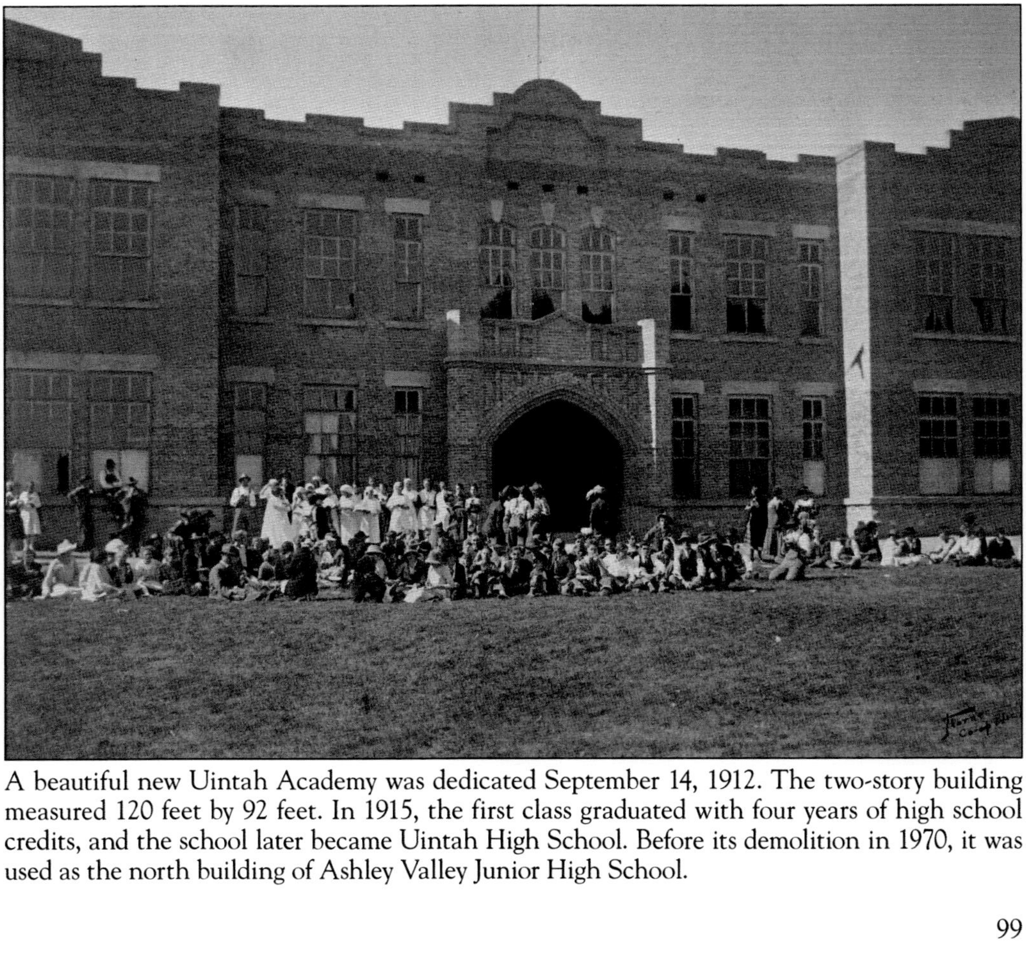

A beautiful new Uintah Academy was dedicated September 14, 1912. The two-story building measured 120 feet by 92 feet. In 1915, the first class graduated with four years of high school credits, and the school later became Uintah High School. Before its demolition in 1970, it was used as the north building of Ashley Valley Junior High School.

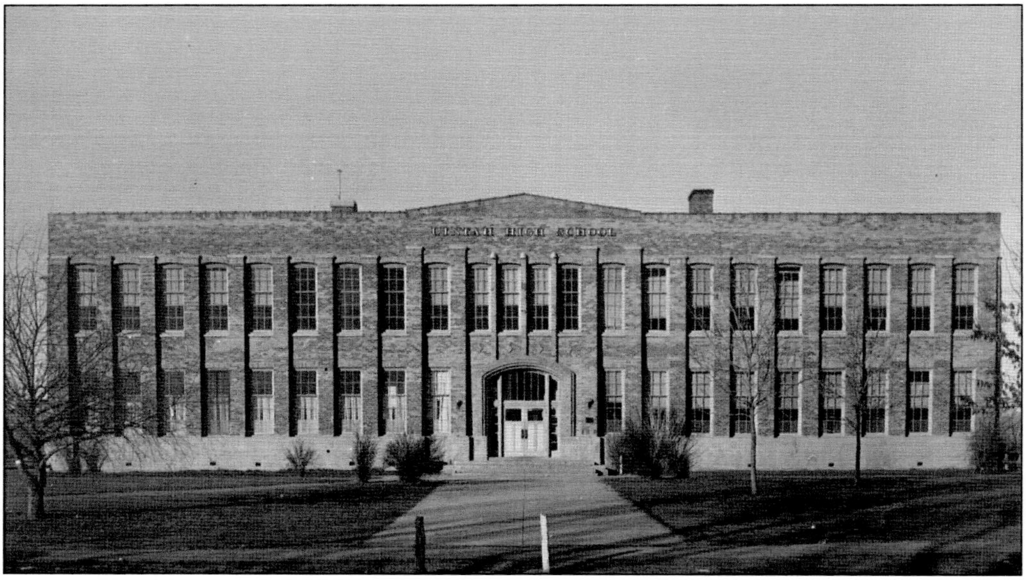

A new Uintah High School was built south of the Uintah Academy in 1923; it was located at 1023 West 200 South. This building was used until the late 1950s, when the new high school was constructed. The former high school was then used as the south building for Ashley Valley Junior High School.

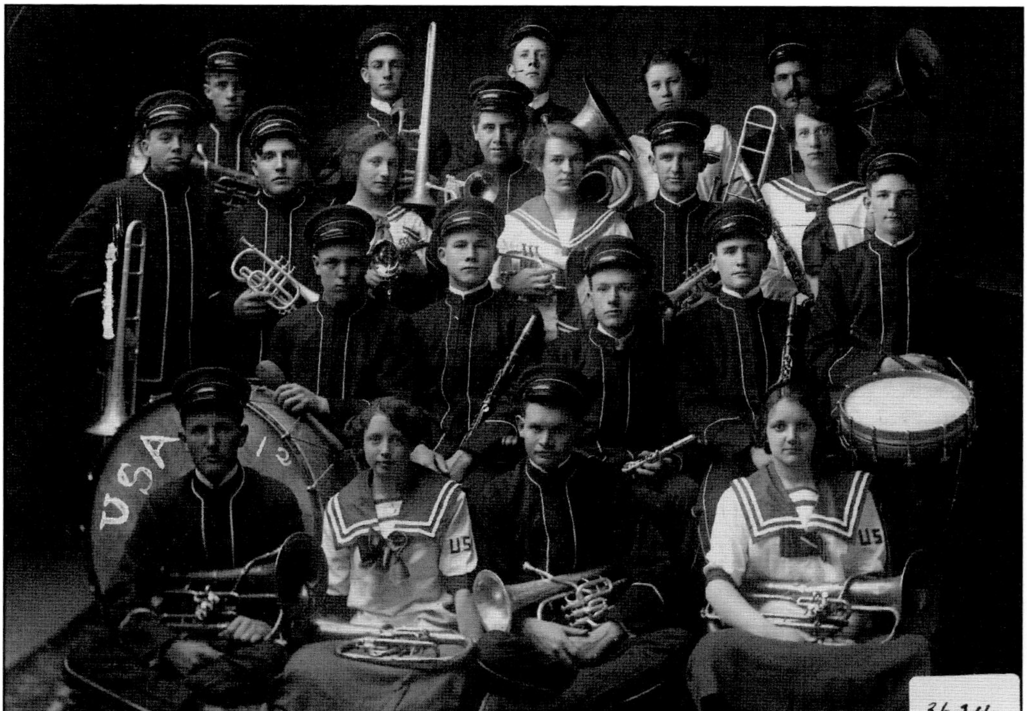

In 1910, the Uintah Stake Academy Band played a few selections on the street corner to the surprise of most businessmen, who were not aware that the band existed. A concert was given at the tabernacle to help with the funds, and the band had earned enough money for new band uniforms by 1912.

Nine

Life is a Celebration

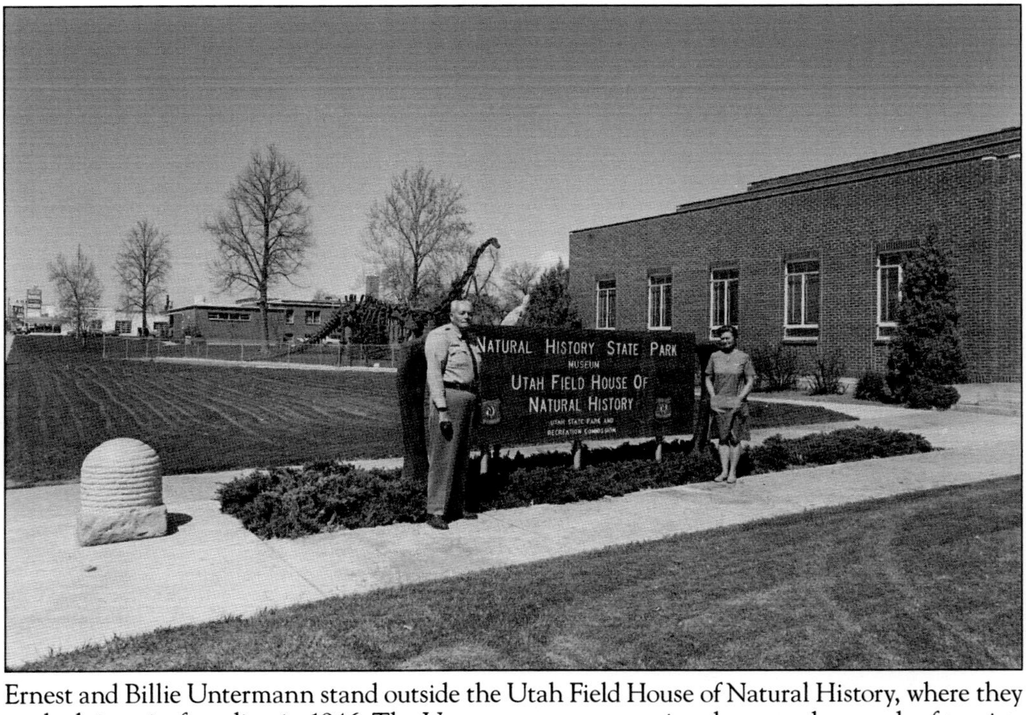

Ernest and Billie Untermann stand outside the Utah Field House of Natural History, where they worked since its founding in 1946. The Untermanns were gracious hosts to thousands of tourists visiting the museum each year. Dippy, the 76-foot-long skeleton of the dinosaur diplodocus, can be seen in its prominent location in front of the museum, where it was placed in 1957. Dippy now stands inside a new, modern museum at 500 East Main Street.

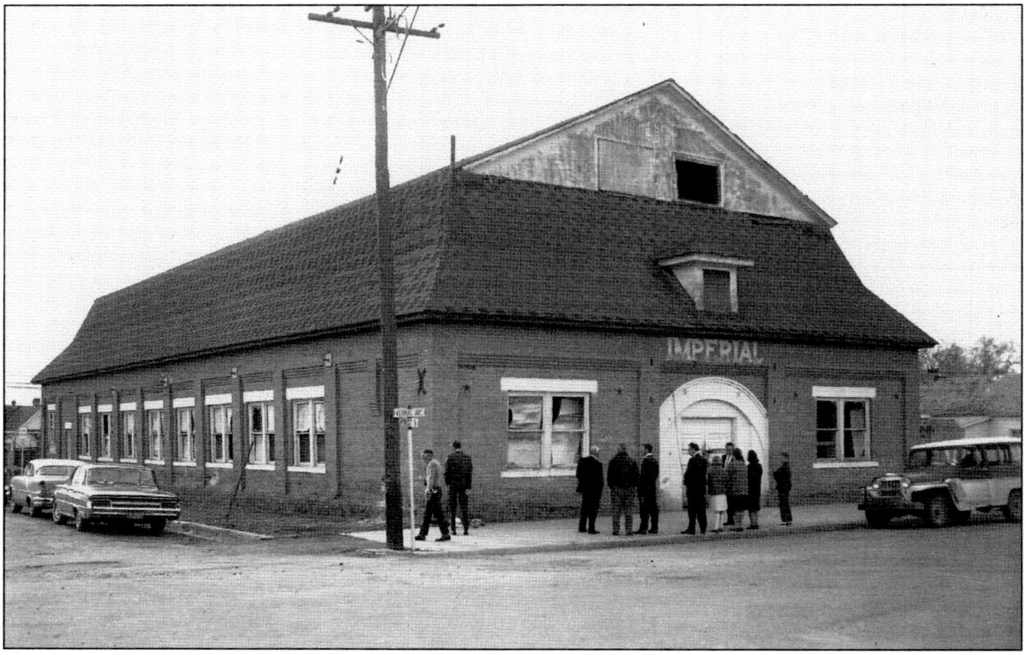

A group gathers in front of the Imperial Hall for a fond farewell prior to its razing in April 1965. The Imperial Hall was known as the Orpheus when it opened its doors in 1912. Andrew King, Clarence Showalter, N.J. Meagher, and Grant Carpenter owned the hall. Before the Vogue Theater was built, the first moving pictures were shown at the Orpheus. The hall was used for movies, plays, dancing, skating, boxing, basketball games, and many other social events. The Uintah Stake purchased the building in 1925, and in 1928, the Orpheus had a new name. The Imperial Hall was the social center of the valley.

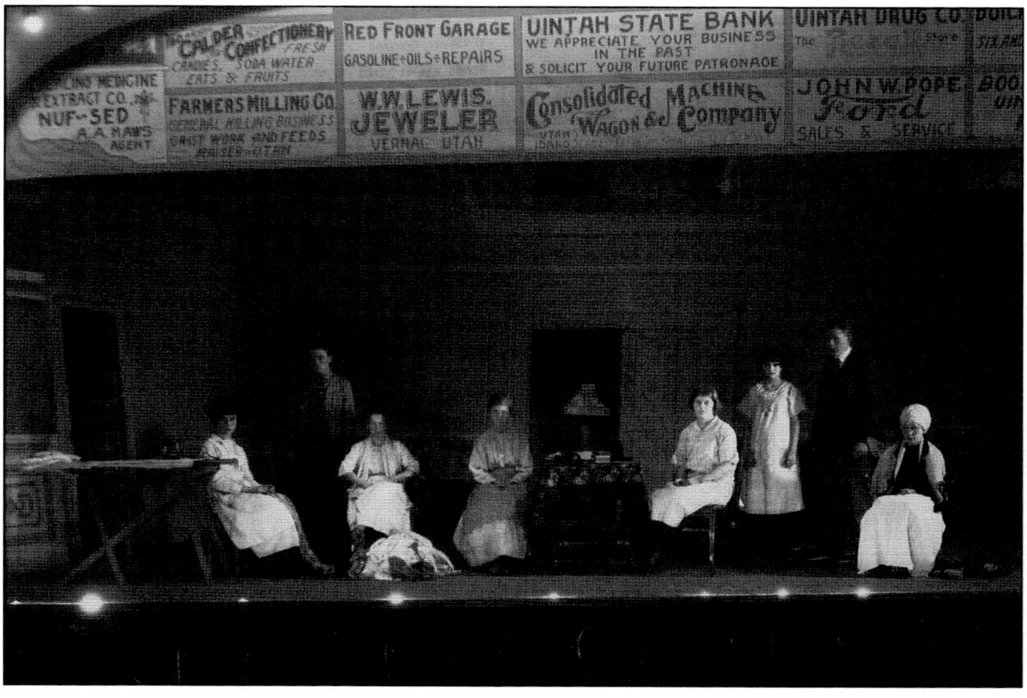

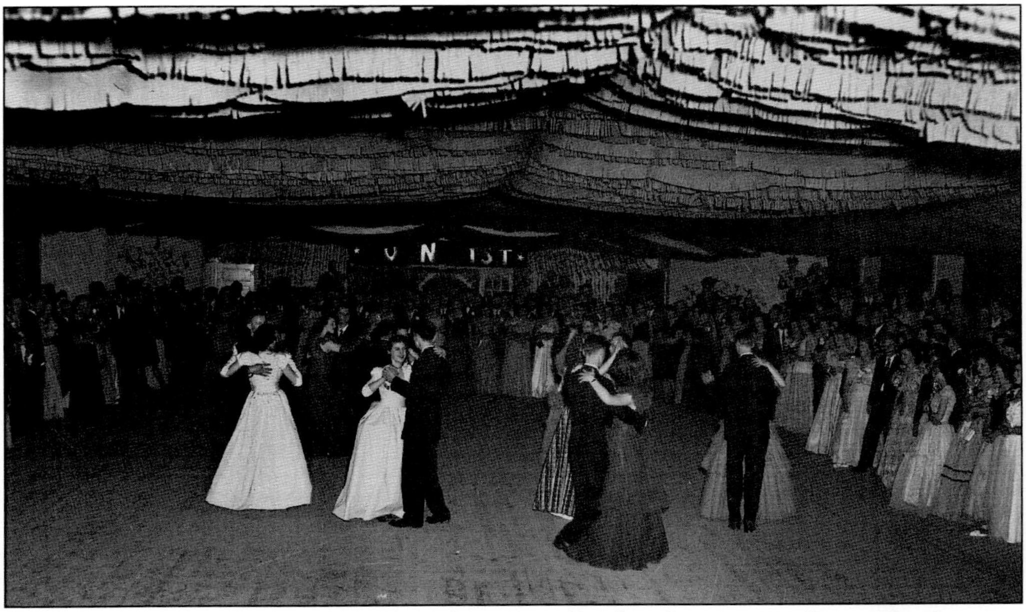

There was no better place to dance than the Imperial Hall with its springy floors. The floor was constructed over cement piers, each equipped with large springs that moved up and down to the movement of the dancers. This junior prom, which took place in 1947, was one of many held at the hall. Another popular dance held at the Imperial was the Gold and Green Ball sponsored by the Uintah Stake.

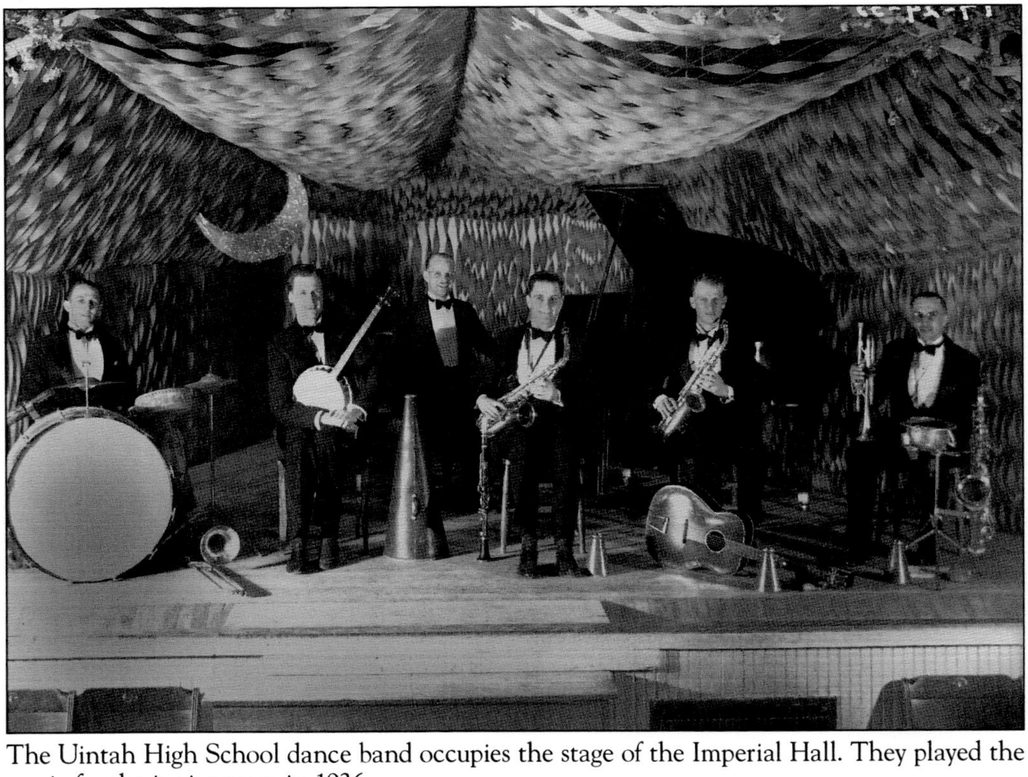

The Uintah High School dance band occupies the stage of the Imperial Hall. They played the music for the junior prom in 1936.

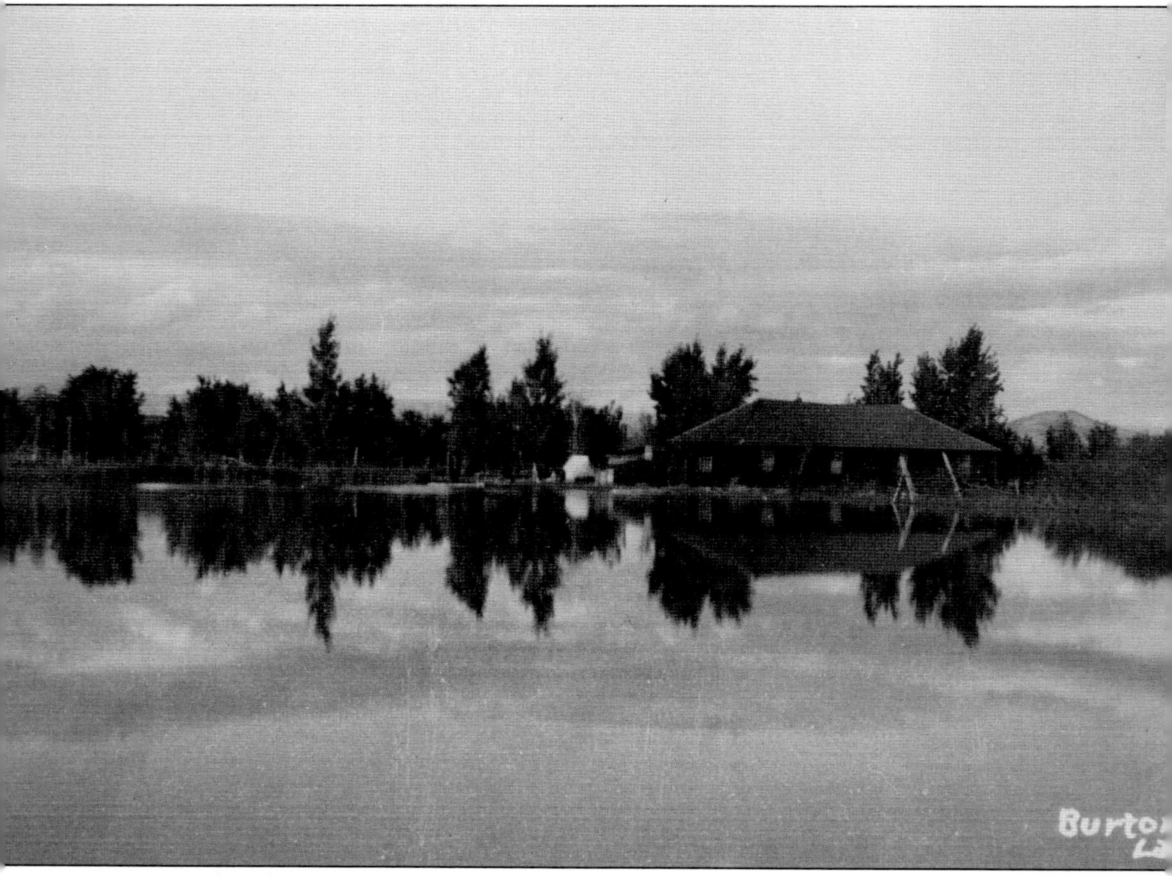

Ira Burton bought 160 acres southeast of Ashley Town and built Burton's Resort on this property in 1900. He constructed a house on the property along with a man-made lake that was fed by Ashley Creek. He also built a dance hall and a racetrack on 40 acres of his property. The lake was stocked with fish and was used for swimming and boating in the summer and ice-skating in winter. Ira built a bathhouse where swimming suits and boats were rented. The dance hall was 36 feet by 82 feet and located next to the lake. Large groups always enjoyed a weekly dance with a live band. A concession stand offered candy, ice cream, sandwiches, soft drinks, and beer. Crowds gathered from all over the basin to enjoy baseball games, horse racing, rodeos, dances, and different events at the resort. On special occasions, fireworks were shot from rafts on the lake.

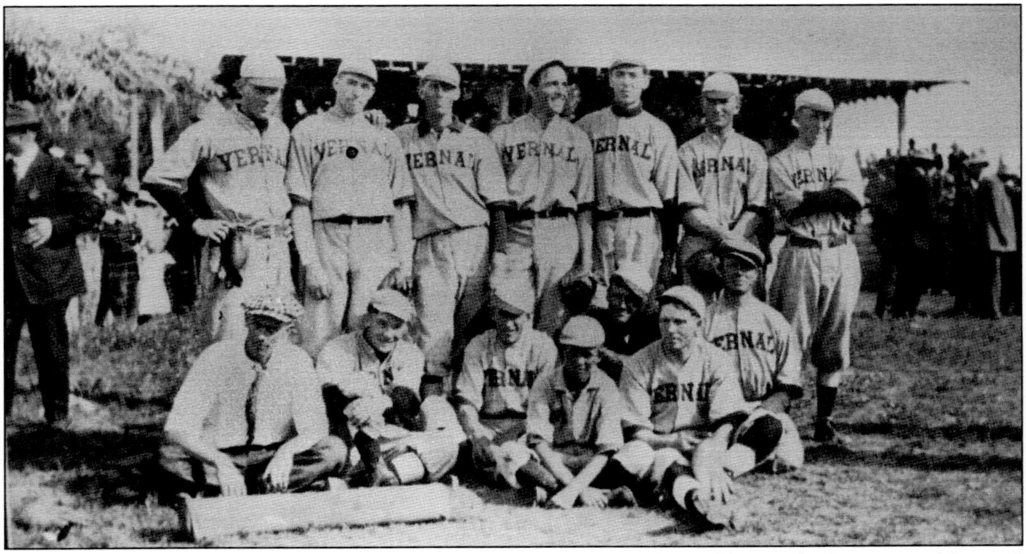

Baseball was an important event for the early settlers. Teams from all over the basin would travel back and forth, from town to town, to play each other. Ball games were part of every celebration. The players are identified, from left to right, as (first row) Harold Reader, Dave Curry, Vern Simmons, Manfred Martin, Bill Watkins, Clark Elmer, Rebeau Calder, and L.W. Curry; (second row) Jim Mease, ? Deprease, ? Teaples, Ray Dillman, Charlie Dawson, Clive Davis, and Ralph Lloyd.

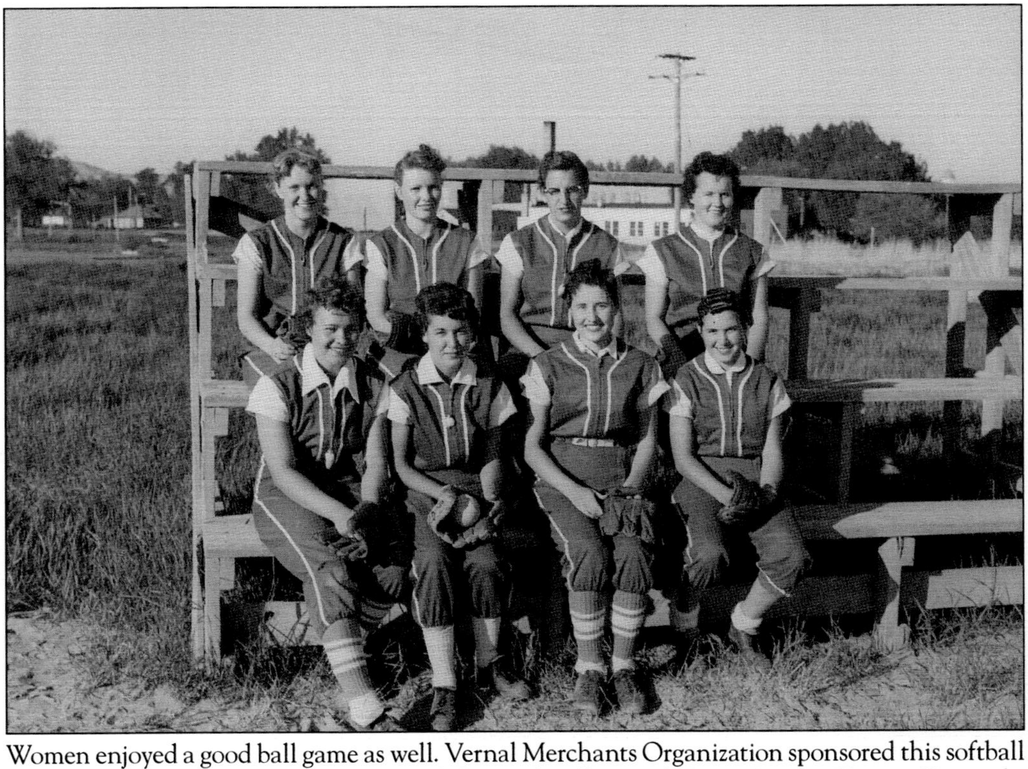

Women enjoyed a good ball game as well. Vernal Merchants Organization sponsored this softball team in June 1959. The players are, from left to right, (first row) Diane Lyman, Bonnie Danniels, Twila Rasmussen, and Rose Mary Bigelow; (second row) Joyce Gingell, Margie Meiure, Helen Gross, and Carma Hacking.

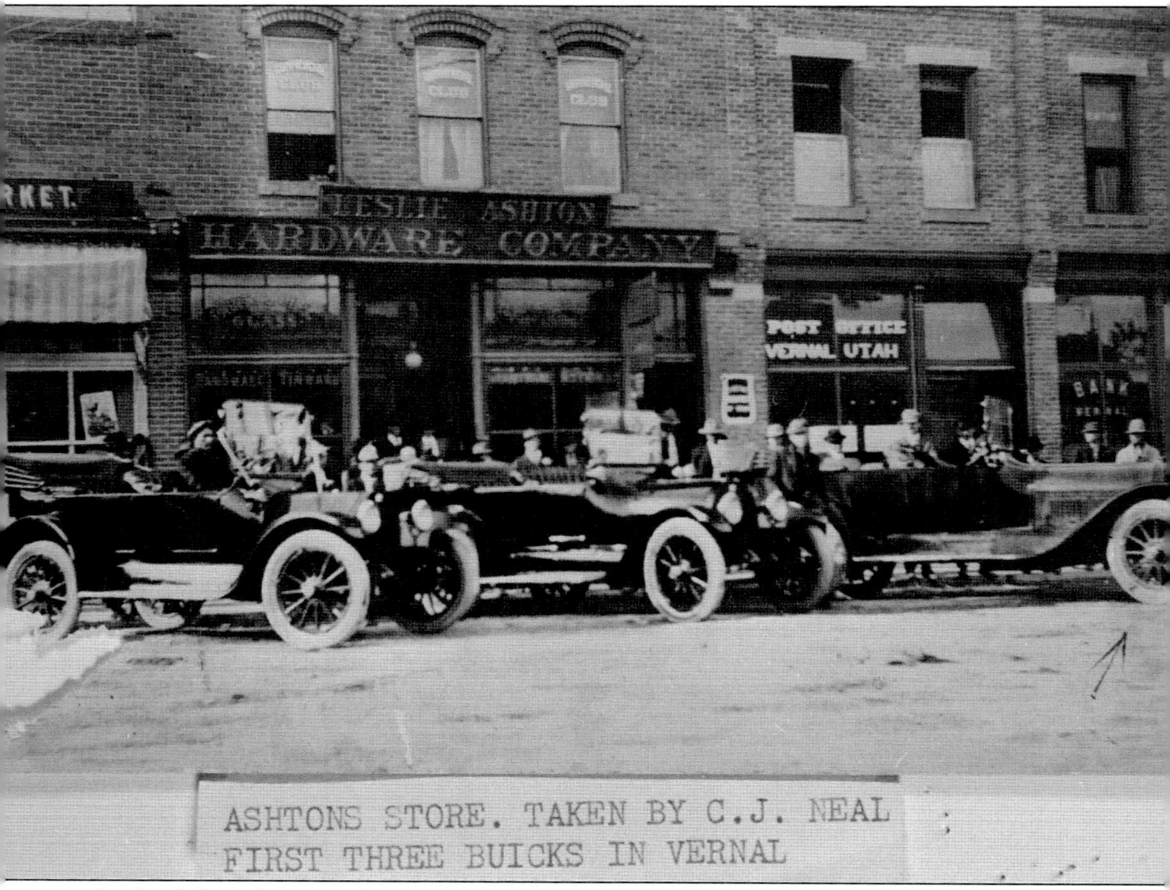

Leslie Ashton became the second local owner of a six-cylinder Buick touring car. On July 10, 1914, it was reported that a new record was made in overland travel in Utah. For the first time in history, a man had left Vernal after the sun was up and had reached Salt Lake City before the sun went down. Leslie Ashton's Buick made the run, and Bert Newell, one of the most competent drivers of the West, drove the car. When it pulled out of Vernal at 5:00 a.m., those on board were Newell, Mr. and Mrs. Leslie Ashton, Clarence Ashton, Lowe Ashton, and Mayor Edward D. Samuels. Two suitcases, a satchel, and a lunch basket constituted the baggage. The car and travelers reached Salt Lake two minutes before 6:00 p.m; the time was two minutes less than 13 hours. The distance was 209.8 miles, and the average time was approximately 16 miles per hour. When the car left Vernal, there was a streamer on it, which made the bold statement, "To Salt Lake before sundown today or bust."

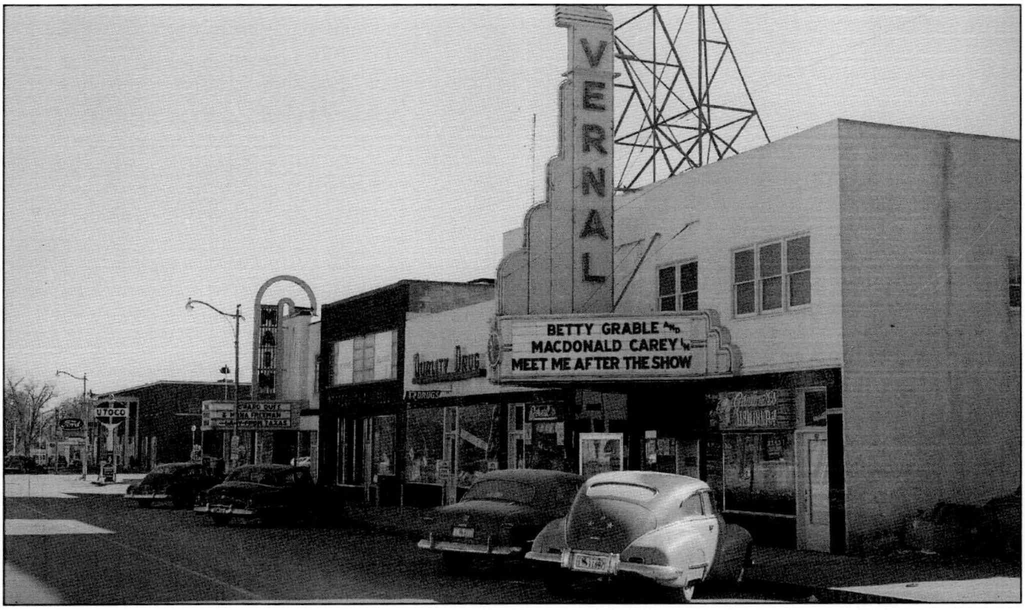

The Vernal Theater and the Main Theater were both located along the south side of East Main Street. This photograph was taken shortly after the Vernal Theater had its grand opening on March 29, 1946. The Shiner family built and owned the Vernal Theater, and Tom Karren and Francis Feltch constructed the Main Theater.

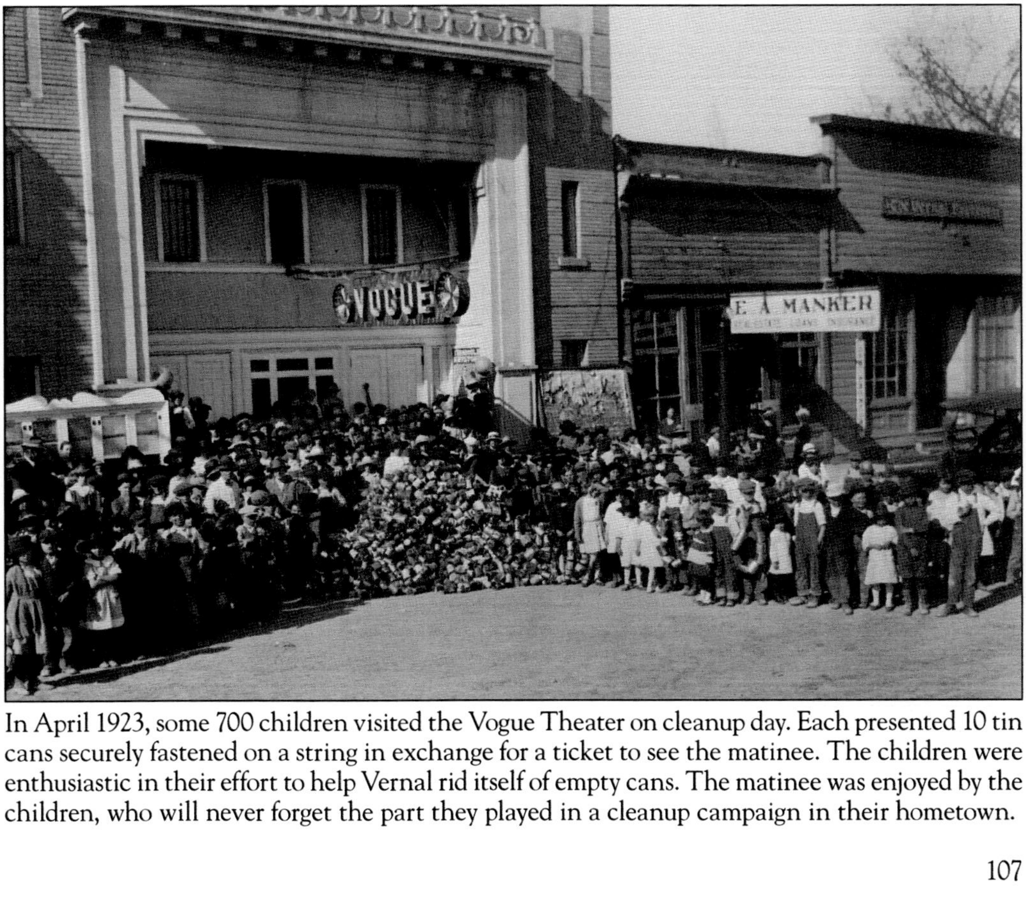

In April 1923, some 700 children visited the Vogue Theater on cleanup day. Each presented 10 tin cans securely fastened on a string in exchange for a ticket to see the matinee. The children were enthusiastic in their effort to help Vernal rid itself of empty cans. The matinee was enjoyed by the children, who will never forget the part they played in a cleanup campaign in their hometown.

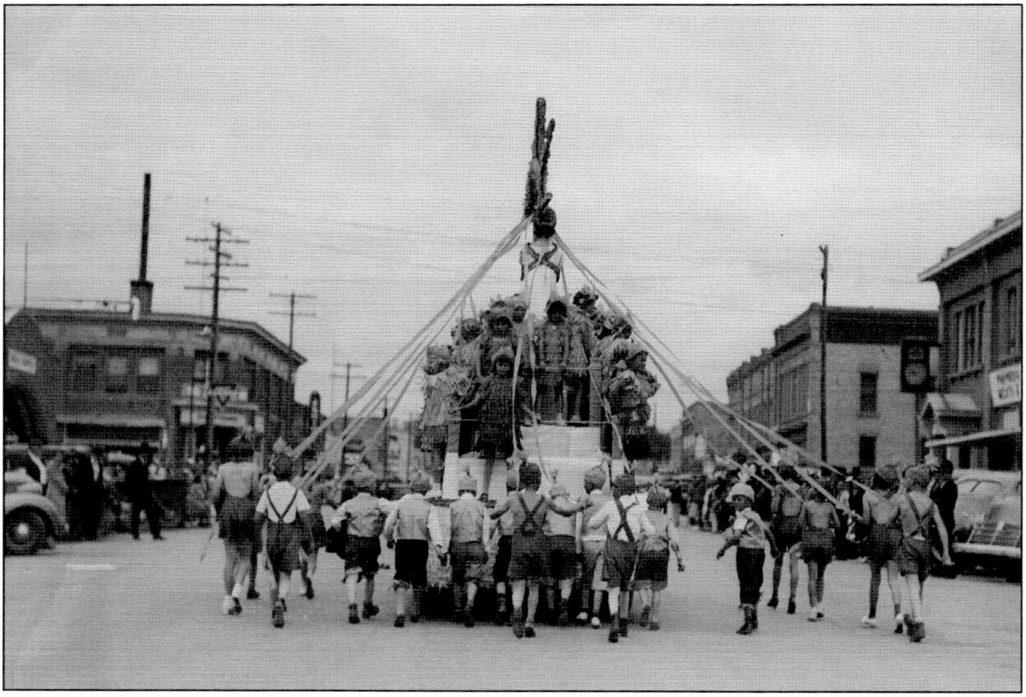

The Ashley Valley celebrated nearly every event with a parade. This one was during the second annual Health Day Celebration in 1938. The float represents the braiding of the maypole. Boys walk beside the float holding the streamers while the girls ride. The buildings in the background are, from left to right, the Bank of Vernal, Ashley Co-op, and Uintah State Bank.

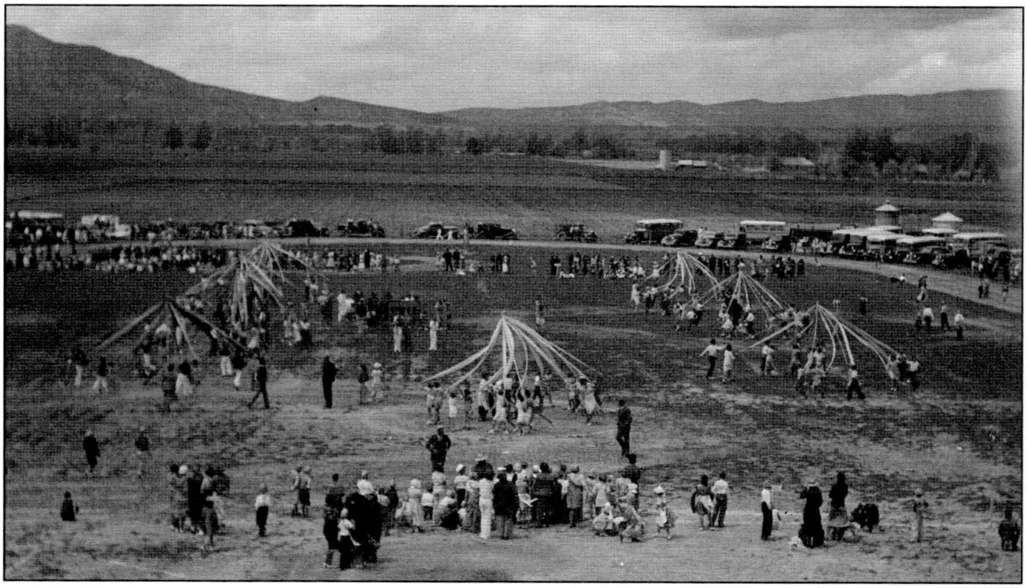

In May 1938, Uintah School's second annual health day was a huge success, as 3,500 Uintah District schoolchildren participated in the countywide event. The day began with a parade ending at the Uintah High School field. Elementary school groups performed dances, and the braiding of the maypole took place in the center of the high school track. Following the program, field and contest sports began between the schools.

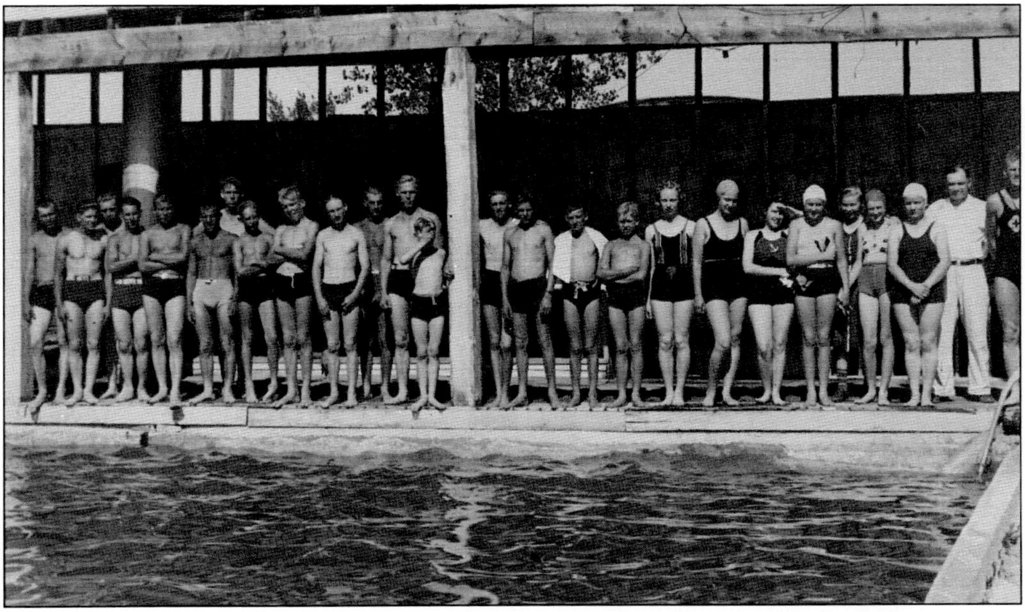

Crystal Baths was the first swimming pool to open in the valley in 1928. It was located two blocks north of Main Street, just off Vernal Avenue. It was a heated, 40-foot-by-70-foot pool with a diving board and had dressing rooms and showers. In 1938, the Red Cross held its lifesaving class at the Crystal Baths. Standing on far right with class participants are Dr. J.W. Stevens (left) and Preston Q. Hale.

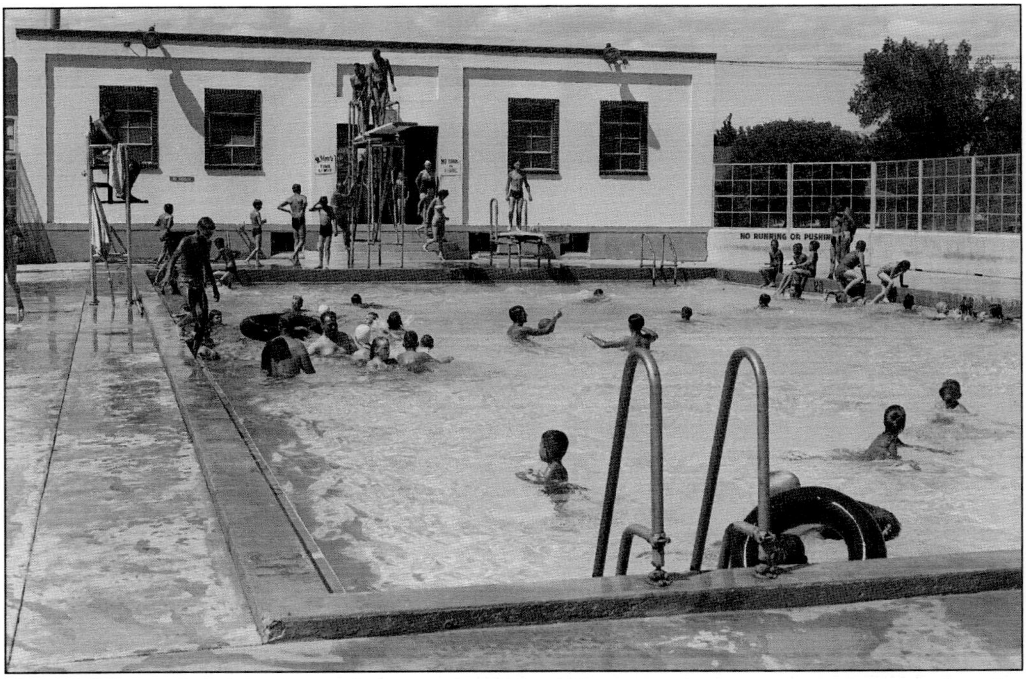

Acres of flaming red, sunburned skin among Vernal's young citizens was a sure sign that the swimming pool season had finally commenced. The long-awaited Vernal swimming pool opened in May 1951, at 155 East 100 North. Water in the pool and showers was heated, and the main pool had floodlights at night.

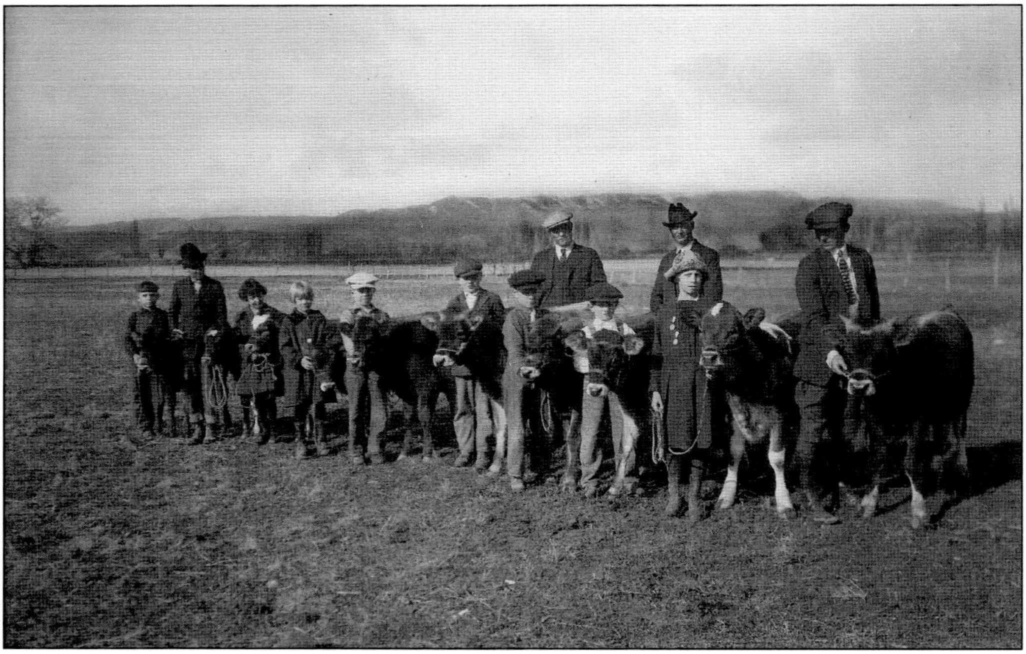

The first annual County Boys and Girls Club fair ever in the state of Utah was successfully held in Vernal in 1926. This fair replaced the county fair, which was not held that year. These children exhibit their calves proudly. Uintah County was said to have the largest Boys and Girls Club of any county in the state. No one in this photograph is identified.

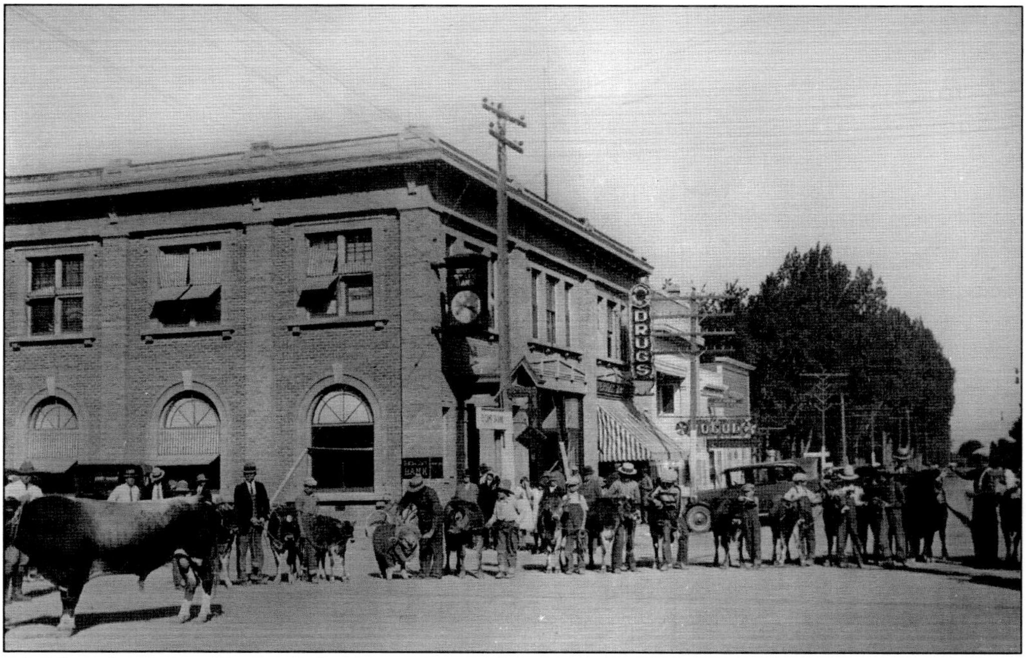

Children line up in front of the Uintah State Bank with their livestock. To stimulate the dairy industry, Uintah State Bank offered a purebred bull calf to the calf club in Uintah County that compiled the best record. In October 1923, the bank made its presentation to the 11 members of the Maeser Calf Club for their success in raising livestock.

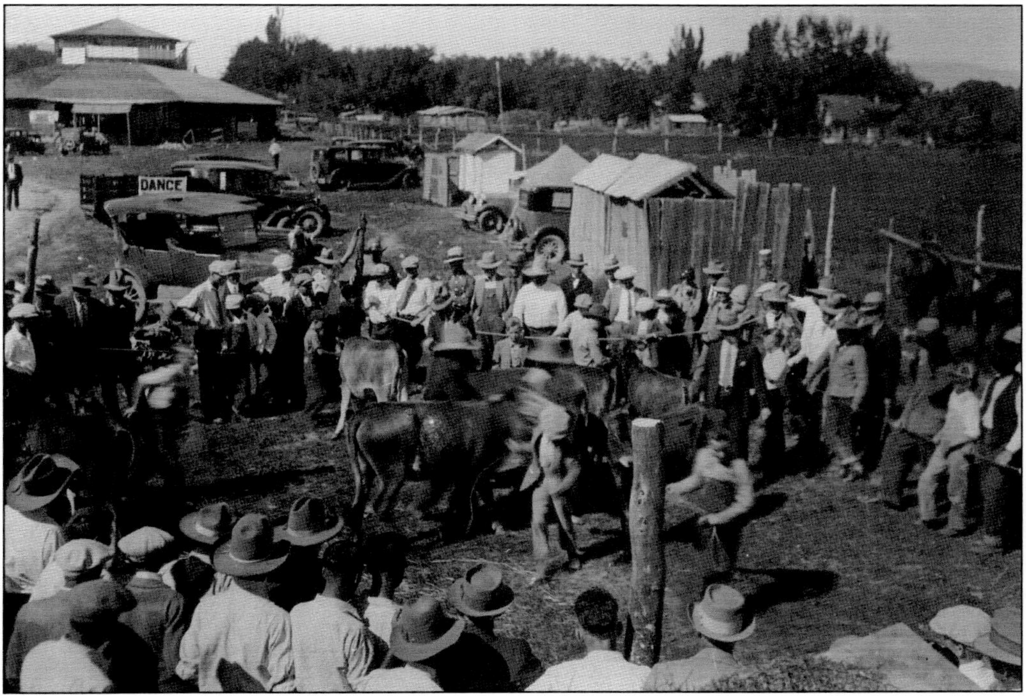

The new fairgrounds were built southeast of Vernal near 300 East 200 South. The round building housed fair exhibits as well as the dinosaur fossil exhibits from the Dinosaur Quarry. This photograph was taken in the early 1920s. The fairgrounds have remained in this location but have had many improvements over the years. A grandstand was built for large crowds to enjoy horse races and rodeos. The Vernal Rodeo–Dinosaur Roundup Rodeo became a big event in the community. In 1948, the livestock show building replaced the round exhibit building and became home to the Junior Livestock Show.

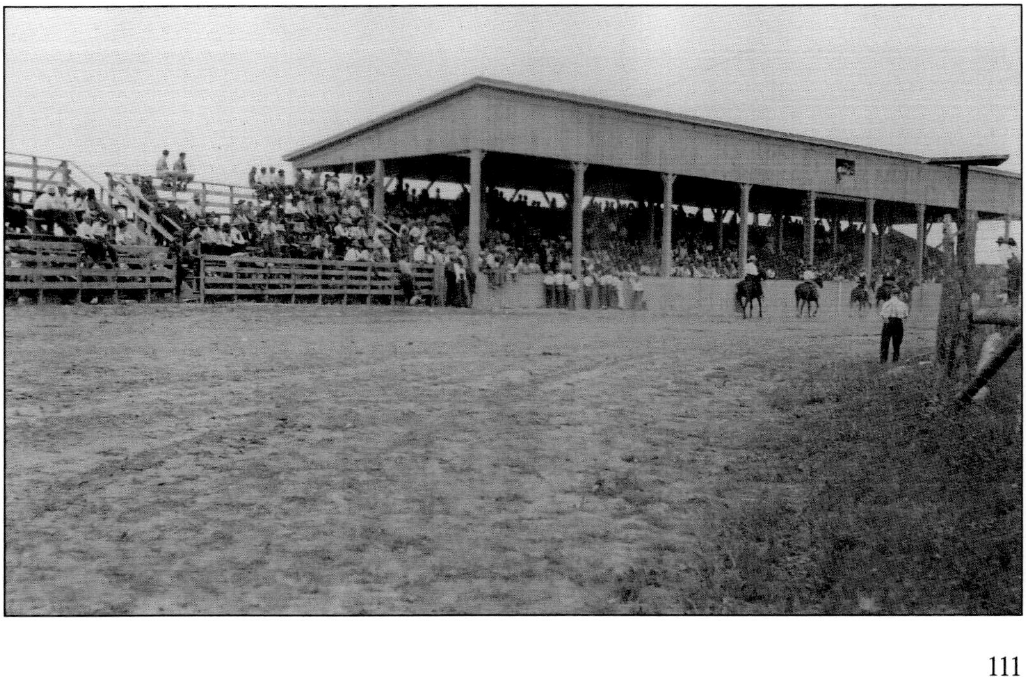

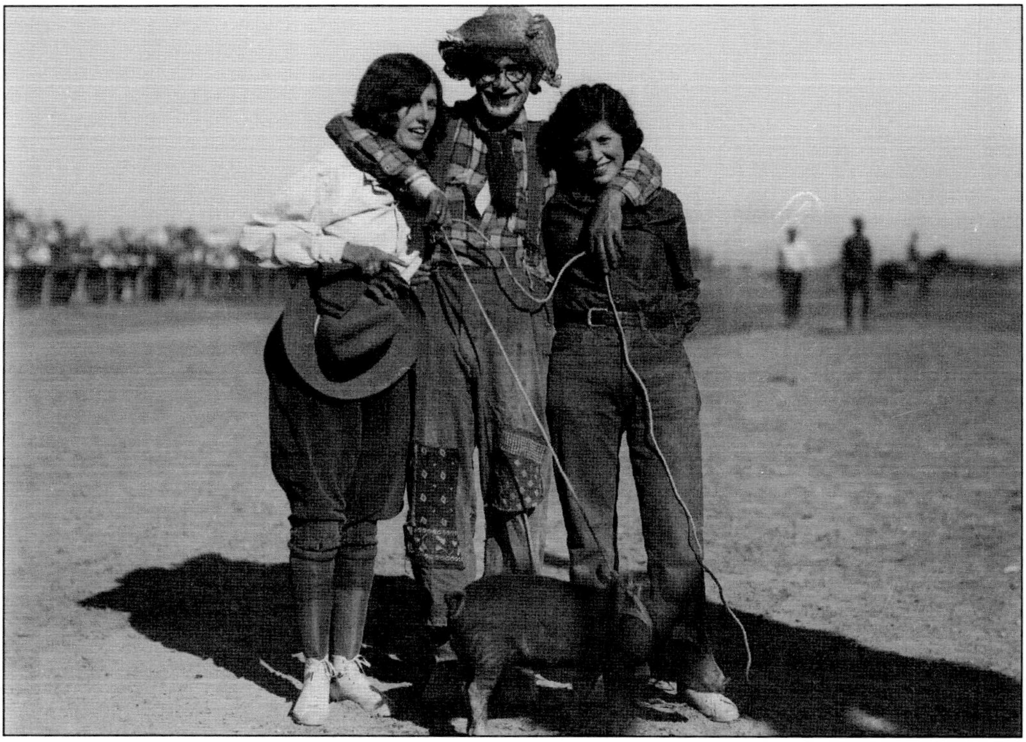

In 1936, the Vernal Rodeo was said to be the most enjoyable and successful show in eastern Utah, with 5,000 people in attendance on the first day of the event. On the last day, there were record crowds of nearly 10,000 people. Two local cowgirls pose with the rodeo clown.

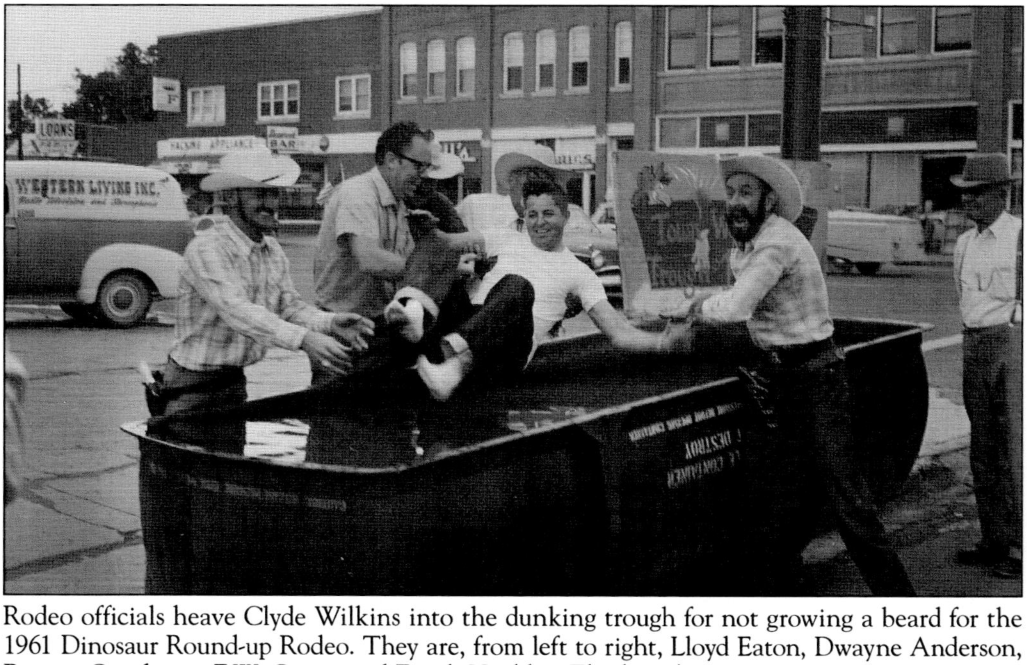

Rodeo officials heave Clyde Wilkins into the dunking trough for not growing a beard for the 1961 Dinosaur Round-up Rodeo. They are, from left to right, Lloyd Eaton, Dwayne Anderson, Barney Goodman, E.W. Coon, and Frank Heckler. The beard-growing contest was a popular event during rodeo season.

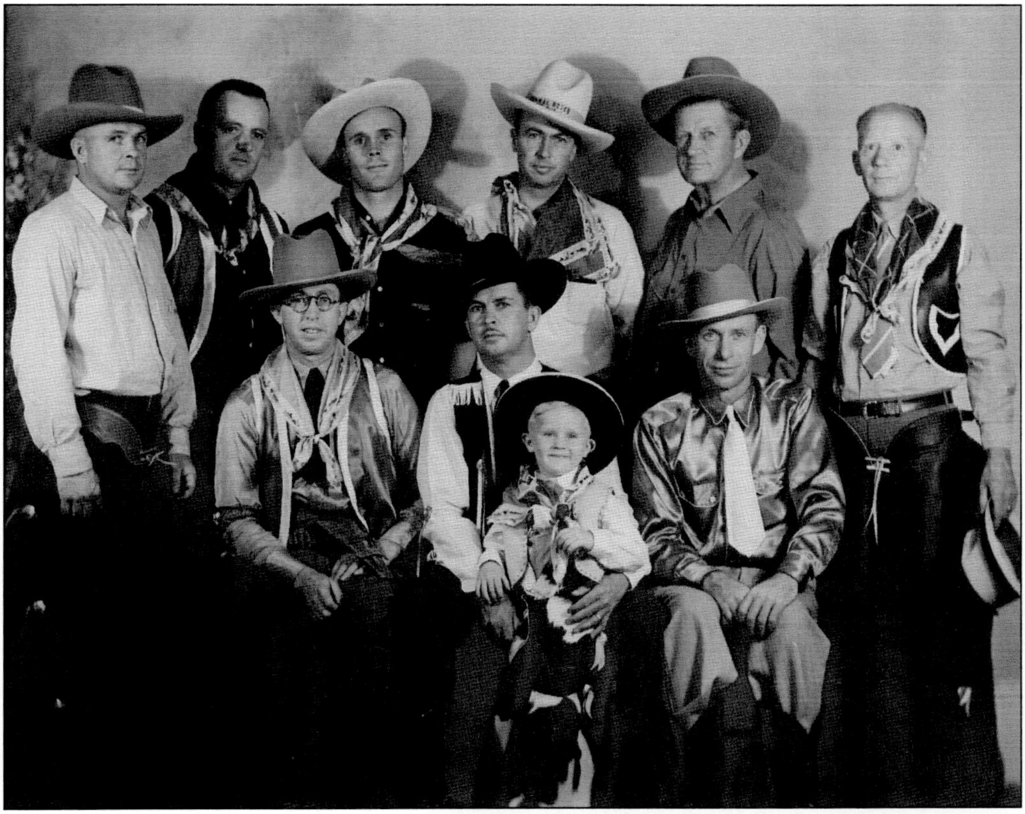

The Vernal Rodeo has been going strong since the early 1900s. It has been organized and planned by the Vernal Rodeo Association since the 1920s. The 1937 Rodeo Committee from left to right consists of (first row) Alvin Weeks, Howard Caldwell, Lee Bennion, and Donnie Barr; (second row) Austin White, DeVere Carroll, Paul Lyman, P.L. Cowan, John Jorgensen, and J.C. Anderson. In 1957, the Vernal Professional Rodeo became known as the Dinosaur Roundup Rodeo. The four-day event still draws crowds of people every July.

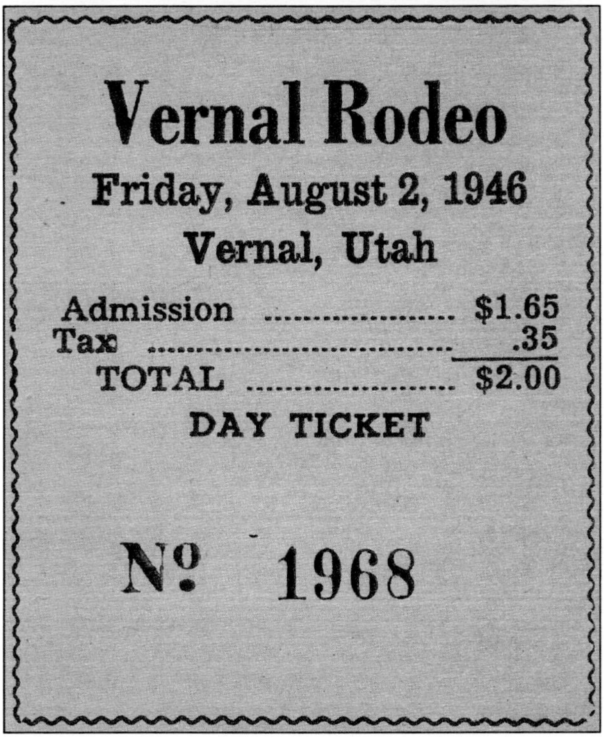

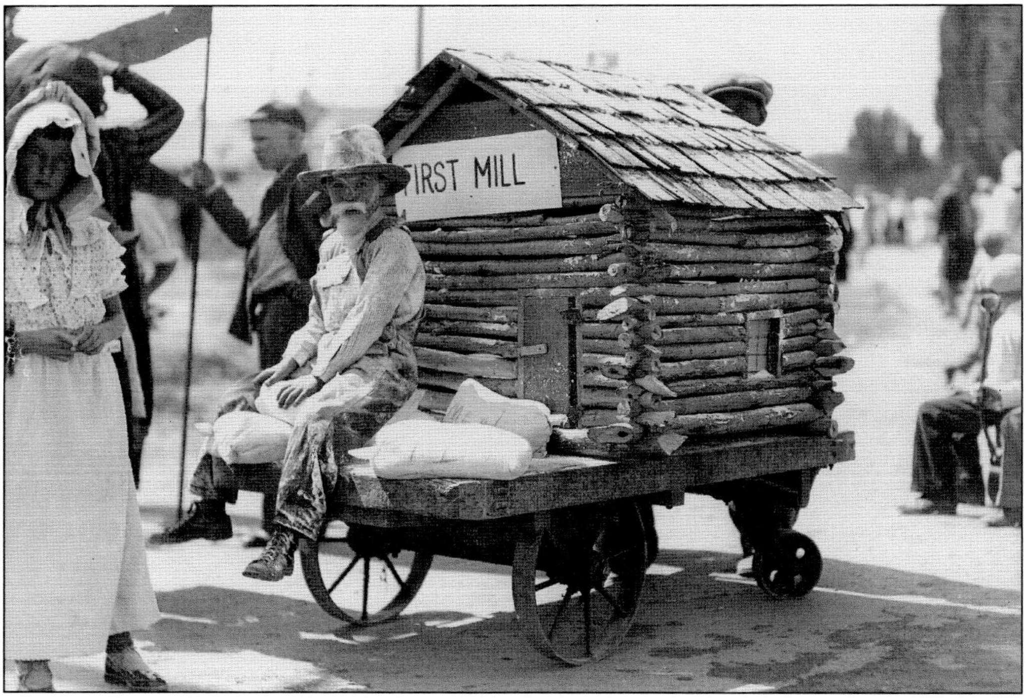

The 1929 Pioneer Day Parade was presented by Primary children from throughout Ashley Valley. In the entry above, a boy portrays the first miller, William Reynolds, in front of the first mill. Below, adorable girls represent Miss Uintah. The *Vernal Express* states that this was the best parade ever witnessed in Vernal and that as many as 3,000 people came from out of the area to attend.

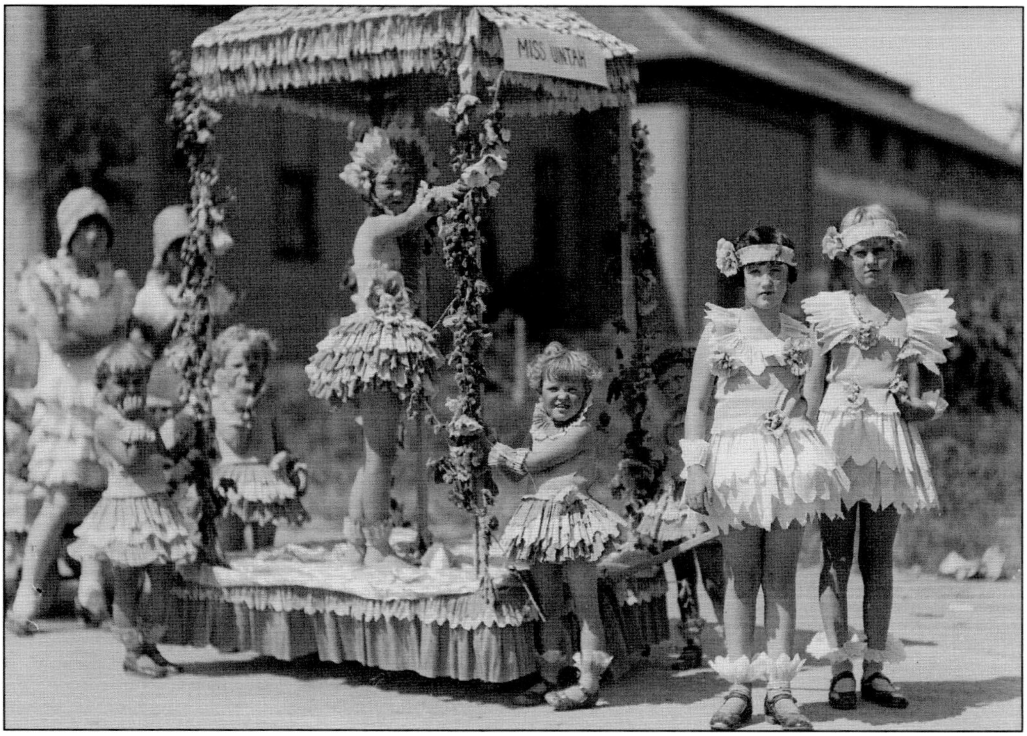

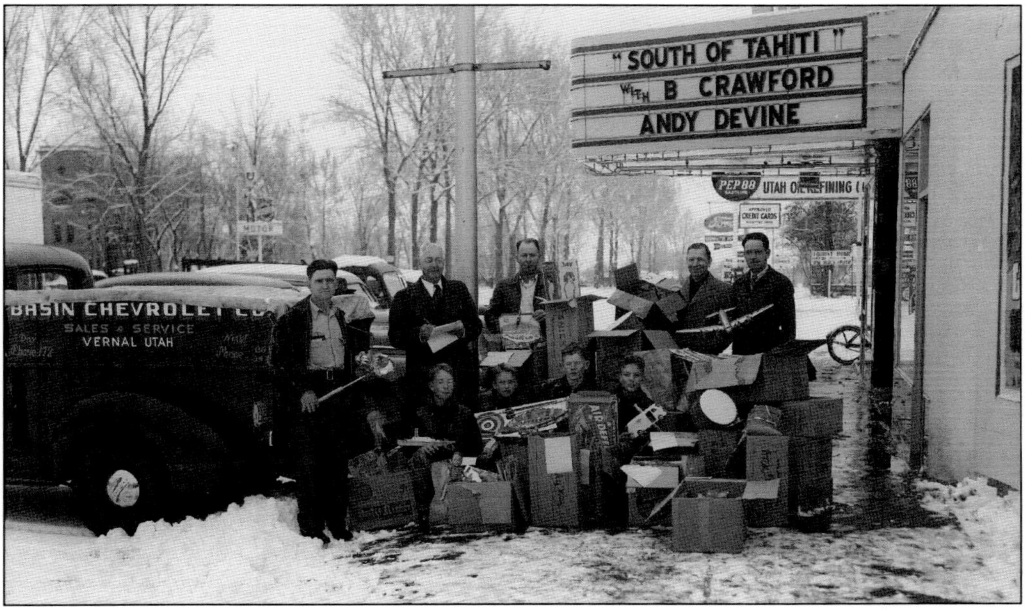

The Christmas Cheer Committee of the Vernal Lions Club, with the help of some local boys, collects toys for the less fortunate. They are photographed in front of the Main Theater prior to delivering the toys. The Lions Club members in the second row are, from left to right, Henry Schaefermeyer, William S. Henderson, two unidentified men, and Fran Feltch. The boys in the first row are unidentified.

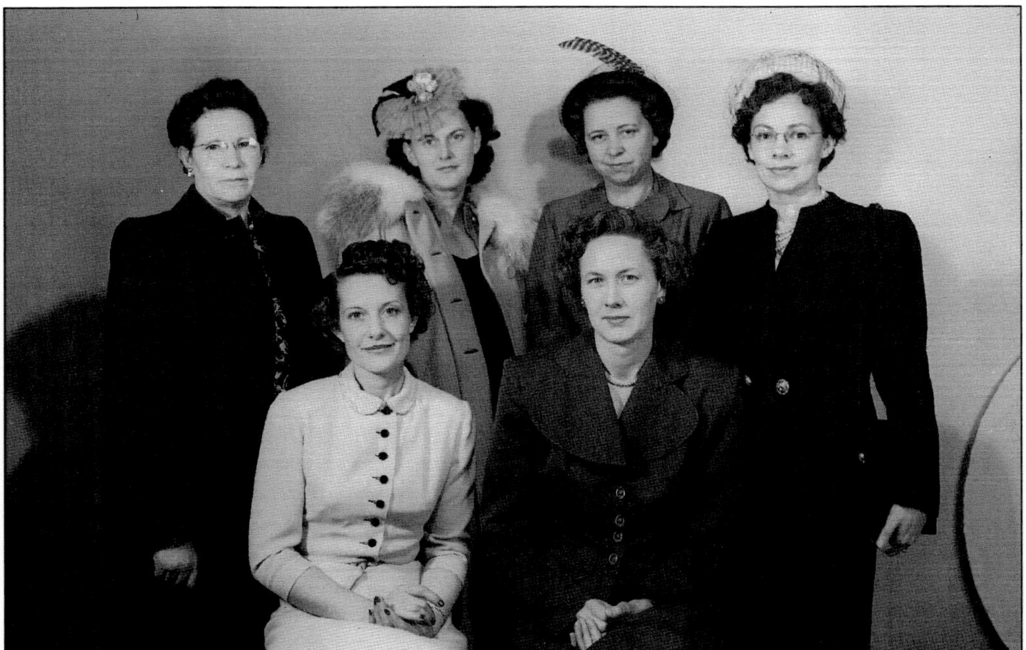

In 1941, the Federated Women's Club was organized locally. The club helped with civic projects, such as supporting the troops locally and abroad. The 1949 club officers are, from left to right, (first row) Mrs. Robert Olsen and Mrs. Tenney Johnson; (second row) Sarah Jones, Mrs. Wilson Gutzman, Mable Calder, and Maruine Anderson.

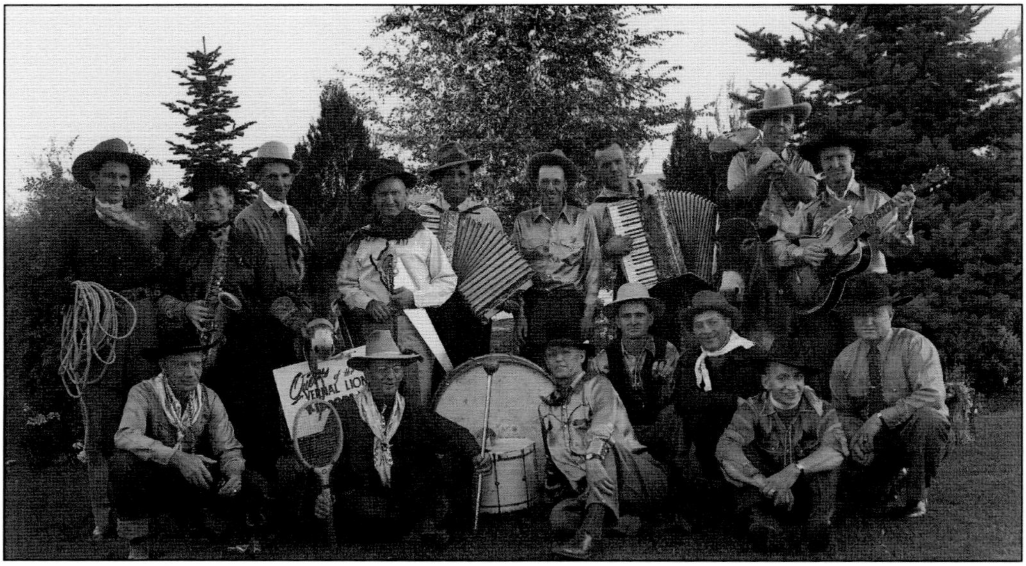

The Vernal Lions Club Band, the Kidoodlers, made any kind of music from the corniest rhythms to the hottest swing. Several of the Kidoodlers were vocalists and interspersed their instrumental numbers with solos, quartets, and close harmony. The 1941 Kidoodlers are, from left to right, (first row) J.C. Anderson, Ray Stringham, C.P. Lewis, Henry Schaefermeyer, Earl Chivers, S. Don Hacking, and Ernest Caldwell; (second row) Earl Calder, George P. Roth, Rulon Hacking, A.A. Call, Reese Timothy, Ken Stringham, Merle Campbell, Hap Wise, and Chellus Caldwell.

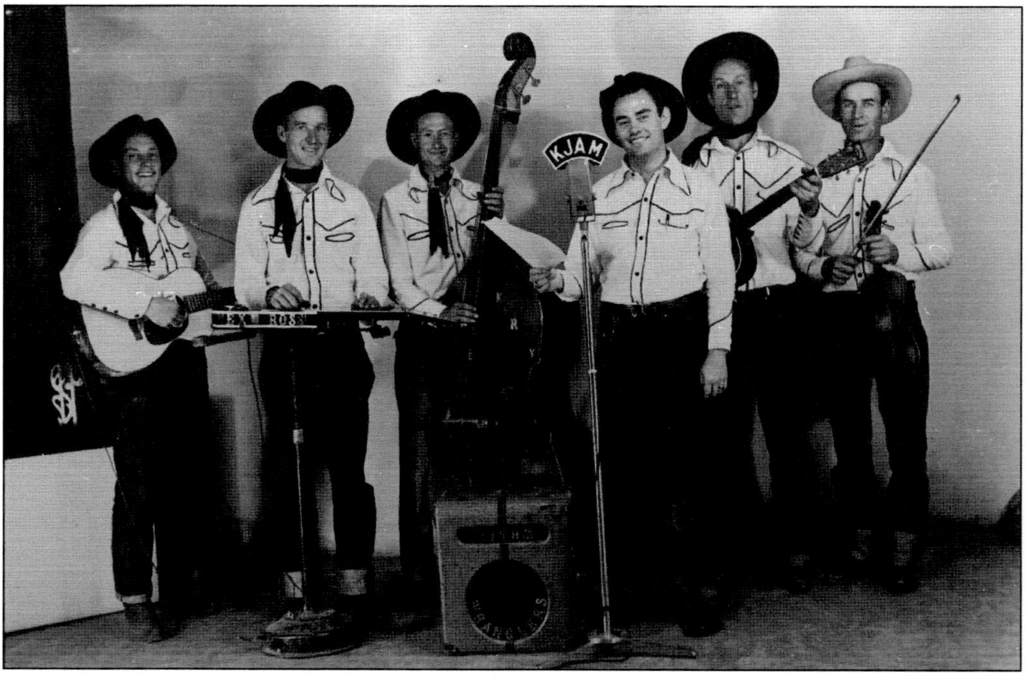

Tex Ross and the Rhythm Wranglers Band had a weekly show on radio station KJAM. They were also a local favorite for dances and weddings. The band members are, from left to right, Ted McKowen, Tex Ross, Kurly Stanley, Lee Walker (KJAM announcer and manager), Marr "Slim" Ross, and Melvin "Cy" Ross.

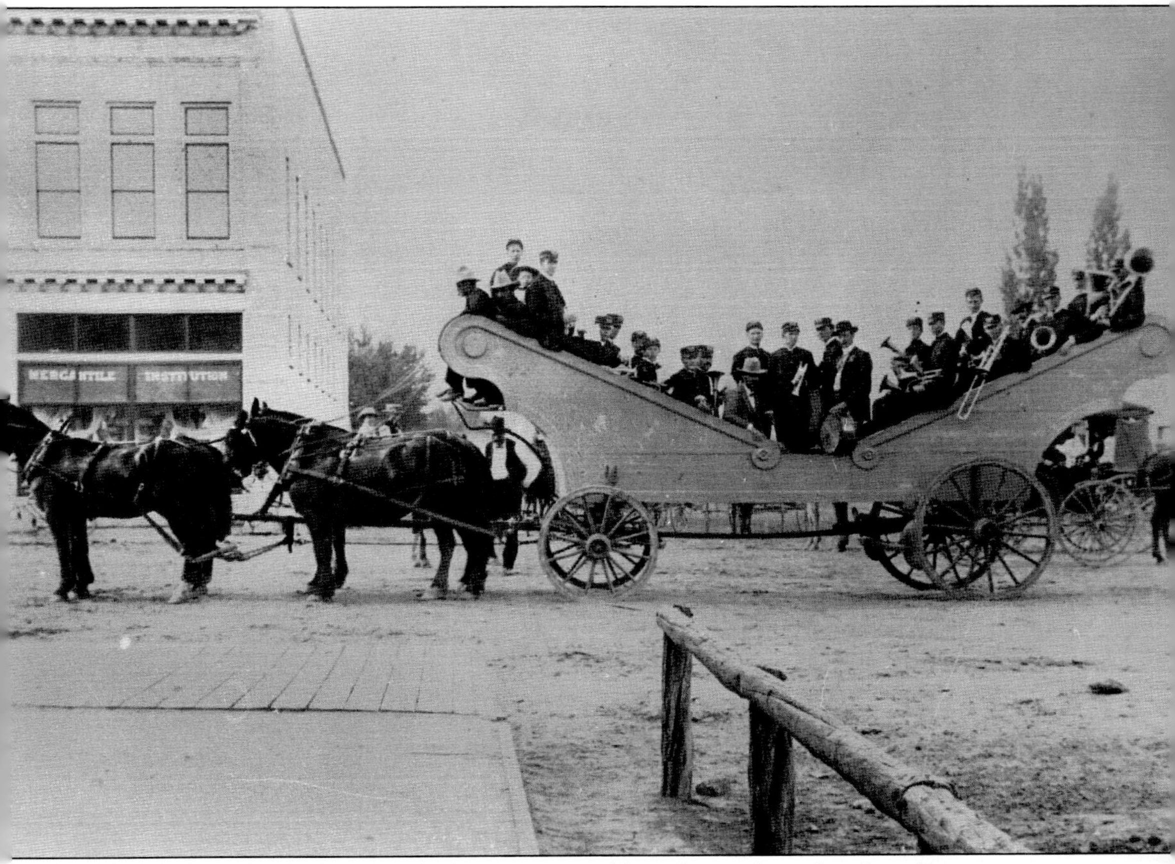

In 1891, George Adams wondered why citizens could not have a brass band in the community. He said, "We should be pleased to hear from those wishing to assist in accomplishing this end." In 1893, the Adam's Cornet Band was formed and began practicing. In 1900, a bandwagon was built, and uniforms were bought. Members were fondly known as "the boys." The band performed for many occasions and was always part of the local parades. Those in the band were George E. Adams, S.P. Hansen, Richard Jensen, J. Couple, L. Sorenson, Ed F. Harmston, George Bartlett, Leslie Ashton, Augustus C. Emert, H. Meadows, J. Merkley, Curtis Hadlock, Stanley Ashton, Howard Belcher, Bart Mowrey, M. Pope, Richard Pope, W. Higley, John Pope, W. Turcher, Joseph Ritter, and Ashley Bartlett.

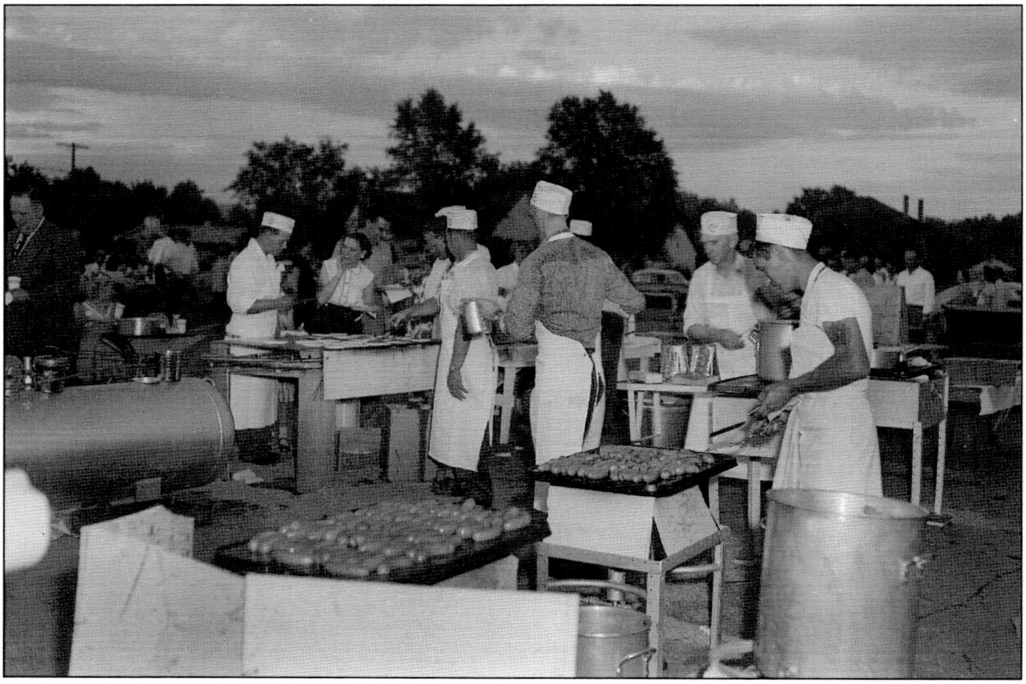

The Chuck Wagon Dinner and Festival at the Uintah Stake Center raised $4,000 towards a new seminary building in 1953. More than 1,700 people attended the event, which began Pioneer Day celebrations in the area. Those who attended were served hotcakes, wieners, eggs, and trimmings by LaRell Anderson and the Uintah Stake Relief Society. LaRell used a special large pancake cooker that he perfected. Thousands of people still attend the July 24 breakfast that is now a fundraiser and support for the local Boy Scouts of America.

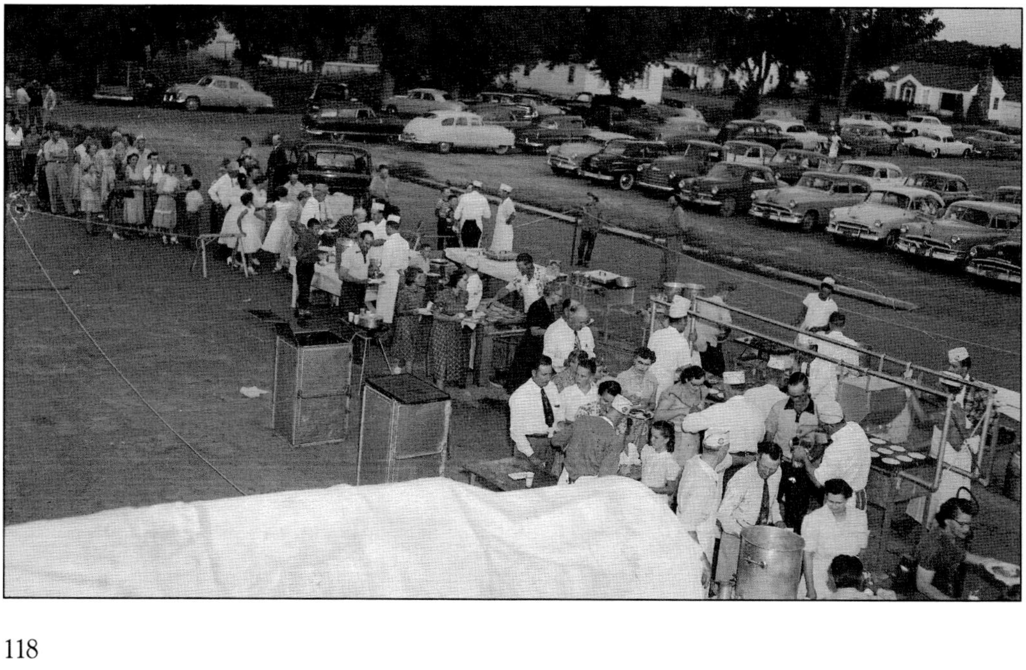

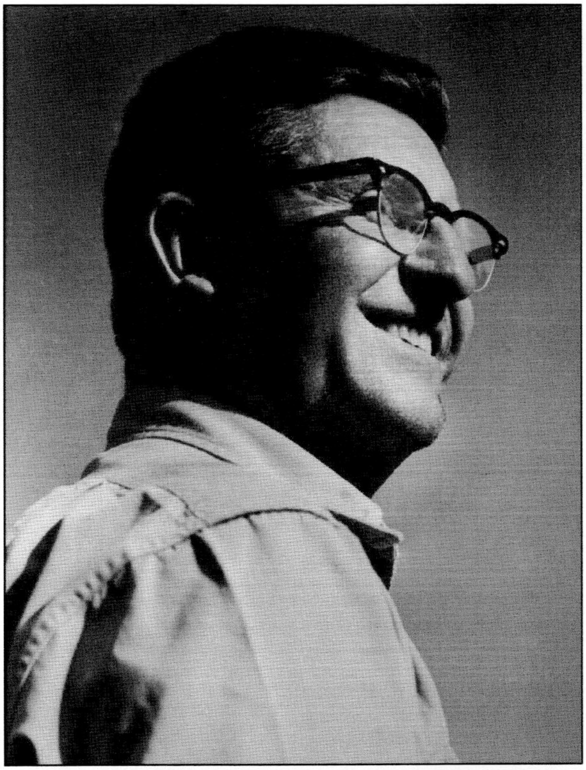

Bus Hatch, founder of Hatch River Expeditions, started running rivers in the early 1930s. Thousands of people experienced their first glimpse of the beauty and excitement of a river canyon while floating with Bus. He had a fearless personality, and his boating skills were among the best. He was a carpenter and built his own boats, made his own oars, and drew his own maps. Bus was inducted into the Utah Tourism Hall of Fame in 1987, twenty years after his death. After he passed away in June 1967, at 65 years old, his son Don carried on the family business. Many famous people have experienced river running with Hatch River Expedition, including Sen. Ted Kennedy and his family. Senator Kennedy is seated to the back of the raft.

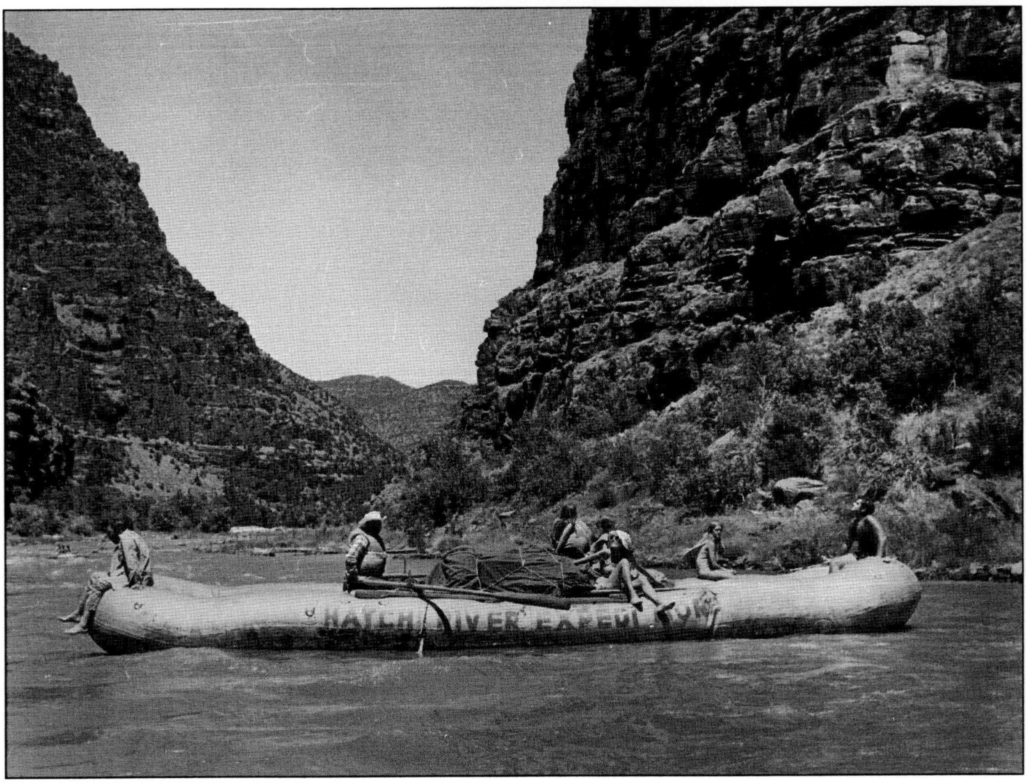

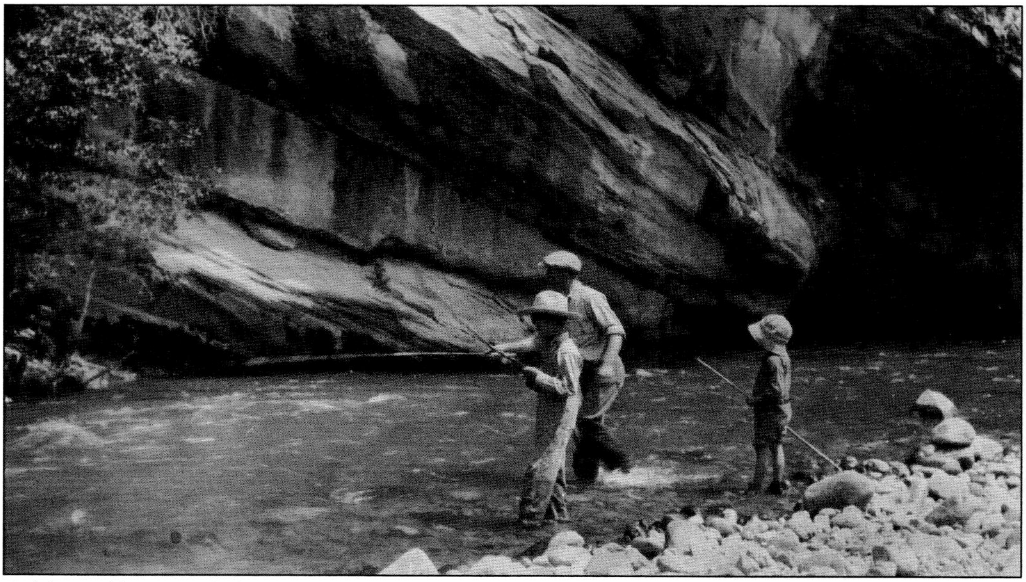

Ashley Valley provided many recreational opportunities for residents. The Uinta Basin is renowned for its lakes, rivers, streams, and reservoirs, which feature some of the largest and tastiest trout and bass. Catfish was a great source of food for the early settlers and could be found in nearby Green River. Two young children, Keith and Ila Wellman, enjoy fishing with Don Wall on the Green River.

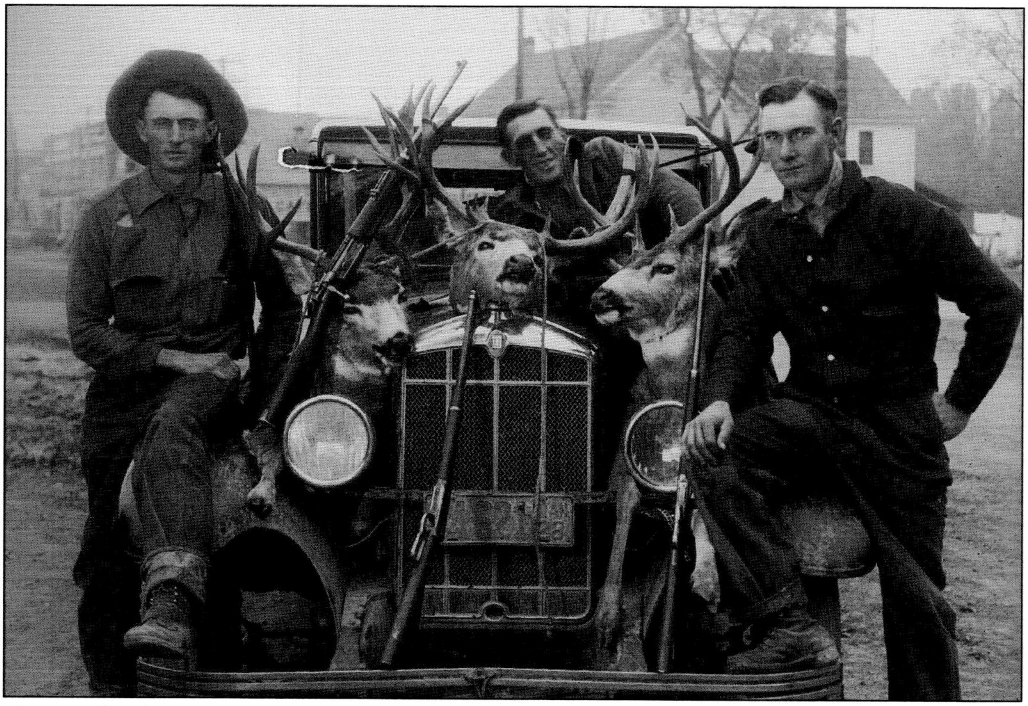

Hunting has been an important part of recreation for Ashley Valley residents since early times. Deer have always been the most hunted animal in the area. Other hunted wildlife includes elk, moose, and various small game. Ben (left) and Jed Luck (center), along with Lindsay Oaks, show the deer they killed during the hunting season in 1928.

Ten

ON THE EDGE

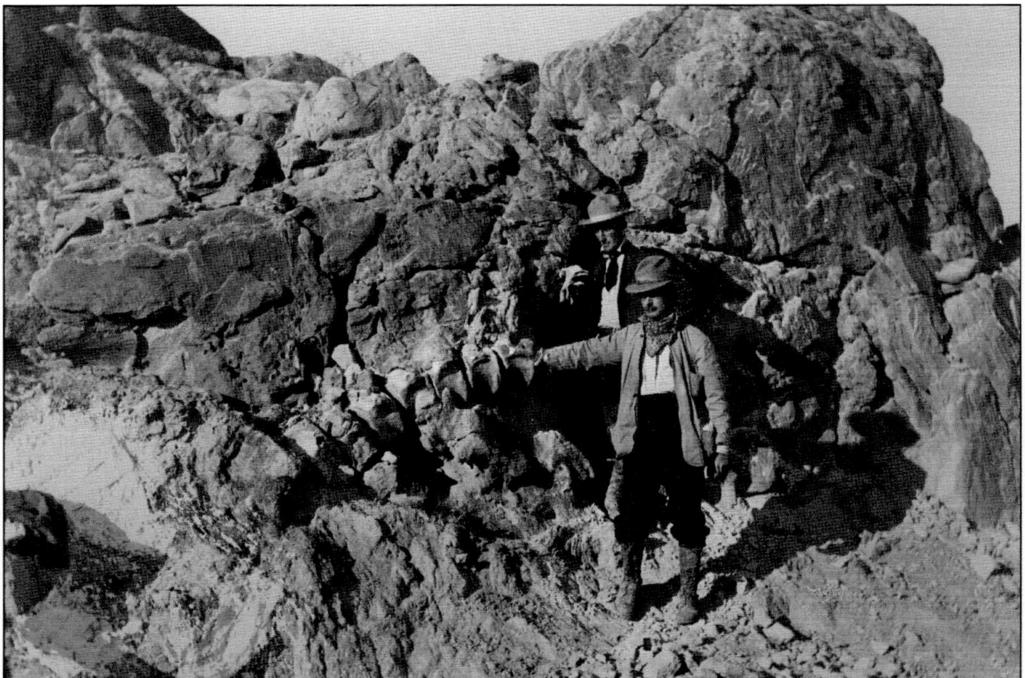

Earl Douglass stands next to dinosaur fossils protruding from a hillside near Jensen, Utah. Historian George Long said that young Johnny Powell discovered the large fossils before Douglass came to the area. Douglass became known for the discovery and was responsible for the Dinosaur Quarry at Dinosaur National Monument.

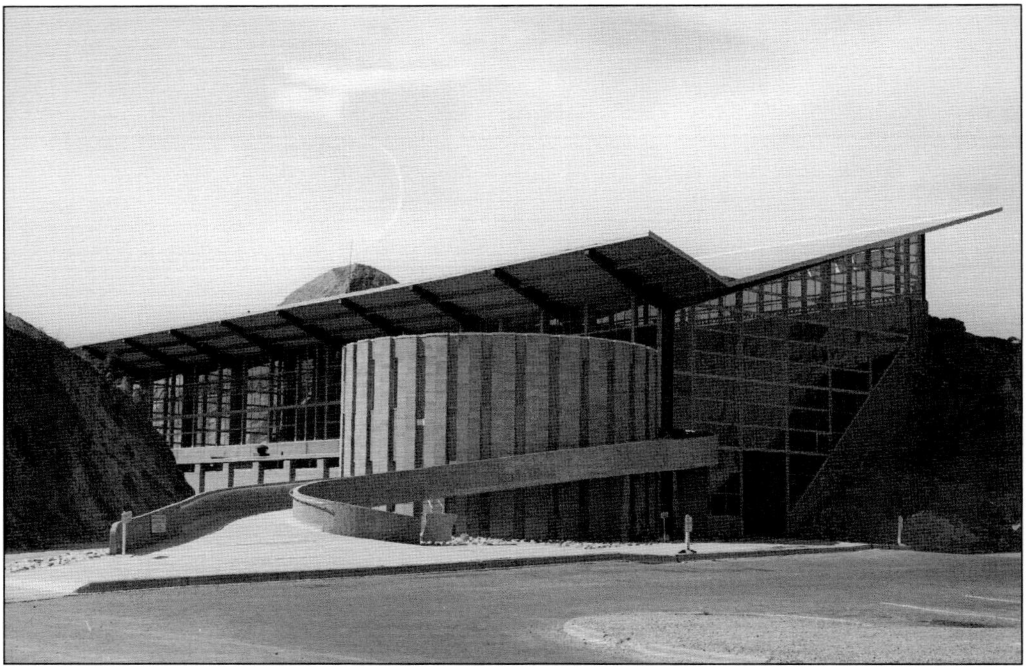

In 1958, a large, modern structure, partially of glass, was built over the hillside with embedded fossils that Earl Douglass had unearthed half a century before. One wall of the quarry forms a side of the building with in-place exhibits of bones and extinct dinosaurs that once roamed the area. The quarry has become a popular site for tourists through the years. Millions of visitors have watched Frank McKnight and other technicians chip around the bones inside the quarry. The foundation began to crack several years ago, and a new quarry is being constructed in 2011.

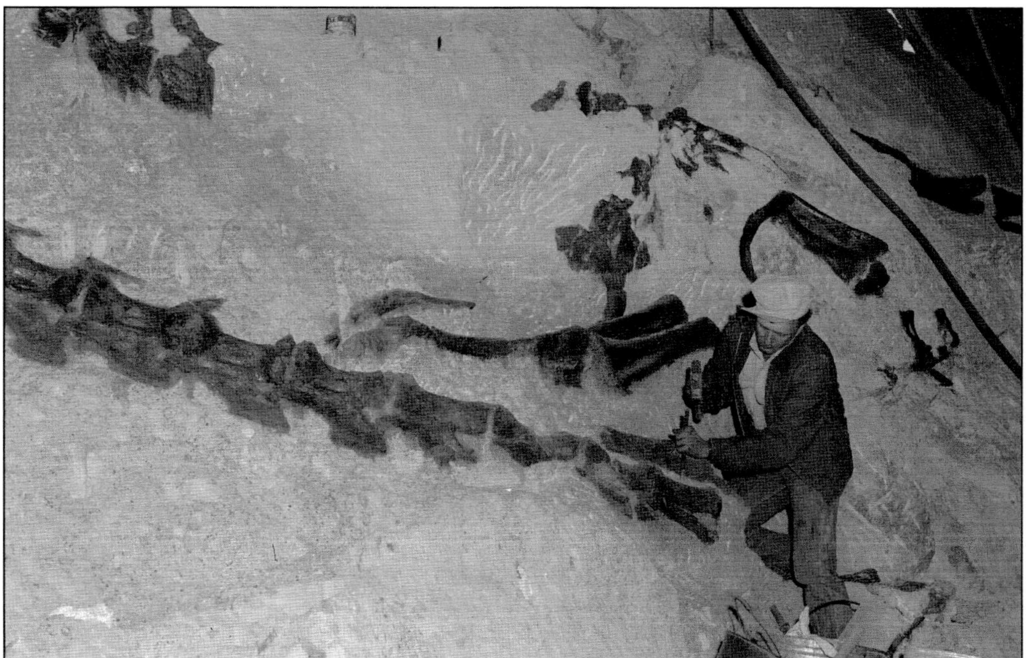

The Great Stone Face, a few miles north of Vernal, was one of many formations resembling figures and faces in the surrounding landscape of the Ashley Valley. It was explained that the sentinel was becoming a hazard to traffic because of deteriorating soil at its base. It was blasted to make gravel fill when Steinaker Reservoir was being built in the early 1960s.

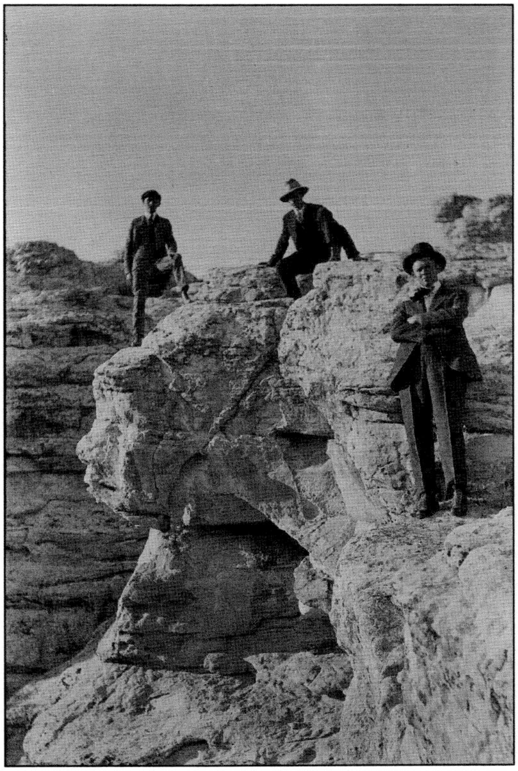

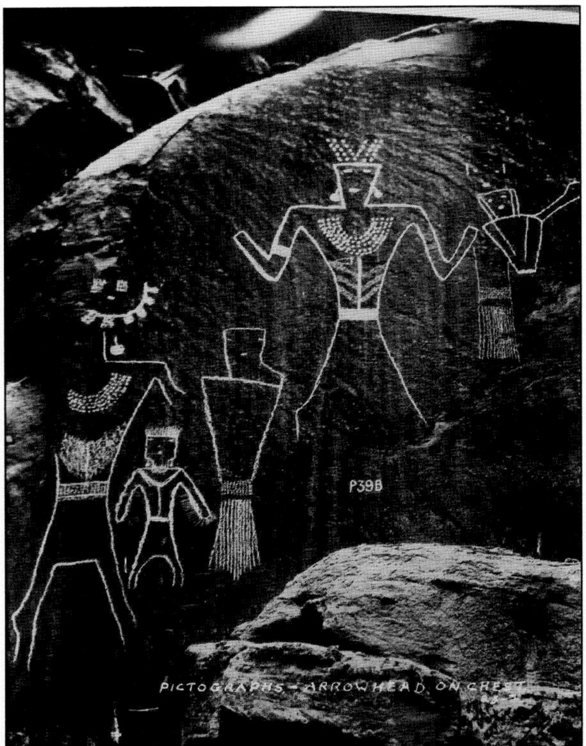

The people known as Fremont Indians left their markings on the cliff walls in the Ashley Valley long before settlers came into the valley. Many of the petroglyphs are located in Dry Fork Canyon, including this panel at the McConkie Ranch. Each panel was numbered, chalked, and photographed by Leo Thorne.

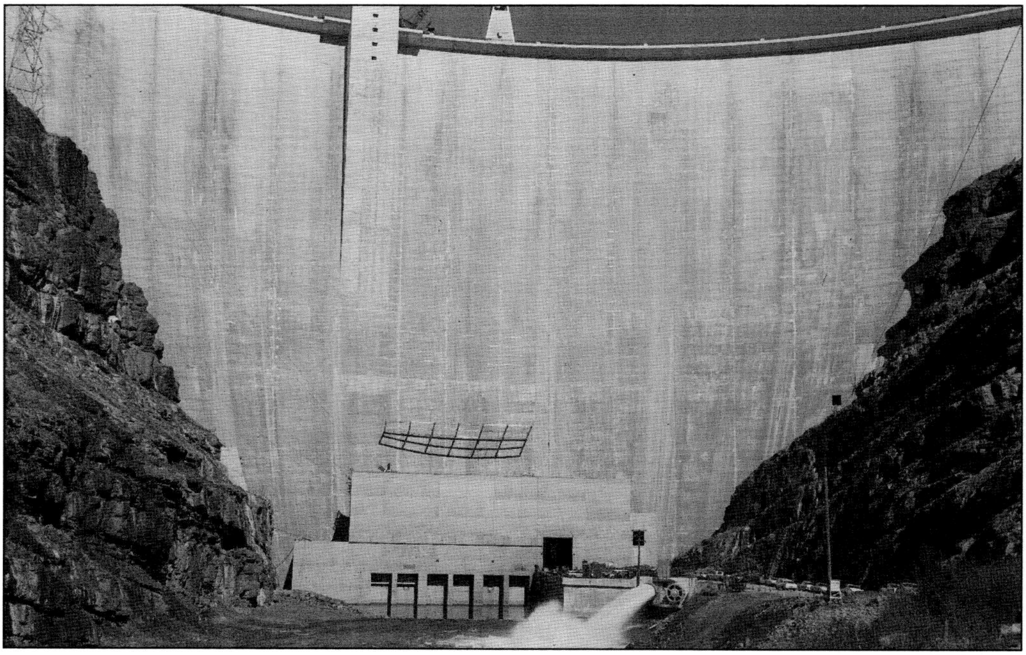

The Flaming Gorge Dam and power plant on the Green River was completed on November 15, 1962. It is 502 feet high with a crest length of 1,285 feet and contains nearly one million cubic yards of concrete. Inside is a maze of stairways and tunnels. The 91-mile-long reservoir has nearly four million acre-feet of water. The small powerhouse building generates a total of 108,000 kilowatts of electricity. The released water operates three turbines each with a capacity of 50,000 horsepower, which operate three generators. Power from the first generator was started in September 1963. Cost of the massive project was over $70 million dollars. In August 1964, Lady Bird Johnson, Utah senator Frank E. Moss (left), and Wyoming senator Gale W. McGee, attended the unveiling of a plaque at the dedication of the dam.

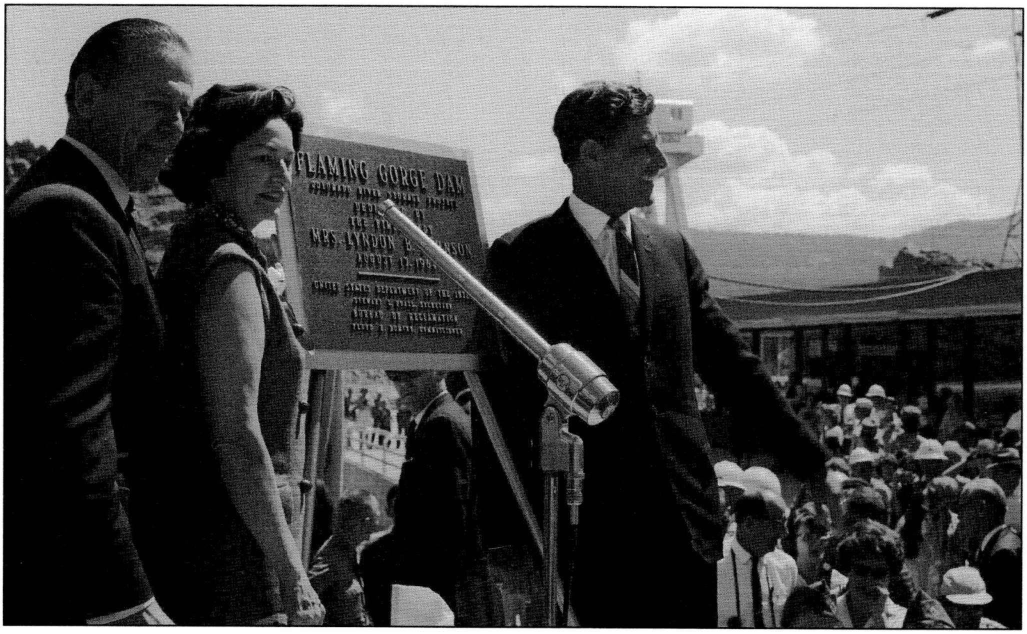

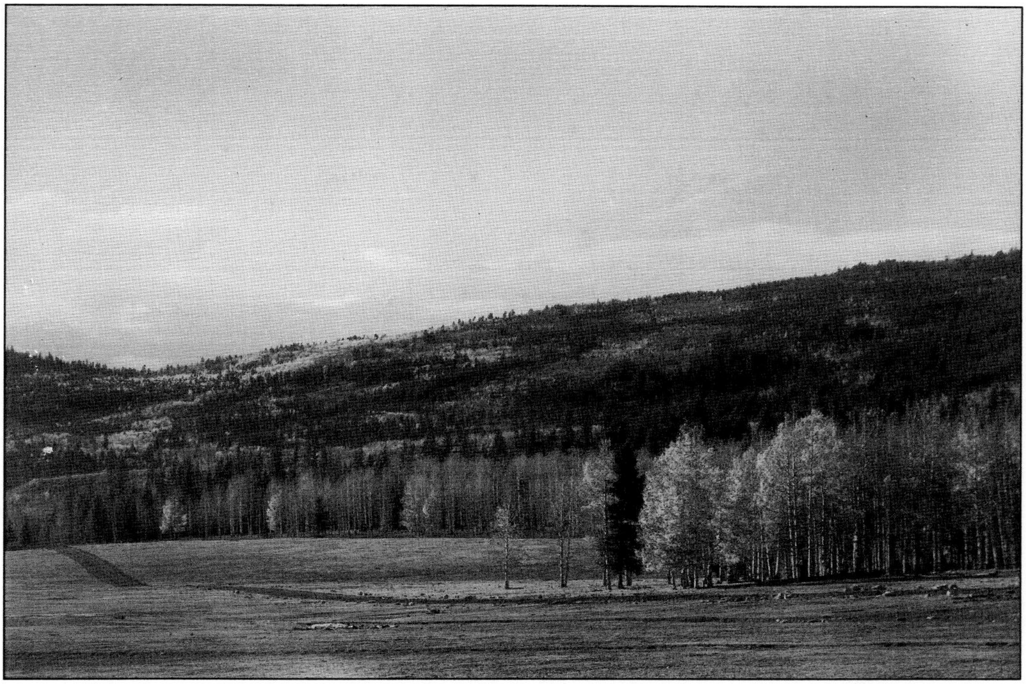

Mountains surround the Ashley Valley on all sides. The Ashley National Forest lies to the north as part of the Uinta Mountains. It offers a variety of activities for the outdoorsman, such as fishing, boating, hunting, camping, hiking, and a beautiful place for a Sunday drive.

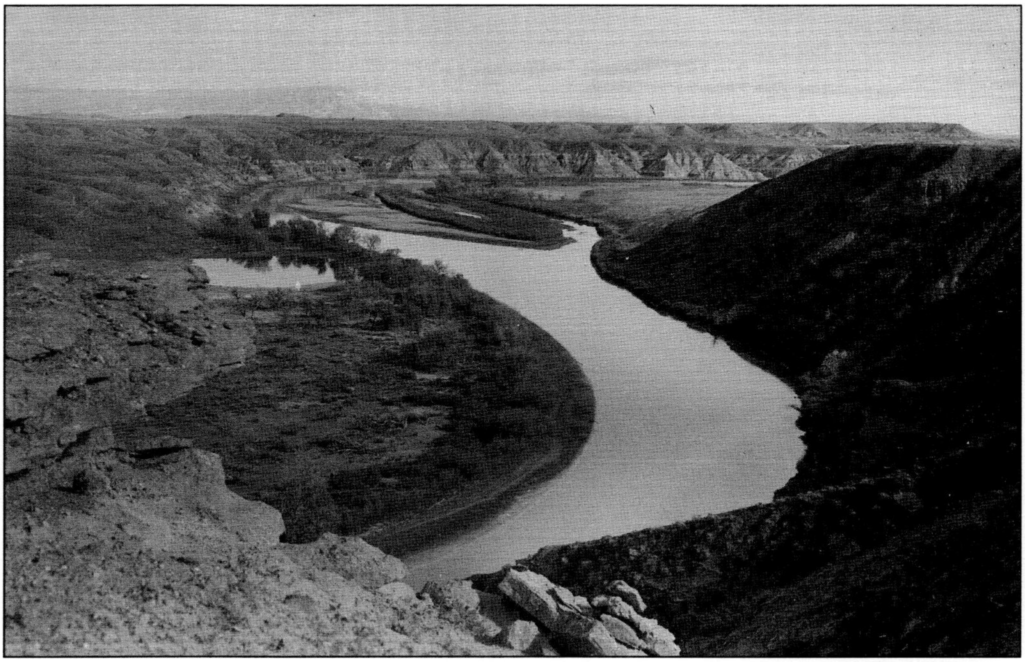

The majestic Green River flows from the Uinta Mountains and enters the valley in the Jensen area. The river hugs the edge of the Ashley Valley on the east and the south sides as it continues its southerly course out of the area. This portion of the river is on the south end of the valley and is referred to as Horseshoe Bend.

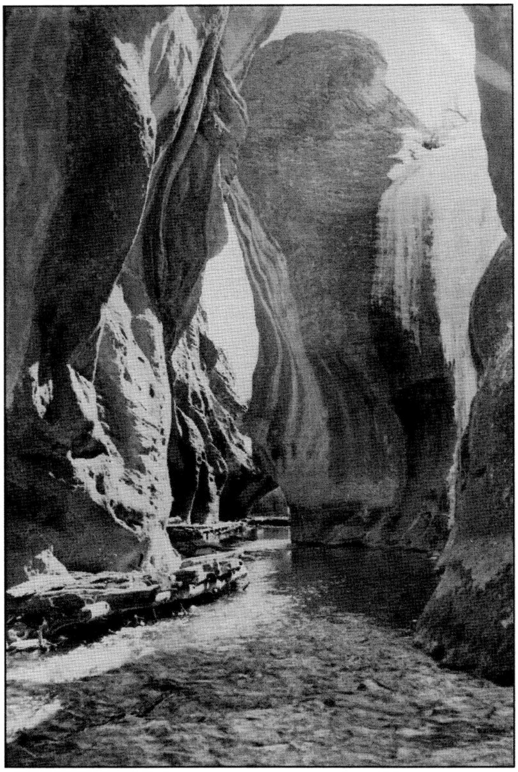

Humphrey's Park was a large meadow at the mouth of Brush Creek Gorge. Brush Creek ran through high cliffs in the gorge with no banks and was inaccessible until Wallace Calder built a wooden boardwalk around the cliff above the water. This walk led to an open area where picnic tables were located and provided by Wallace Calder. This fascinating landmark was once located where the phosphate plant stands now, but it has since then been buried.

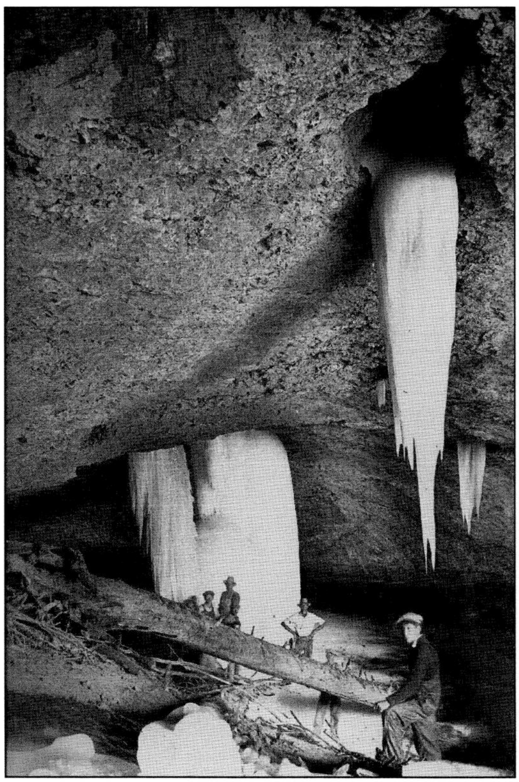

Big Brush Creek Cave is sometimes called the ice cave, because of the big ice stalactites that hang down in the entrance and inside the cave. The cave is located approximately one mile below Red Cloud Loop Road. This tremendous cave is known for its bottomless pits, sudden ledges, endless caverns, and its maze of tunnels.

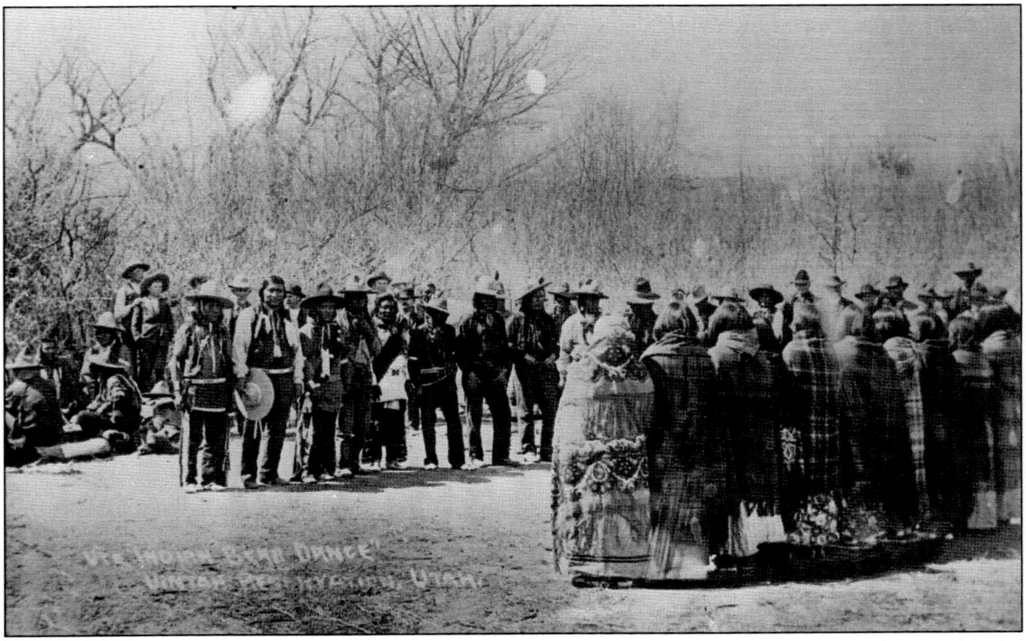

The Ute tribe lives on the reservation at Fort Duchesne, only 20 minutes west of Vernal. The Utes are a big part of the history and settlement of the Ashley Valley. One activity the Ute people enjoy participating in is the Bear Dance. The Utes and other surrounding communities gather together to enjoy the four-day festivities. The dance represents the ways of the bear. It commemorates the coming of spring and expresses hope for a plentiful season. Pictured below are Oakanus and Pootquas, two sisters weaving baskets, which is one of the many handicrafts the Ute tribe is known for.

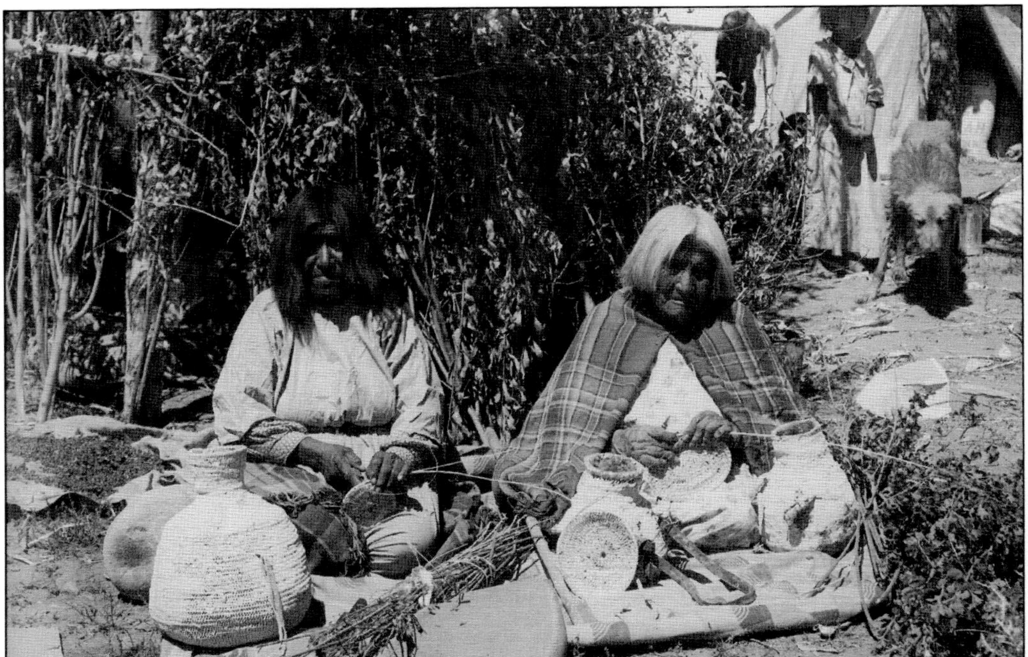